"This excellent and accessible book shows us why a focus on children's rights is both necessary and achievable, through a close examination of the discourses and practices around this issue. The prominence given to children's voices in the book is to be welcomed and demonstrates the commitment of the authors to put children at the centre of practice, policy making and research."

**Professor John Devaney**, *University of Edinburgh, UK*

"This timely and authoritative volume offers a compelling, rights-based framework for contemporary social work practice. Bringing together critical theory, legal analysis, and practice wisdom, it powerfully centres children's voices, while engaging seriously with protection, participation, and provision. It offers an invaluable resource for practitioners, educators, and students seeking to embed children's rights meaningfully and ethically within everyday social work decision-making and service delivery."

**Lisa Bunting**, *Professor of Child and Family Social Work, Queen's University, Belfast, Northern Ireland*

"This book offers a comprehensive exploration of children's rights within social work, emphasising theory, protection, participation, and provision. It centres children's voices and experiences to inform social work practice and promote children's well-being and does so from a strong research-based perspective. As such this work is invaluable not just for social work professionals and researchers, but for everyone working with children across education and children's services."

**Daniel Muijs**, *Professor of Education and Head of the School of Social Sciences, Education and Social Work, Queen's University, Belfast, Northern Ireland*

# Children's Rights in Social Work Practice

This book provides a thorough examination of children's rights, focusing on key themes and objectives that contribute to their understanding, implementation, and advocacy.

Written by academics both in the UK and internationally, and with each chapter containing two illustrative case studies, this volume will increase awareness and knowledge among social workers, enhancing professional practice whilst fostering empowerment and addressing systemic issues. Chapters are divided into four main themes: understanding theory that promotes children's rights, protection from harm, participation, and provision of services. Each section delves into the fundamental concept of children's rights, including the United Nations Convention on the Rights of the Child, and highlights the role of social workers in actively promoting and protecting these rights. In doing so, this collection emphasises the importance of safeguarding children, identifying and responding to abuse, neglect, and exploitation, as well as problematising the balancing act of realising children's rights in the modern context of child welfare.

By providing practical strategies and techniques for promoting and protecting children's rights, this book serves as a concise and informative resource for practitioners, students, and academics working in the field of social work, as well as scholars of child protection, safeguarding, and social policy more broadly.

**Paul McCafferty** is Reader of Social Work at Queen's University Belfast in Northern Ireland. Paul has expertise in child welfare, with a strong focus on risk, assessment, and decision-making in social work. His interests extend to evidence-based and informed practices, as well as the acquisition and utilisation of knowledge in the field. He is particularly passionate about children's rights, especially their participation rights within the child welfare system.

**Esther Mercado García** is a Reader Professor at Complutense University of Madrid in Spain. Her research focuses on social work practice and family welfare, with a particular interest in children's rights in people with intellectual and learning disabilities, and qualitative methods. She has published work on children's rights and participation, contributing to the development of child-centred approaches in social work, and is involved as deputy-director for the special interest group Children's Rights in Practice.

**Davy Hayes** is Professor of Child Protection and Safeguarding at Queen's University Belfast in Northern Ireland. His research focuses on service user experiences of child protection, involving children and family members in child protection processes, and the practice and experiences of professionals operating in the child protection system. He is Chair of the Northern Ireland branch of the British Association of Social Workers, and a Board member of the Northern Ireland Social Care Council.

**Gerry Marshall** is a Lecturer in Social Work at Queen's University Belfast in the School of Social Sciences, Education and Social Work. His research focuses on children and young people who are looked after, particularly in the context of residential child care, and on identity formation for those growing up in care. Gerry's work also extends to exploring the use of immersive virtual reality technology as a tool for social work education and training.

# Children's Rights in Social Work Practice

## Theory, Protection, Participation, and Provision

**Edited by Paul McCafferty, Esther Mercado García, Davy Hayes, and Gerry Marshall**

Routledge
Taylor & Francis Group
LONDON AND NEW YORK

Designed cover image: Getty Images / FamVeld

First published 2027
by Routledge
4 Park Square, Milton Park, Abingdon, Oxon OX14 4RN

and by Routledge
605 Third Avenue, New York, NY 10158

*Routledge is an imprint of the Taylor & Francis Group, an informa business*



*British Library Cataloguing-in-Publication Data*
A catalogue record for this book is available from the British Library

*Library of Congress Cataloging-in-Publication Data*
Names: McCafferty, Paul editor
Title: Children's rights in social work practice : theory, protection, participation, and provision / edited by Paul McCafferty, Esther Mercado García, Davy Hayes, and Gerry Marshall.
Description: Abingdon, Oxon ; New York, NY : Routledge, 2026. | Includes bibliographical references and index.
Identifiers: LCCN 2026010319 (print) | LCCN 2026010320 (ebook) | ISBN 9781032949260 hardback | ISBN 9781032949253 paperback | ISBN 9781003582410 ebook
Subjects: LCSH: Children's rights | Child welfare | Social work with children
Classification: LCC HQ789 .C46436 2026 (print) | LCC HQ789 (ebook)
LC record available at https://lccn.loc.gov/2026010319
LC ebook record available at https://lccn.loc.gov/2026010320

ISBN: 978-1-032-94926-0 (hbk)
ISBN: 978-1-032-94925-3 (pbk)
ISBN: 978-1-003-58241-0 (ebk)

DOI: 10.4324/9781003582410

Typeset in Times New Roman
by SPi Technologies India Pvt Ltd (Straive)

For my mum, who believed in me, and whose love and encouragement made my life full of joy and happiness.

To my wife, Martina, who has been my inspiration ever since we were kids ourselves.

And to my children, Pól Óg, Dúalta, and Mólly—being your dad has been my greatest happiness.

Dr Paul McCafferty

To my parents, my greatest inspiration, for every quiet sacrifice and for giving me wings to dream.

To my dad, forever in my heart and in all that I am. We will keep moving together through infinite space.

To my mom, for her sustaining love, her guiding strength, and her unwavering support.

Dr Esther Mercado García

For my mum, Annie Mary (Nan) Hayes née Moore, who has always encouraged and supported me, and who is still going strong at 103 years of age! And for my wife Nuala, and our three children, Ellen, Sarah, and Owen, who bring joy and laughter to my life every day.

Professor Davy Hayes

To my fabulous daughter Francesca. The fount of hope, light, and life.

Dr Gerry Marshall

# Contents

# Tables

# Boxes

# About the Editors

**Paul McCafferty** is Reader of Social Work at Queen's University Belfast in Northern Ireland. Paul has expertise in child welfare, with a strong focus on risk, assessment, and decision-making in social work. His interests extend to evidence-based and informed practices, as well as the acquisition and utilisation of knowledge in the field. He is particularly passionate about children's rights, especially their participation rights within the child welfare system. Additionally, Paul is engaged in various aspects of social work education, training, and practice learning.

**Esther Mercado García** is a Reader Professor at Complutense University of Madrid in Spain. Her research focuses on social work practice and family welfare, with a particular interest in children's rights in people with intellectual and learning disabilities, and qualitative methods. She has published work on children's rights and participation, contributing to the development of child-centred approaches in social work and is involved as deputy-director for the special interest group Children's Rights in Practice at The European Social Work Research Association. Her work is driven by values that promote children's rights, voices, and inclusion in decision-making.

**Davy Hayes** is Professor of Child Protection and Safeguarding at Queen's University Belfast in Northern Ireland. His research focuses on service user experiences of child protection, involving children and family members in child protection processes, and the practice and experiences of professionals operating the child protection system. He is Chair of the Northern Ireland branch of the British Association of Social Workers, a Board member of the Northern Ireland Social Care Council, and he sits on the editorial board of the journal *Child Abuse Review*. His research aims to identify how the experiences of those delivering and receiving child protection services can be improved.

**Gerry Marshall** is a Lecturer in Social Work at Queen's University Belfast in the School of Social Sciences, Education and Social Work. His research focuses on children and young people who are looked after, particularly in the context of residential child care, and on identity formation for those growing up in care. Gerry's work also extends to exploring the use of immersive virtual reality technology as a tool for social work education and training. He has extensive experience from his previous roles as a practitioner, manager, and inspector in children's residential care services.

# Contributors

**Ravit Alfandari** is a Senior Lecturer at University of Haifa in Israel. Her research focuses on decision-making and risk assessment in child protection and children's rights, with a particular interest in children's participation in research and practice in the context of child protection. She has published work on participatory research on child maltreatment and is the convener of the European Social Work Research Association's special interest group on decision, assessment, and risk (DARSIG). Her work is driven by a commitment to promoting children's voices and advancing rights-based practice.

**Andrés Arias Astray** is Professor of Social Work at Complutense University of Madrid in Spain. He is a member of the Research Group 'Psychosocial Factors and Social Intervention' (Complutense University) and the Institute of Knowledge Technologies (UCM-ITC). His research interests are diverse, with a current focus on the following: epistemology of social work; social work with groups, especially with online groups; digital inclusion; gender violence; and factors in the detection and assessment of cases of child sexual abuse by the professionals in child welfare systems.

**Jo Dillon** is Head of Social Work at University of Chester in England. Their research focuses on participation in child and family social work, with a particular interest in how children can influence actions taken on their behalf and services provided for them. They have published work on children's rights, participation, and co-written a practice tool for Research in Practice designed to embed creative participatory methods when working with children and families. Their work is driven by a commitment to further children's understanding about the roles of social workers in their lives and encourages practitioners to design bespoke and unique resources.

**Linda Ducca Cisneros** is Lecturer of Social Work at Complutense University of Madrid in Spain. Her research focuses on social work with groups and participation, with a particular interest in adolescents and youth. She has published work on youth participation, social work intervention with groups, and art as a technique for social intervention and is involved in as International Association for Social Work with Groups and a board member and member of the Research Group 'Psychosocial Factors and Social Intervention' (Complutense University). Her work is driven by a commitment to the values of social work with groups and critical social work.

**Kristina Edman** is a postdoctoral researcher at the Department of Health Services Research at Akershus University Hospital in Norway and affiliated with the Department of Care Science at Malmö University in Sweden. Her research focuses on communication in institutional settings, with a particular emphasis on children's participation. She has published work on how children exercise participation and how social workers and other practitioners may facilitate it. She is also active in the Swedish Association for Family Therapy, where she serves as Scientific Secretary. Her work is driven by a commitment to bridging the gap between practice, research, and education, with a focus on using practice-near datasets that capture how practice unfolds in situ.

**Mandi MacDonald** is Professor of Child and Family Social Work at Queen's University Belfast in Northern Ireland. Her research focuses on supporting families, assessing and enhancing parenting, and the needs and rights of children and young people who are in out-of-home care or adopted, especially their experiences of family life. Mandi has published work on each of these areas of social work practice and has used arts-based methods for co-creating knowledge with care-experienced youth as research partners. As Co-Director of the Centre for Child, Youth and Family Welfare at Queen's University, and a member of the European Family Support Network, her work is driven by a commitment to collaborative research that addresses real-world needs and priorities for children and families.

**Simone McCaughren** is an Assistant Professor at Trinity College Dublin in Ireland. She is an interdisciplinary scholar whose research is grounded in a strong human rights ethos, contributing significantly to areas such as adoption practice, post-adoption contact, foster care to adoption, and parental contact post-separation. Simone has presented nationally and internationally and led a major 2022 study that produced guidelines for contact with children aged 0–6 in custody and access cases. She is currently leading a national study on Intercountry Adoption for the Adoption Authority of Ireland.

**Mary McColgan** is Emerita Professor of Social Work at Ulster University in Northern Ireland. Their research focuses on Safer Staffing in Social Work and Children's Rights, with a particular interest in participation of young people in decision-making. They have published work on safer staffing in social work with a particular focus on children's services and survivors' perspectives of intimate partner violence, and they are involved in the British Association of Social Work's International Committee for Social Work and Commonwealth Organisation of Social Workers (COSW). Their work is driven by a commitment to social work values, promoting children's voices, and improving social work education.

**Shiran Reichenberg** is the Executive Director of the Clinical Legal Education Center and the Clinical Director of the "Sherf-Ulman Rights of Youth at Risk Clinic" at the Faculty of Law, Hebrew University of Jerusalem. Through her clinical teaching, she works to advance children's rights and youth participation through direct advocacy, legal education, and policy engagement. Shiran's research examines access to justice for youth at risk, the welfare and residential care systems, children's rights as human rights, and the structural intersections between gender, vulnerability, and state intervention. She is currently developing comparative research on procurement and outsourcing in child welfare services, and another research project on the design of youth-centred justice systems.

**Liz Tanner** is Social Work Development Lead at Southern Health and Social Care Trust in Northern Ireland and is doing a part time PhD in social work at Queen's University Belfast. Their research focuses on social work retention with a particular interest in mid- to late-career social workers. They have published work on factors that support social work retention, and student social workers commencing their assessed year in employment, and are involved in promoting social work retention within their current role. Their work is driven by a deep commitment to supporting the social work workforce, ensuring that every professional feels valued, inspired, and motivated. They strive to foster fulfilment, well-being, and longevity in the profession, enabling social workers to deliver compassionate, high-quality and values-led services that truly make a difference.

# Preface

We sought to involve children and young people as fully as possible in the development of this book. When offered the opportunity to choose their area of contribution, they selected the theme they felt most passionate about—participation. This choice goes to the heart of what matters most to them: being actively involved in decisions, policies, research, and civil society, not only in relation to their lives but also in shaping the world around them.

For children and young people, participation is more than simply being included—it is an affirmation of their value, agency, and right to be recognised as independent actors with a voice. This aligns directly with Article 12 of the United Nations Convention on the Rights of the Child, which affirms the right of children to express their views freely in all matters affecting them, and with Article 13, which guarantees their right to seek, receive, and impart information and ideas of all kinds.

These rights challenge long-standing assumptions about who holds knowledge and whose perspectives are valued. Knowledge production should not be the preserve of academics or elites; rather, it must be a democratic process in which access to knowledge—and the opportunity to create it—is shared. Involving children and young people in this process recognises that they are not merely subjects of research or policy but co-creators of knowledge and active contributors to social change. Through their participation, they help to democratise knowledge itself—making it more inclusive, relevant, and reflective of lived experience. We hope that at some point children and young people will take a larger part in the next book by agreeing to write a full chapter.

I'd personally like to thank the following children for working with Caoimhe McCormick (my hardworking and dedicated PhD student) to write this preface. Each of your contributions have made a significant impact on the book. I would also personally like to acknowledge the contribution of Voice of Young People in Care (Northern Ireland) for agreeing to allow us as editors to work with the children and young people named here: Michelle Chapman, Jay Hyndman, Lita Gallagher, Thomas Magee, and Kenzie McCracken-Long.

## What the Young People Said

*Young people feel participation is important because it gets them actively involved with an equal chance and opportunity to be heard and listened to while also trying to inspire change. This is important because it allows individuals to contribute their ideas towards common goals or other outcomes.*

*It is important to use the power of words to make a difference—for example, in legislation and policy: We want to use our voice to share our ideas and opinions and help adults to see things from our perspective. This empowers young people to stand up and make a difference for other young people.*

*With participation, it's important that young people feel welcomed and safe—for example, bringing drinks and snacks, having someone there that the young people recognise and trust, and checking in with young people.*

*Building rapport with young people is the best way to form a working relationship and get the most accurate results in research. This may also make young people more comfortable and trusting to share their opinions. It's important to explain to young people that everything they say is confidential—and why you might have to break confidentiality.*

*Creating a contract with the young people during the first session is very important because it allows everyone to create rules for sessions and helps ensure everyone is a part of the group. Outlining what should not be discussed in this contract creates a more trusting relationship. Acting as an equal is important for developing rapport, and part of that rapport is based on respect. Some young people would describe respect as being treated as an equal and a street that goes both ways; if you show respect, you get respect back.*

*We feel you should treat us as normal people rather than treating us like we are damaged. You should also show respect by having a good tone, showing proper body language, and having good presentation in your work. Respect is also shown if you are there and actively engaged in the activity at hand. Some young people think it's important how their support workers dress around them because if they come in dressed in a suit or something really fancy, it would lead some young people to feel insecure or feeling lower compared to the support worker. This is why it's important for support workers to dress casually—because it helps emphasise that the workers are equal to the young people involved.*

*Participation helps people by helping grow their confidence. Young people definitely see a big improvement in their confidence when they are actively participating. It is also a chance for young people to make new friends for life when they meet other people who are doing the same thing as them. Many people see making friends as a challenge, so when it comes to participation, it makes it easier for the young people. Another way participation helps young people in care is that it helps give them something to do, other than drinking and taking drugs.*

*Participation forums really benefit young people by not only giving them the option to try and change things for the better—e.g., through legislation or influencing other organisations or agencies—but also by helping young people know more about themselves through things like mental health workshops and by helping them with basic life skills through things like peer support. Participation forums cover everything a young person needs for their mental and physical health.*

*In addition, we have the right to participate in different groups that help shape our future for the better. Participation forums give young people the chance to voice their opinions on issues that directly impact them or that could directly impact them in the future. It also gives those in power an opportunity to hear from those directly affected by legislation or policy so that they can see in person how it would actually affect the part of the public towards which the legislation or policy is directed. We want to demonstrate how we feel: The participation forums that young people go to give them the opportunity to do as the United Nations Convention of the Rights of the Child says they should be able to in accordance with the convention; Article 12 gives us the right to have our say on the issues that affect us, and we have communicated how best to do this. It is now up to you to take it seriously.*

# Acknowledgements

We would like to acknowledge Queen's University Belfast and Complutense University Madrid for their significant support during the writing of this book. Without the backing of our respective institutions, we would not have been able to dedicate the time and commitment required to bring this work to completion.

# Abbreviations

| | |
|---|---|
| ASD | Autism Spectrum Disorder |
| UNCRC | United Nations Convention on the Rights of the Child |
| WHO | World Health Organization |

# Introduction

*Paul McCafferty*

## Overview

I was a child when I first noticed how society made children feel small. Not in size but in significance.

Where I grew up, turning 11 meant sitting the 11+ exam—a test that split children into two tracks: Those who passed went to grammar schools, and the rest went to secondary schools. Grammar schools were held up as the place for the "brightest and best," with a clear path to university and white-collar careers. For kids like me, who didn't make the cut, the message was equally clear: We weren't seen as academic or "good enough," and blue-collar work was assumed to be our natural destination. It wasn't only a test; it was a judgement on your worth and your future. It felt deeply unfair. Even at that age, I knew something *just wasn't right*. Being judged and sorted by a system designed entirely by adults stirred a quiet fury in me—one I didn't yet have the words for but could feel intuitively.

I saw the adults around me often speaking for me, about me, and over me—but rarely with me. And this wasn't only something that happened in school. It seemed to be everywhere—in family conversations where decisions were made without my input, in community settings where children were expected to be seen and not heard, and in services that were supposedly designed to support us but where our voices were nowhere to be found. It was as if childhood came with an automatic assumption of silence, as though our experiences were not valid until filtered through an adult's interpretation. Even when the issues directly affected me, my perspectives were treated as optional, if they were acknowledged at all. Over time, this persistent marginalisation began to feel normalised, but it also sparked a growing sense of unease and awareness in me: Something about the way society regarded children just wasn't right. These early experiences, though unnamed at the time, started a conviction that would shape my life's work.

That conviction led me into social work, a profession with a powerful mandate to support the vulnerable and promote social justice. It was no surprise, then, that I chose to work in child welfare, an arena where the stakes are high and the need to respect children's voices is especially urgent. During the next

DOI: 10.4324/9781003582410-1

35 years, I committed myself to this work, beginning in children's residential care, then moving into specialist roles with adolescents. Later, I worked with adult perpetrators of domestic violence and child sexual abuse—complex and often personally painful work that further deepened my understanding of the systems meant to protect children. I went on to deliver training in child protection before eventually moving into academia.

Through it all, one thing stayed with me: the belief that children deserve better.

That belief became even more personal when I became a father. It changed everything for me. Suddenly, the abstract became real, the professional became personal. I found myself asking: What kind of dad do I want to be? What messages do I want to give my children, not only through my words and actions but also through the kind of world I help shape? What kind of society do I want them growing up in?

These weren't mere abstract thoughts; they became daily reflections. How do my wife and I encourage our children to be confident and kind, to speak up and listen? How do we support them in discovering who they are while also helping them understand the responsibilities they carry in the world? How do we involve them in decisions that affect them in ways that are respectful and age-appropriate? And how do we set boundaries—not to control but to guide—so that they feel safe, valued, and respected?

These are not easy questions, but they matter deeply. Because for me, parenthood isn't only about love and care (though it is absolutely about that). It's also about being consistent with the values we hold—ethically, morally, and politically. It's about walking the talk. The way I raise my children must align with the same beliefs I've spent my professional life defending—that children are not possessions or projects but full human beings with thoughts, feelings, and rights of their own. If I want a society that values children, I must begin in my own home, with how I show up, how I respond, and how I role model. And perhaps that's what this book is really about, too—not only rights on paper but rights in practice. Not just what we say we believe but how we live it—at work, at home, and everywhere in between.

And yet despite everything we claim to stand for, despite all the professional codes, legal frameworks, and public commitments, I've seen how many children's agency is still routinely brushed aside. Their voices are too often ignored or minimised, their perspectives doubted, and their rights treated as optional extras rather than non-negotiable entitlements. For me, this isn't only something that happens in isolated cases or outlier institutions—it's widespread, embedded in both our public systems and our private relationships.

I've seen it in boardrooms and classrooms, courtrooms and care homes, churches and community centres. It cuts across class, religion, ethnicity, and culture. It happens in affluent households and in families struggling to make ends meet. It happens in social work offices, schools, youth justice systems, and even in well-meaning spaces where people genuinely believe they are doing what's best for children. The problem is not always malice or neglect; it's often a deep-rooted adultism, a cultural instinct to assume we know best simply because we're older. We speak for children, over them, and about them but not often enough with them. And when we do, it's often on adult terms, in adult-designed systems that filter, sanitise, or dilute what they really want to say.

This failure to honour children's agency is not only a professional oversight—for me, it's a moral and societal failure. Because when we sideline children's voices, we teach them that their perspectives don't matter. We reinforce a hierarchy where adult power is protected and children's voices are conditional.

That's why I've written this book with my friends and colleagues—not only to name the problem but also to offer a call to conscience and a call to act. The main philosophical tenet of our book that you will soon see in the coming pages is that until we centre children's moral worth in the present—not only as future adults—we are bound to fail, no matter how sophisticated our tools or intentions.

So, at the heart of our call lies a simple but urgent truth: Children's rights should not be negotiable. It should be beyond question that children are entitled to protection from harm, to be heard and taken seriously, to be involved actively in decisions that shape their lives, and to be recognised and valued as individuals in their own right. These are not radical or aspirational demands; they are the most basic expressions of dignity and justice. They are also the core commitments enshrined in the United Nations Convention on the Rights of the Child (UNCRC), which marked a fundamental shift in how the world is meant to regard children—not as incomplete adults or passive recipients of care but as full human beings with inherent rights, evolving capacities, and moral worth.

Yet despite the clarity of these commitments, the lived reality for many children tells a very different story. The global evidence is not merely sobering—it is damning. In context after context, across low-, middle-, and high-income nations alike, children's rights are celebrated in rhetoric but routinely violated in practice. Although laws may invoke their protection and institutions may cite their participation, the daily lives of children are shaped by systems that exclude, marginalise, and control. In every critical domain—poverty, health, education, protection from violence, and meaningful participation—our collective performance falls short.

Children's rights may be enshrined in legal frameworks, but in practice, they are persistently disregarded. This dissonance between paper and practice speaks to a troubling gap between institutional promises and lived experience. Around the world, for example, children continue to go hungry, encounter systemic obstacles to accessing the most basic services, suffer abuse that too often remains hidden, and are denied equal opportunities to learn and thrive. They feature prominently in policy rhetoric yet rarely as active participants in shaping the decisions that affect them. They are more frequently spoken about than genuinely listened to. The vision of the UNCRC remains unrealised not because of a lack of knowledge or capacity but because political will and institutional priorities continue to neglect the value of children's lives in the here and now. The gap between the rights we claim to uphold and the conditions children actually face is not a technical oversight—it is a moral failure. Addressing this gap requires more than symbolic commitments; it demands urgent, sustained, and systemic transformation.

Take poverty, for example—a stark and persistent violation that exposes the hollowness of our commitments. One in six children globally lives in extreme poverty (UNICEF, 2023), a figure that is not merely a statistic but a direct breach of their right to an adequate standard of living as outlined in Article 27 of the UNCRC, which recognises every child's right to a standard of living adequate for their physical, mental, spiritual, moral, and social development. Even in wealthy nations, millions of children go without food, safe housing, or heating—conditions that contravene Article 6, which guarantees the right to life, survival, and development, and Article 24, which affirms children's right to the highest attainable standard of health. In the United Kingdom, for example, more than 4 million children live below the poverty line—a situation characterised by UN Special Rapporteur Olivier De Schutter (2025) as the outcome of political choice rather than inevitable economic forces. Such conditions do not merely reflect economic hardship; they represent a systematic failure to uphold children's most basic human rights. Take Mary (a fictionalised example), who juggles three exhausting jobs and still faces the indignity of standing in line at a local food bank simply to put food on the table for her three children.

These patterns are reflected in health outcomes, too. Globally, mental health disorders among children and adolescents are climbing: Approximately 1 in 7 (14%) young people aged 10–19 now experience a mental health condition, making it the third leading cause of disease burden in this age group (World Health Organization [WHO], 2025a, 2025b). Lifetime prevalence of self-harm and suicidal behaviours is a major concern, yet mental health services remain critically underresourced: Countries on average allocate less than 2% of their health budgets to mental health, and in low-income nations, there may be fewer than 0.01 child mental health workers per 100,000 people (WHO, 2025a). Practitioners across settings report escalating mental health crises, trauma exposure, and self-harm among young people, but services are frequently fragmented, underfunded, and gatekept, delaying early intervention and often failing to respond adequately (WHO & UNICEF, 2024). This widespread systemic failure constitutes a clear breach of children's rights as set out in the UNCRC—most notably Article 24, which guarantees every child the highest attainable standard of health, including mental health, and Article 39, which obliges states to ensure appropriate care, recovery, and reintegration for children who have experienced trauma (Office of the United Nations High Commissioner for Human Rights & UNICEF, 2013; WHO & UNICEF, 2024). The continued lack of access to timely, coordinated, and adequately resourced services directly undermines these rights and reflects a profound neglect of the legal and ethical obligations owed to children. Take Ava (fictionalised), a 14-year-old who has been secretly cutting herself for months. When her school finally refers her for help, she is told the waiting time for a psychiatric assessment is more than 6 months. In the meantime, she is handed a leaflet and encouraged to stay strong.

In education, although global enrolment in education has expanded significantly in recent decades, issues of quality and equity remain deeply entrenched. According to UNESCO (2024), approximately 250 million children and youth are still out of school worldwide, and learning poverty remains widespread. These challenges are especially acute among marginalised groups. For example, children affected by crisis and conflict are disproportionately affected, with 1 in 3—around 103 million—lacking access to education (Save the Children, 2024). In this group, girls and children with disabilities face even greater barriers: Nearly 52% of out-of-school children in crisis contexts are girls, and an estimated 20% are children with disabilities (Global Partnership for Education, 2024)—like Amina (fictionalised), a 10-year-old girl in a conflict zone who dreams of returning to the classroom but now spends her days scavenging for food and water instead.

These figures underscore ongoing global failures to uphold children's rights under the UNCRC—particularly Article 28, which guarantees the right to free and compulsory primary education for all, and Article 29, which emphasises the development of each child's full potential. Although progress has been made in expanding access, meaningful inclusion, equality, and quality education remain out of reach for many of the world's most vulnerable children, in direct contravention of these rights. Their right to education and to achieve their full potential is not fulfilled—it is eroded.

Violence against children remains pervasive and normalised. Globally, up to 1 billion children aged 2–17 years experience physical, sexual, or emotional violence or neglect each year (WHO, 2022). In schools, nearly half of all students aged 13–15—around 150 million—report having experienced peer-to-peer violence, including bullying and physical fights, often compounded by corporal punishment and unsafe learning environments (UNICEF, 2019). The rise of digital technology has introduced new forms of harm, with approximately 1 in 3 young people across 30 countries reporting that they have been victims of cyberbullying and nearly 20% saying it caused them to miss school (UNICEF, 2019). Meanwhile, online grooming and sexual exploitation are increasing, enabled by anonymous digital platforms and inadequate safeguards (UNICEF, 2025). Consider Jake (fictionalised), a 13-year-old who becomes the target of relentless cyberbullying after a private photo is shared without his consent. The messages flood in day and night. He stops going to school, too ashamed and anxious to face his classmates. Despite repeated reports, little action is taken, and the harm continues unchecked. These forms of violence occur across settings—homes, schools, communities, institutions, and online—but are too often hidden, normalised, or minimised (UNICEF, 2024). Their persistence represents a direct violation of children's rights as enshrined in the UNCRC, particularly Article 19 (protection from all forms of violence) and Article 34 (protection from sexual exploitation and abuse; United Nations, 1989).

What unites these patterns is not only systemic failure; it is a deeper societal truth: We do not truly value children.

We value their future productivity more than their present personhood. We prioritise control over curiosity, protection over partnership, and compliance over contribution. This imbalance is not limited to education systems, political rhetoric, or public policy—it runs through the very institutions that claim to serve children's best interests. And social work is not exempt from this indictment.

Take, for example, the domain of children's participation in social work decision-making, a principle enshrined in law, policy, and professional rhetoric. On paper, it appears universally accepted that children should be involved in matters that affect their lives. In reality, however, participation is frequently conditional, marginalised, or absent altogether. Social workers may consult with children before case conferences or reviews, but their contributions are often paraphrased, diluted, or selectively conveyed to fit institutional agendas. When children express dissent, frustration, or fear, these responses are not always treated as legitimate expressions of experience and insight. Instead, they are too often pathologised—as immaturity, emotional dysregulation, or resistance to help.

This recurring disconnection between principle and practice is not simply a failure of individual practitioners—it reflects a broader systemic flaw embedded in the structures and culture of social work. For me, despite its radical origins, social work has become entangled in a risk-averse, adult-centric culture that too often reinforces the very inequalities it seeks to dismantle. In this milieu, participation is too often treated as a procedural requirement rather than a relational and political commitment. It becomes something to be recorded, not respected; something to be demonstrated, not deeply embedded. Beneath this sits a more fundamental issue: Social work, despite its professed commitment to being child-centred, often struggles to see children as credible social actors in their own right. Children are too frequently viewed through a lens of vulnerability and risk, rather than as people with perspectives worth engaging. This ingrained adultism shapes professional judgement and institutional responses, subtly reinforcing the idea that children's views are secondary, unreliable, or inconvenient. Even when children are technically involved, their views may be sidelined, particularly when they challenge adult authority, professional risk narratives, or dominant assumptions about what constitutes a "reasonable" contribution. Take Anne (fictionalised), a 14-year-old in care who repeatedly asks to stay with her aunt rather than be moved to yet another foster placement. Her social worker notes her preference but presents it in the meeting as "a reluctance to accept necessary change." Her words are filtered, softened, and ultimately sidelined. When she grows upset, her response is labelled as "emotional volatility" rather than understood as a legitimate plea to be heard and taken seriously. In such contexts, the adult-centric framing of "what's best for the child" goes unquestioned, and decisions are routinely made for children, not with them.

The result is a troubling dynamic. We are more invested in children's cooperation than in their contribution. We accept their voices when they reinforce established plans but resist them when they reveal systemic failings or demand institutional change. In doing so, social work practice risks becoming a carefully choreographed performance of inclusion—one that maintains rather than redistributes control. Participation becomes symbolic: present in discourse, absent in substance.

Crucially, the failures surrounding participation are not isolated; they are symptomatic of a deeper struggle in social work to operationalise its core commitments across the board. The same structural and cultural conditions that marginalise children's voices also compromise the profession's ability to deliver on protection, prevention, and early intervention. When children's rights are treated as optional or conditional—subject to bureaucratic convenience or institutional risk-aversion—genuine child-centred practice becomes impossible. Participation, in this sense, is the litmus test: It reveals how far we are willing to go to recognise children not only as recipients of care but also as rights-holders whose views, experiences, and agency must shape every facet of practice. That we continue to fall short speaks not only to procedural gaps but also to an enduring ambivalence in how the profession values children—and whose voice is ultimately allowed to count.

This ambivalence is not accidental; it is rooted in a deeper moral architecture that governs adult–child relations. Children are caught in a moral order designed by and for adults, whereby their needs must not inconvenience, their views must not disrupt, and their pain must not complicate professional routines. In this order, rights are not guaranteed—they are contingent. They are spoken about more than they are honoured, and more often positioned as ethical ideals than operational mandates.

This is particularly troubling given social work's foundational commitment to social justice, dignity, and advocacy. These values should demand that we act in radical solidarity with children, not paternalistically manage their lives. Yet too often, the profession reproduces the very power imbalances it seeks to challenge. We speak of being child-centred yet rarely act in sustained partnership. We invite voice but do not yield power. We assess vulnerability but overlook agency. In cultures of risk aversion and bureaucratic pressure, we replace meaningful engagement with scripted procedures, offering checklists where we should offer connection. We ask but do not act. We listen but do not change.

And yet we are not lacking in frameworks. The UNCRC offers a clear, comprehensive, and legally binding foundation for children's rights. Various models provide practical guidance on how to operationalise participation in meaningful ways. Bronfenbrenner's (1979) ecological systems theory urges us to see the child in a broader web of influences, and the sociology of childhood challenges outdated assumptions by positioning children as active social agents. Bourdieu's (1986) work on social capital deepens our understanding of how inequality and power shape access to rights in practice.

We have the theory. We have the tools. We have the evidence. But none of it will matter if we do not truly value children. Our repeated failure to uphold children's rights is not due to a lack of guidance—it is the product of a deeper societal disregard. These models are only as effective as the attitudes that underpin them. When children are not seen as full human beings in the here and now—when their agency is dismissed, their insight discounted, and their personhood deferred to some imagined future adulthood—then even the most progressive frameworks become hollow. The problem is not one of knowledge but one of will. Until we confront the fact that children are still not regarded as equal moral subjects, the gap between what we profess and what we practise will persist. The failure is not theoretical—it is ethical, cultural, and deeply political.

This failure is not only societal, however; it is replicated and reinforced in the very institutions tasked with promoting children's welfare. Social work today is increasingly shaped by risk management, compliance culture, and performance metrics. These pressures can crowd out rights-based practice. Practitioners are overburdened, systems are defensive, and creativity is stifled. This culture breeds caution, especially when working with children. We worry about liability, reputation, and procedure. And in doing so, we may default to protective paternalism rather than authentic engagement. This shift towards proceduralism and managerialism doesn't only constrain creativity—it colonises the moral language of practice. Over time, values such as care, trust, and reciprocity are replaced with measurable outputs, compliance checklists, and defensive documentation. In such a climate, ethical courage becomes the exception, not the norm. But rights are not a luxury to be considered when time allows. They are the foundation of ethical practice. When we sideline rights in favour of speed or safety, we risk doing more harm than good.

So, what does all this mean for us as social workers, educators, policymakers? It means that children's rights cannot be treated as an optional framework, an ethical extra, or a specialised concern. They must form the foundation of how we understand, teach, and practise social work. Rights-based practice calls on us to listen differently, not only hearing children's words but also valuing their knowledge; to act differently, translating participation into real influence; to think differently, challenging our assumptions about capacity, protection, and authority; and to work differently, pursuing structural change alongside individual support.

This is not an abstract challenge. It is deeply personal. As I reflect on my journey—from child to practitioner to academic—I return to the same simple but powerful truth: Children know more than we think they do, and they deserve far more than they are given. Their rights are not aspirational goals for the future; they are moral imperatives for the present.

This book begins with a call to conscience—not merely to recall the promises we have made to children but to honour them through action. As social workers, we are entrusted with power. We must choose to use it wisely, justly, and accountably. The chapters that follow explore how children's rights can be realised across diverse contexts and challenges in child protection. But let this introductory chapter remind us why we do this work: because every child matters, every voice counts, and every right must be upheld.

To explore this commitment in depth, the book is structured around four key themes that reflect the fundamental rights of children in social work: theory, protection, participation, and provision. These themes are not abstract categories; they are the terrain on which the profession must struggle, reflect, and evolve if it is to remain true to its ethical foundations. Each section draws on both academic theory and real-world practice to examine what these rights mean, where we fall short, and how we can do better. It is a vision of hope—but not a naïve one. The hope offered here is grounded in critical reflection, honest analysis, and a refusal to look away from the structural and cultural failings that continue to deny children their full rights. We must grapple with tough concepts—power, control, adultism, risk aversion, and professional complicity—and this book does not shy away from that challenge. Instead, it embraces the complexity of children's rights in both practice and theory, offering readers a space to think critically, act ethically, and imagine differently. Through each chapter, the reader is invited not only to understand children's rights but also to feel the urgency of realising them—and to see their implementation as both a professional duty and a moral imperative.

What sets this book apart is its refusal to treat children's rights as a bolt-on to standard practice. Instead, it argues that rights must form the core ethical compass of social work. This is not a manual of compliance or a celebration of best practice; it is a critical reappraisal of our professional responsibilities, informed by theory, driven by evidence, and motivated by conscience.

## Book Contents

### *Section I: Critical Social Theory Regarding Children's Rights in Social Work*

We start by grounding ourselves in critical social theory. This first section asks: What can theoretical frameworks offer us in rethinking how we understand and enact children's rights in social work? I open this section by applying Axel Honneth's theory of recognition to Article 12 of the UNCRC. He argued that social work needs a relational approach that respects children's love, rights, and solidarity if we are serious about participation.

Jo Dillon then takes us into the world of Pierre Bourdieu, showing how the concept of *illusio*—the hidden rules of the game—shapes power relations in child protection. Her chapter calls for greater transparency and shared understanding between social workers and the families with which they work.

To round off the section, I return with a chapter on the sociology of childhood. I challenge the traditional view of children as passive dependents and instead encourage us to see them as active social agents whose intersecting identities must be accounted for in practice.

### *Section II: Children's Rights to Protection from Harm*

Protection is at the heart of social work—but it's not always as straightforward as it seems. This section explores the complexities of upholding Article 19 of the UNCRC, especially when child protection and family support are treated as competing rather than complementary.

Davy Hayes argues that this binary needs to be broken down. His chapter explores how integrating child protection and family support can help us better meet children's rights to safety and stability. Ravit Alfandari and Shiran Reichenberg offer a case study from Israel, examining how legal frameworks can sometimes prioritise protection without guaranteeing service provision—a tension that weakens the overall impact of child protection systems.

Mandi MacDonald and Simone McCaughren explore the complex terrain of adoption, identity, and postadoption contact. They argue that open adoption, although challenging, offers a way to reconcile children's right to protection with their rights to identity and family connection.

### *Section III: Children's Rights to Participate in Decisions That Affect Their Lives*

Participation is often spoken about but less often realised. This section turns to Article 12 of the UNCRC, exploring how children's voices can be meaningfully included in decisions that shape their lives.

Esther Mercado García and I open with an expansion of our systematic review of systematic reviews—a comprehensive synthesis of what we know about participation in child welfare. We identify and further develop three key themes: the consistent sidelining of children's voices, the centrality of relationships, and the importance of context.

Kristina Edman and I offer a practical model: a 6-point compass for understanding different types of participation. Our work encourages social workers to reflect not only on how much participation is happening but also on the kind of participation that is taking place.

Finally, Linda Ducca Cisneros and Andrés Arias Astray draw on qualitative research with young people in Madrid, Spain. Using art-based methods, they explore how adolescents define and experience participation in their own terms, offering insights into what participation looks like when young people are in the lead.

### *Section IV: Children's Rights to the Provision of Services in Social Work*

The final section turns to the rights that enable children to thrive: the rights to services, support, and a fair chance. This section explores how social work can be a vehicle for delivering not only protection and participation but also provision.

Gerry Marshall and I revisit Honneth's recognition theory to explore how identity formation takes place in residential care. We argue that provision isn't merely about services—it's also about relationships, dignity, and belonging.

Mary McColgan and I take a global view, assessing how well services promote well-being across different contexts. Our analysis reveals both progress and persistent gaps, especially for the most marginalised children.

Liz Tanner, Davy Hayes, and I close the section with a hard truth: You can't uphold children's rights without a stable, supported workforce. Our chapter explores the link between staff retention and rights-based service delivery, arguing that without safe staffing children's rights to protection and provision will always be compromised.

## Conclusion

The book concludes with a powerful call to conscience. As social workers, educators, and policymakers, we are entrusted with power—power that can either silence or amplify, exclude or include, marginalise or empower. This final chapter challenges us to reflect critically on how that power is exercised and urges us to use it wisely, justly, and accountably. Children's rights are not abstract ideals or optional extras to be considered when time and resources allow. They are real, urgent, and non-negotiable. In this conclusion, I argue that if we are serious about reclaiming social work as a rights-based profession, then we must begin not with frameworks, checklists, or performance metrics but with values—especially those that centre children's humanity, dignity, and agency. And we must begin now. This is a vision grounded in hope, but it is also one that requires us to confront hard truths, grapple with tough concepts, and resist the pull of complacency. This book does just that, offering both critique and possibility and reminding us that meaningful change begins with the courage to act differently.

We invite you to engage with this book not as a collection of chapters but as a conversation—one that spans theory and practice, critique and hope, challenge and possibility. Whether you're a student, practitioner, policymaker, or academic, we hope these pages prompt reflection, inspire action, and affirm the importance of placing children's rights at the heart of social work. Dip in, read deeply, make notes, question what you find, and above all—enjoy the journey.

## References


Bourdieu, P. (1986). The forms of capital. In J. Richardson (Ed.), *Handbook of theory and research for the sociology of education* (pp. 241–258). Greenwood.

Bronfenbrenner, U. (1979). *The ecology of human development: Experiments by nature and design*. Harvard University Press.

De Schutter, O. (2025). *Report of the Special Rapporteur on extreme poverty and human rights (A/80/138)*. United Nations. https://docs.un.org/en/A/80/138

Global Partnership for Education. (2024). *Education data highlights*. https://www.globalpartnership.org/results/education-data-highlights

Office of the United Nations High Commissioner for Human Rights & UNICEF. (2013). *General Comment No. 15 (2013) on the right of the child to the enjoyment of the highest attainable standard of health (art. 24)*. https://www.ohchr.org/en/documents/general-comments-and-recommendations/crccgc15-general-comment-no-15-right-child-highest

Save the Children. (2024). *One in three children in conflict and fragile countries out of school – new analysis*. https://www.savethechildren.net/news/2024-review-one-three-children-conflict-and-fragile-countries-out-school-new-analysis

UNESCO. (2024). *250 million children out of school: What you need to know about UNESCO's latest education data*. https://www.unesco.org/en/articles/250-million-children-out-school-what-you-need-know-about-unescos-latest-education-data

UNICEF. (2019). *More than a third of young people in 30 countries report being a victim of online bullying*. https://www.unicef.org/press-releases/unicef-poll-more-third-young-people-30-countries-report-being-victim-online-bullying
UNICEF. (2023). *Child poverty: Global trends*. https://www.unicef.org/documents/child-poverty-trends
UNICEF. (2024). *Violence against children: Types and contexts*. https://data.unicef.org/topic/child-protection/violence/
UNICEF. (2025). *Measuring technology-facilitated violence against children in line with ICVAC*. https://data.unicef.org/wp-content/uploads/2025/03/ICVAC-Tecnical-Brief-3_17.pdf
United Nations. (1989). *Convention on the rights of the child*. https://www.ohchr.org/en/instruments-mechanisms/instruments/convention-rights-child
World Health Organization. (2022). *Violence against children: Key facts*. https://www.who.int/news-room/fact-sheets/detail/violence-against-children
World Health Organization. (2025a). *Adolescent mental health fact sheet*. https://www.who.int/news-room/fact-sheets/detail/adolescent-mental-health
World Health Organization. (2025b). *Children and young people's mental health: The case for action*. https://www.who.int/news-room/commentaries/detail/children-and-young-people-s-mental-health--the-case-for-action
World Health Organization & UNICEF. (2024). *Mental health of children and young people service guidance*. https://www.who.int/news/item/09-10-2024-who-and-unicef-launch-guidance-to-improve-access-to-mental-health-care-for-children-and-young-people

Section I

# Critical Social Theory Regarding Children's Rights in Social Work

# 1 Children's Participation in Child Protection Decision-Making

## A Framework Based on Honneth's Recognition Theory

*Paul McCafferty*

### Introduction

#### *Recognition of Children's Participation Rights*

Children's participation in decision-making processes in child protection systems is crucial for upholding their rights and safeguarding their well-being. The United Nations Convention on the Rights of the Child (UNCRC; United Nations, 1989) establishes these rights, underscoring the significance of children having a voice in decisions that affect their lives. Article 12 of the UNCRC is particularly notable because it requires that children's views be given due weight according to their age and maturity, thus recognising children as autonomous individuals capable of meaningful contributions.

However, despite these legal provisions, children's participation in child protection systems remains inconsistent. Social workers encounter considerable obstacles in fully realising children's participation rights, including ingrained professional attitudes, organisational limitations, and systemic barriers that restrict children's meaningful involvement in decision-making processes (McCafferty & Mercado García, 2024). This chapter posits that Axel Honneth's recognition theory offers a valuable framework for enhancing children's participation and addressing the challenges that social workers face in the contested space where children's rights and social work practice converge.

Honneth (1995) outlined three key forms of recognition—love, rights, and solidarity—that are essential for fostering self-confidence, self-respect, and self-esteem. These forms of recognition are particularly significant in child protection systems, where emotional, legal, and social recognition play a crucial role in empowering children and ensuring their voices are acknowledged. Honneth's recognition theory provides a useful framework for understanding how individuals, including children, can develop a positive sense of self and participate actively in society (Marshall et al., 2020). According to Honneth (1995), recognition through love, rights, and solidarity is critical for personal identity development, supporting self-confidence, self-respect, and self-esteem. For children in child protection systems—many of whom have experienced trauma—such recognition is essential for enabling their participation in decision-making processes that directly affect their lives (McCafferty, 2024).

DOI: 10.4324/9781003582410-3

This chapter employs Honneth's recognition theory to emphasise the significance of children's participation in child protection decision-making, focusing on how the recognition of children's rights and dignity can dismantle barriers to effective participation. Providing a deeper exploration of Honneth's theory, the chapter applies each dimension of recognition directly to the context of children's participation rights in child protection. It examines how these forms of recognition can be practically implemented to encourage meaningful engagement, thereby enhancing the agency and voices of children in processes that directly affect their welfare and protection.

***Emotional Recognition Through Love: Building Self-Confidence***

The first dimension, love, is about emotional recognition in intimate relationships, such as those between children and their social worker in child protection settings. Honneth (1995) emphasised the importance of emotional recognition in developing self-confidence. When children feel valued and cared for, they are more likely to develop a secure sense of self and confidence, which is crucial for participating meaningfully in decisions that affect their lives. This is particularly important in child protection contexts, where many children may have faced neglect or abuse, leaving them with diminished self-confidence and trust in adults (Patmisari et al., 2024).

For these children, emotional recognition is not only desirable but also necessary for their reintegration into meaningful decision-making processes. Emotional recognition is synonymous with the care and affection that children need to rebuild trust in those responsible for their care. Bainbridge (2015), for example, highlighted the importance of emotional security in fostering children's self-confidence, enabling them to voice their opinions and participate actively in decisions about their welfare. Aligning closely with attachment theory, particularly Donald Winnicott's (1965) concept of the "good enough parent," children need consistent and reliable emotional support to develop emotionally and psychologically. In turn, secure attachments foster confidence, making children more likely to express their views and participate in decisions that affect them. Consequently, children who feel emotionally supported by their social workers are more likely to engage, and their participation is more authentic and meaningful.

However, emotional recognition is often not prioritised in child protection systems due to the demands on social workers, who are often overburdened with heavy caseloads (Hansen et al., 2024). This lack of time can limit their ability to build the trusting relationships necessary for emotional recognition (Bessell, 2011). As a result, children may feel alienated and perceive their participation as superficial or tokenistic, which can cause them to withdraw from decision-making processes altogether (Lindahl, 2021). This marginalisation of children's voices perpetuates a cycle of disengagement and further emotional detachment (Mitchell, 2021), which must be avoided.

***Legal Recognition: Upholding Children's Rights and Fostering Self-Respect***

The second dimension of Honneth's theory, rights, pertains to legal recognition. Legal recognition acknowledges individuals, including children, as rights-bearing members of society with the capacity to influence decisions that affect them. This form of recognition fosters self-respect because it affirms individuals' status as moral agents capable of making significant contributions (Honneth, 1995). For children in the child welfare system, legal recognition is particularly important in ensuring their voices are heard and respected in decision-making processes (Mitchell, 2022) such as case conferences or court proceedings. In social work, Article 12 of the UNCRC enshrines children's right to express their views in legal proceedings, mandating that these views be given due weight based on the child's age and maturity. Similarly, many national legal frameworks (e.g., the Children Act [1989] in the United Kingdom) emphasise the importance of considering children's views in all matters affecting their welfare (Dillon et al., 2016).

However, despite these legal protections, the practical realisation of children's participation rights remains limited, with research indicating that children's voices are often marginalised in decision-making processes and social workers often make decisions on their behalf without fully considering their views (Berrick et al., 2015). This failure to recognise children's legal rights diminishes their self-respect and erodes trust in the system. One main obstacle in this regard is the perception that children, particularly younger children or those with developmental disabilities, lack the capacity to participate meaningfully in decision-making (Toros, 2021). This mistaken and reductive assumption can lead to tokenistic consultation, whereby children are technically included in the process but don't have the opportunity to contribute meaningfully (Kennan et al., 2018). For example, in some cases, children may be invited to meetings but do not receive the necessary supports, such as advocates or interpreters, to help them fully engage.

***Solidarity: Participation as Social Recognition and Fostering Self-Esteem***

The third dimension of Honneth's theory of recognition, solidarity, refers to the social acknowledgement of individuals based on their contributions to a community. This recognition is crucial in fostering self-esteem, helping individuals feel valued and appreciated for their unique roles in society (Honneth, 1995). In the context of child protection systems, solidarity is particularly significant for children because it relates to their participation in decision-making processes (Niemi, 2021). By being actively involved in decisions that affect their lives, children experience a sense of solidarity because they are recognised as meaningful contributors to these important decisions. This recognition can help promote their sense of self-worth and belonging, highlighting their value as active participants rather than passive recipients of care. In doing so, solidarity can contribute to enhancing children's participation rights, ensuring their voices are heard and respected in the system (Shuttleworth, 2023).

However, research has shown that children in child protection systems often feel their participation is tokenistic, with little impact on final decisions (Bouma et al., 2018). This lack of social recognition can lead to frustration and disempowerment because children perceive their contributions are not valued (Nunes, 2021). Marginalisation in decision-making processes, therefore, discourages children from participating in the future, perpetuating a cycle wherein their voices remain unheard (Kosher & Ben-Arieh, 2020).

## Mutuality in Children's Participation Rights

At the core of Honneth's recognition theory is the concept of mutuality, which emphasises reciprocal relationships among individuals, the state, and society. Honneth (1995) argued that recognition is a fundamental human need, and individuals develop a healthy sense of self only through interactions with others. As shown in Box 1.1, this concept of mutuality is especially relevant to children's participation rights, challenging the traditional power dynamics in child protection systems in which adults often dominate decision-making, with practice implications for social work.

This approach calls for a holistic, reciprocal perspective on professional–child relationships, whereby children are not only recipients of care but also givers of care, rights-respecters, and active members of their communities (Warming, 2015). Recognising children in this way enables them to develop the self-confidence, self-respect, and self-esteem necessary to participate meaningfully in their lives and in society, and Honneth's recognition theory provides a powerful framework for doing so in child protection (McCafferty, 2024). By emphasising love, rights, and solidarity, Honneth's theory offers a holistic approach to fostering children's emotional security, legal agency, and social belonging, thereby

**Box 1.1 Reflective Questions for Social Workers: Supporting Children in Child Protection**

How do I currently approach building emotional recognition (love) with children in my care, and what specific actions could I take to ensure they feel valued and supported, particularly when they have experienced trauma?

In what ways can I ensure that children understand their legal rights in the child protection system, and how can I advocate accommodations that empower them to participate meaningfully in decision-making?

How do I actively involve children as contributors in their welfare decisions, in order to foster a sense of solidarity and belonging, rather than viewing them solely as recipients of support?

Reflecting on the concept of mutuality in Honneth's recognition theory, how can I balance power dynamics in my professional–child relationships to create reciprocal and empowering interactions?

enhancing their sense of worth. For social workers, then, this framework underscores the importance of recognising children's emotional needs, legal rights, and social contributions, ensuring that children are not only heard but also valued as active participants in decision-making processes (Houston, 2015).

By creating environments in which children feel emotionally supported, legally empowered, and socially valued, social workers can help children develop the self-confidence, self-respect, and self-esteem necessary to engage meaningfully in decisions affecting their lives (Thomas, 2012). This approach not only upholds children's participation rights but also contributes to their well-being and development as active members of society. Ultimately, Honneth's recognition theory highlights the potential of child protection systems to contribute to a more just and equitable society where all individuals, including children, receive the recognition they deserve (Hansen et al., 2024).

## Empowering Participation in Child Protection: Supporting Mary's Voice in Decision-Making

The following case study illustrates the potential of Honneth's framework to enhance participation in child protection decision-making.

### *Background*

Mary, a 10-year-old in the child protection system, was removed from her home due to neglect and emotional abuse. Mary's history of trauma left her with low self confidence and distrust of adults, creating barriers to her participation in case conferences. Recognising the importance of empowering Mary and honouring her participation rights, her social worker, Jenny, employed Honneth's dimensions of recognition—love, rights, and solidarity—to build a relationship in which Mary could feel secure, respected, and valued in decisions about her future.

### *Emotional Recognition (Love)*

Jenny focused on fostering a safe and supportive relationship with Mary, demonstrating consistent care and attention to her emotional needs. During their sessions, Jenny encouraged Mary to express her feelings about her situation, listened without judgement, and offered validation of Mary's emotions. This emotional recognition built Mary's self-confidence, enabling her to feel secure enough to share her thoughts and preferences during meetings. Jenny's approach aligned with the attachment theory principle of providing a "good enough" relationship, which helped Mary rebuild trust in adults.

### *Legal Recognition (Rights)*

To affirm Mary's status as a rights-bearing individual, Jenny explained her right to participate in decisions that affect her life, drawing from Article 12 of the UNCRC. She ensured Mary understood that her opinions mattered and that they would be taken seriously. Recognising that the legal framework supported Mary's voice, Jenny advocated accommodations, such as having an advocate present to help Mary articulate her thoughts during case conferences. This recognition of Mary's legal rights fostered her self-respect, helping her see herself as an active participant rather than only a recipient of care.

#### *Social Recognition (Solidarity)*

Jenny worked to build a sense of solidarity by involving Mary in discussions about her placement and educational needs. She encouraged Mary to explore how she might contribute to her well-being by identifying her strengths and aspirations. Through this acknowledgement of her unique perspective and contributions, Mary began to feel valued as part of the decision-making team. This social recognition reinforced Mary's self-esteem, promoting a sense of belonging and purpose.

#### *Outcome*

Through these efforts, Mary gradually became more engaged in her case conferences, confidently expressing her preferences for placement and school. Jenny's holistic application of Honneth's recognition theory transformed Mary's experience from one of passive involvement to active participation, providing her with the confidence, respect, and self-worth necessary for meaningful engagement in her life decisions.

This case study demonstrates that applying Honneth's recognition theory in child protection practice can profoundly influence a child's ability to participate meaningfully in decisions affecting their life. By prioritising emotional, legal, and social recognition, Jenny helped Mary rebuild trust, self-confidence, and a sense of agency. This approach not only upheld Mary's rights but also empowered her as an active contributor in her care, highlighting the transformative potential of recognition-based social work in fostering children's participation and well-being.

### Barriers to Participation and Recognition: Insights from Honneth's Recognition Theory

As stated, Honneth's recognition theory offers a powerful lens for understanding barriers that prevent the full participation and recognition of children in child protection systems. According to Honneth, social recognition is fundamental to individuals' self-esteem and their ability to act as valued contributors in their communities. For children, particularly in the context of child protection, meaningful participation affirms their status as moral agents capable of influencing decisions about their lives (Woodman et al., 2022). However, numerous barriers hinder this process of recognition and solidarity and are worthy of reflection.

***Conceptual Barriers: Attitudes Towards Children's Participation***

One primary obstacle to children's participation is the prevailing attitude among social workers, who often see children as passive recipients rather than active agents (McCafferty, 2017). Traditional views of childhood reflect a failure to recognise children as moral agents capable of exercising agency and contributing meaningfully to decision-making (McCafferty et al., 2021). This aligns with Honneth's theory, whereby failure to recognise the individual's agency results in the denial of their social value, leading to diminished self-esteem and social standing. For children in child protection, this can manifest in tokenistic forms of participation, such that their views are sought but not genuinely considered (Toros, 2021). Such practices inhibit the recognition of children's capacities and deny them the social solidarity necessary for their development as contributors to decisions affecting their lives.

***Practical Barriers: Lack of Resources and Skills for Meaningful Engagement***

Honneth's theory also points to the importance of material and practical support for social recognition. In child protection, practical barriers such as a lack of time, resources, and training hinder the ability of social workers to engage children meaningfully. High caseloads, limited time, and bureaucratic constraints prevent social workers from developing the trusting relationships necessary for genuine participation. Additionally, many social workers lack the skills or tools required to communicate effectively with children, especially those with developmental disabilities or complex needs (Wilson et al., 2020). From Honneth's perspective, this lack of practical support equates to a failure of solidarity, resulting in the child's need for recognition and participation going unmet.

***Systemic Barriers: Power Imbalances and Structural Invisibility***

Systemic power imbalances are another major barrier to children's participation and recognition. The adult-dominated structure of child protection systems often leaves children feeling invisible in the decision-making process

**Box 1.2 Reflective Questions for Social Workers: Potential Barriers to Participation**

Am I making assumptions about children's capacity to participate based on their age or ability?

How can I challenge my biases or attitudes that might limit a child's voice in the decision-making process?

Do I have the time and resources to build meaningful relationships with the children I work with?

How can I develop my skills to better engage children with diverse communication needs?

(van Bijleveld et al., 2015). According to Honneth, power imbalances reflect a denial of legal and social recognition, whereby individuals are not treated as equal participants. For children, this invisibility diminishes their self-respect and reinforces their disempowerment (Honneth, 1995).

***Bridging Emotional Gaps***

To address the challenges in child protection, professionals should prioritise emotional recognition by creating environments where children feel safe, valued, and heard (Skauge et al., 2021). Effective child-centred communication strategies, such as play, storytelling, and creative activities, provide children with meaningful ways to express their emotions (Husby et al., 2018). Symbolic play techniques are particularly beneficial for younger children because they help them explore their emotions in a non-verbal way. This approach aligns with Winnicott's theory that children frequently use symbolic activities to express themselves. These approaches allow children to share feelings comfortably, fostering emotional recognition.

In addition, comprehensive trauma-informed care training is essential for social workers. This approach emphasises creating emotionally safe environments and understanding the psychological impacts of trauma on children's ability to participate in decision-making. Trauma-informed care equips social workers with the skills to identify trauma signs, adjust interactions to prevent retraumatisation, and respond sensitively to children's emotional needs (Bunting et al., 2019). By fostering trust, respect, and emotional safety, social workers can help children engage more fully and confidently in decisions that affect their lives. Trauma-informed care also encourages collaboration with other professionals to address a child's well-being and any barriers to participation holistically.

Emotional recognition is also fundamental to fostering meaningful participation. Without emotional support and trust, children may lack confidence in sharing their views or engaging in decision-making (McMellon & Tisdall, 2020). Building this trust requires social workers to create nurturing environments where children feel truly heard. This approach equips them with strategies to address emotional barriers that could inhibit participation. By cultivating supportive relationships, social workers help children rebuild the self-confidence needed to engage actively in decision-making processes (McCafferty, 2017). Recognising and addressing children's emotional needs not only enhances individual participation but also supports the broader

**Box 1.3 Reflective Questions for Social Workers: Bridging Emotional Gaps**

How can I build emotional safety and trust with the children I work with?
What creative methods can I employ to help children express their emotions?

goal of ensuring children's voices are respected across child protection systems (Balsells et al., 2017).

Finally, establishing consistent, trusting relationships with children through informal, regular check-ins can help develop these bonds, allowing social workers to understand each child's needs and concerns on a deeper level. Such ongoing support reinforces a child's sense of stability and willingness to participate openly (Bainbridge, 2015).

#### *Ensuring Meaningful Legal Recognition*

To ensure meaningful legal recognition, professionals must challenge assumptions and actively engage children in decision-making processes. This starts by providing children with clear and accessible information about their rights and the processes that affect them, helping them understand the implications of decisions being made (Lundy & McEvoy, 2011). Social workers should also offer developmentally appropriate opportunities for children to express their views (Gal, 2015). Tools like illustrated guides or interactive digital platforms can aid children in understanding complex legal procedures, empowering them to participate more effectively. Legal recognition goes beyond simply listening to children; it involves ensuring that their perspectives are given genuine consideration in decision-making. Social workers need to be ready to adjust outcomes based on children's input, ensuring their participation has a tangible impact (Lundy, 2007). This requires a shift from merely acknowledging children's voices to incorporating them actively into decisions. For instance, research by Schofield et al. (2011) indicated that children are more likely to engage meaningfully in care planning when they believe their contributions will influence the final outcome. By respecting and valuing children's voices, child protection systems can uphold their participation rights and support the development of their self-respect.

Upholding children's participation rights also means actively implementing legal frameworks that guarantee their right to be heard. Social workers must not only recognise these rights but also make concerted efforts to include children's

**Box 1.4 Reflective Questions for Social Workers: Ensuring Meaningful Legal Recognition**

How effectively do I provide clear and accessible information about children's rights and the decision-making processes that affect them, ensuring they understand the implications?

Am I creating developmentally appropriate opportunities for children to express their views, and how do I ensure their input is genuinely considered and reflected in the final decisions?

In what ways do I offer feedback to children about how their contributions influenced the outcomes, and how can I improve this to reinforce their sense of agency and self-respect?

perspectives in the decision-making process (Falch-Eriksen et al., 2021). This involves moving beyond tokenistic consultation, ensuring that children's views are taken seriously and integrated into final decisions. Social workers should provide child-friendly explanations of legal processes, use age-appropriate language, and offer feedback on how children's input influenced the outcome (Schofield et al., 2011). For instance, after a child participates in a case conference, it's important to explain the results to them and clarify how their views were considered in the final decision.

#### *Building Solidarity*

To build solidarity, social workers should ensure that children's participation is authentic and influences the decision-making process in a meaningful way. This requires a cultural shift in child protection systems, ensuring children are seen as active participants with valuable insights rather than passive recipients of care (Barnes, 2012). It is essential for social workers to create environments where children feel their contributions are valued and that their participation truly makes a difference. Key strategies for fostering solidarity include involving children at every stage of decision-making, from assessment to planning and review. Social workers should ensure that children's views are reflected in the final decisions and provide feedback on how their input shaped the outcomes (Schofield et al., 2011). Recognising and valuing children's contributions not only affirms their role as active participants but also enhances their sense of agency and self-esteem (Houston & Montgomery, 2017).

Beyond individual decision-making, social workers can support solidarity through child-led advocacy groups and peer support networks. These groups offer children a platform to express their views collectively, influencing policy and practice in the child protection system. Child-led advocacy empowers children to champion their rights while providing mutual support in the system. Additionally, peer mentorship programmes, in which older children mentor younger ones in care, can reinforce solidarity by fostering a sense of belonging

**Box 1.5 Reflective Questions for Social Workers: Building Solidarity**

How am I ensuring that children's contributions are valued and have a tangible impact on decisions, and what steps can I take to improve their involvement in all stages of decision-making?

Do I provide consistent feedback to children on how their views influenced outcomes, and how can I enhance this process to strengthen their sense of agency and self-esteem?

How can I better support child-led advocacy groups and peer support networks to empower children to influence policy and practice collectively, to foster a stronger sense of community and belonging?

and community. Social recognition, or solidarity, is achieved when children's views are valued and acted on in ways that affirm their role in decision-making (Rossiter, 2014). Ensuring that children's participation has a real impact not only builds their self-esteem but also reinforces their identity as valued participants in their care (Kauhanen & Kaukko, 2020). To create this culture of solidarity, social workers must provide consistent feedback on how children's input influenced decisions, demonstrating that their participation was both meaningful and respected (Toros et al., 2018).

## Breaking Down Barriers: A Case Study of Honneth's Recognition Theory in Practice

### *Background*

Ella, a 12-year-old girl, entered the child protection system due to neglect in her home. Ella's experience in the system initially mirrored many common barriers to meaningful participation: She felt ignored, misunderstood, and saw little influence of her views on the decisions that affected her life. Social workers responsible for her care appeared to view her as too young to contribute to decision-making, limiting her participation to brief, often tokenistic consultations.

### *Conceptual Barriers: Attitudes Towards Children's Participation*

At the beginning of her case, the social workers primarily consulted Ella's parents and other adults, believing Ella was too young to understand fully or contribute meaningfully. This aligns with the traditional view of childhood that sees children as passive recipients rather than capable agents. Ella's input was solicited only occasionally, and even then, it was not genuinely considered in case conferences. This lack of recognition left Ella feeling invisible and unimportant, diminishing her sense of self-worth and agency.

This approach denied Ella the social recognition needed for her development as a moral agent and active contributor, as outlined in Honneth's theory. The failure to recognise Ella's capabilities created frustration and disengagement, with her self-esteem negatively impacted by being sidelined in decisions about her care.

### *Practical Barriers: Lack of Resources and Skills for Meaningful Engagement*

In addition to conceptual barriers, practical challenges further limited Ella's participation. Social workers handling Ella's case were overburdened with high caseloads and constrained by tight deadlines. They did not have the time to engage in extended dialogue with Ella or build the trusting relationships required for her meaningful involvement. Moreover, Ella had a mild learning disability, which complicated communication, and the social workers lacked the training and tools to engage her in a way that was developmentally appropriate.

Without the necessary time and resources, Ella's views were not accurately understood, and she struggled to communicate her feelings. This lack of engagement was a form of practical non-recognition, which, according to Honneth, equates to a denial of solidarity. Ella's capacity to participate was not supported, further reinforcing her feelings of invisibility and disempowerment.

#### *Systemic Barriers: Power Imbalances and Structural Invisibility*

The systemic power imbalances in the child protection system exacerbated Ella's exclusion. Meetings were structured around adult authority, with social workers and caregivers dominating decision-making processes. Ella attended case conferences but rarely had the opportunity to speak, and when she did, her contributions were often overshadowed by the adults in the room.

In line with Honneth's theory, this power imbalance denied Ella the legal and social recognition necessary for her self-respect. Her invisibility in the process left her feeling disempowered, reinforcing her perception that her views were secondary and unimportant. The structural systems in place perpetuated this imbalance, offering few opportunities for Ella to participate as an equal partner in decisions about her care.

#### *Addressing the Barriers*

The turning point in Ella's case came when a new social worker, Diane, joined the team. Diane was trained in child-friendly communication techniques and committed to ensuring children's participation was meaningful. Recognising the conceptual barriers, Diane made a concerted effort to shift the attitudes of her colleagues, emphasising the importance of treating Ella as a capable contributor.

To address the practical barriers, Diane used storytelling and drawings to help Ella express her thoughts and feelings. She also advocated a reduced caseload, allowing her to dedicate more time to building a trusting relationship with Ella. Through regular check-ins outside of formal meetings, Ella began to open up more, and her views became clearer. With the right tools in place, Ella's participation became more meaningful.

Diane also worked to redistribute the power imbalances by ensuring that Ella's contributions received equal weight to those of the adults. She restructured case conferences to allow Ella to speak first, giving her the confidence to share her views without being overshadowed. Diane made sure that Ella received feedback after every meeting, explaining how her input influenced decisions, which helped to rebuild Ella's self-esteem and sense of agency.

#### *Outcome*

Over time, Ella's participation transformed. She became an active contributor to her care plans, and her input was reflected in the decisions made about her future. The shift in professional attitudes, investment in resources and

**Box 1.6 Reflective Questions for Social Workers: Overcoming Barriers**

Conceptual Barriers: How does my attitude towards children's participation influence the extent to which I recognise them as capable contributors in decision-making?
Practical Engagement: What steps can I take to ensure that I have the time and resources needed to engage meaningfully with children, especially those with additional communication needs like Ella?
Communication Techniques: How can I incorporate child-friendly communication tools, such as storytelling or drawings, to help children express their thoughts and feelings more comfortably and clearly?
Addressing Power Imbalances: How can I ensure that children's voices receive equal weight in case conferences or meetings, rather than being overshadowed by adults' opinions?
Feedback and Recognition: How can I provide children with regular feedback on how their input influenced decisions, in order to help them rebuild their self-esteem and sense of agency, as seen in Ella's case?

communication tools, and efforts to balance power dynamics ensured that Ella's voice was recognised and valued. This recognition significantly improved Ella's self-esteem and belief in her ability to influence decisions about her life.

Ella's case highlights how overcoming conceptual, practical, and systemic barriers to participation and recognition can lead to more empowering outcomes for children in the child protection system. By aligning practice with Honneth's recognition theory, social workers can ensure that children like Ella are treated as capable agents, fostering their development as valued contributors to the decisions that affect their lives.

## Implications for Social Work Practice

Honneth's theory emphasises that social work practice must focus on not only children's legal right to participate but also the emotional and social recognition needed to ensure they feel valued and capable. For children in child welfare, this means enhancing:

- **Self-Confidence (Emotional Recognition)**: Offer emotional support to create a safe space where children feel comfortable expressing their thoughts and feelings.
- **Policy and Culture**: Establish environments that consistently encourage and value children's voices.
- **Training and Skill Development**: Equip social workers with the skills needed to engage children meaningfully.
- **Self-Respect (Legal Recognition)**: Regard children as individuals with legal rights who are entitled to have their perspectives considered in decisions that affect them.

- **UNCRC-Aligned Legislation**: Ensure social workers adhere to laws that safeguard children's rights.
- **Inclusive Decision-Making**: Integrate children's input into the outcomes of decisions.
- **Self-Esteem (Social Recognition)**: Recognise children's contributions to bolster their self-esteem and affirm their role as valued members of society.
- **Civic Inclusion and Respect**: Foster a sense of belonging by treating children's contributions with respect and importance.

### Conclusion: A Call for Recognition-Based Participation

Children's participation in child protection decision-making is not merely a legal right but a moral obligation. Honneth's recognition theory offers a valuable framework for understanding the importance of recognising children as active participants in these processes. The need for recognition goes beyond legal entitlements—it extends into emotional and social domains, emphasising that children must be acknowledged not only as legal subjects but as whole people with unique perspectives, feelings, and capacities. Ensuring that children receive emotional, legal, and social recognition allows social workers to create a system in which children are empowered to shape their futures and their voices are genuinely valued (Cashmore et al., 2023). This means not merely allowing children to be present in decision-making spaces but actively encouraging and facilitating their meaningful participation. When children are encouraged to communicate in ways that are comfortable for them, their participation becomes more authentic, increasing the likelihood that their voices will shape the outcomes of the decisions being made.

For participation to be meaningful, it must be rooted in a genuine recognition of children's abilities, rights, and contributions (Keddell, 2023). This requires a profound shift in both mindset and practice. Social workers need to move beyond viewing children as passive recipients of protection and instead embrace their role as facilitators of children's participation. This helps them build trust and gives children the opportunity to clarify any concerns or preferences they may have. Such practices foster an environment where children's views are respected and their agency is acknowledged.

Moreover, recognition-based participation means creating structures in which children are not only heard but also integral to the decision-making process. This tangible involvement demonstrates that their input is not only valued but also central to shaping decisions. These practices exemplify a commitment to moving away from tokenistic approaches that treat children's participation as a checkbox exercise and towards a system that treats children as legitimate partners in determining their future.

Only through recognition-based approaches can we avoid tokenism and build a child protection system that genuinely respects and incorporates children's voices. Recognition enables social workers to create a space where children are not only heard but also have a tangible influence on decisions regarding their care. By integrating recognition into the core of child protection practices, social workers can build a more equitable system. This shift is not merely about policy reform or new procedural standards but also about transforming the culture in child protection services to ensure that every child is recognised as a vital contributor to shaping the outcomes of their lives. Only then can we truly fulfil the promise of children's rights and create a system in which their participation is respected, valued, and impactful (McCafferty & Mercado García, 2024).

## References

Bainbridge, A. (2015). Pedagogy of recognition: Winnicott, Honneth and learning in psychosocial spaces. *Journal of Pedagogic Development*, *5*(3), 9–20.

Balsells, M. Á., Fuentes-Pelaez, N., & Pastor, C. (2017). Listening to the voices of children in decision-making: A challenge for the child protection system in Spain. *Children and Youth Services Review*, *79*, 418–425. https://doi.org/10.1016/j.childyouth.2017.06.055

Barnes, V. (2012). Social work and advocacy with young people: Rights and care in practice. *British Journal of Social Work*, *42*(7), 1275–1292. https://doi.org/10.1093/bjsw/bcr142

Berrick, J. D., Dickens, J., Pösö, T., & Skivenes, M. (2015). Children's involvement in care order decision-making: A cross-country analysis. *Child Abuse & Neglect*, *49*, 128–141. https://doi.org/10.1016/j.chiabu.2015.07.001

Bessell, S. (2011). Participation in decision making in out-of-home care in Australia: What do young people say? *Children and Youth Services Review*, *33*(4), 496–501. https://doi.org/10.1016/j.childyouth.2010.05.006

Bouma, H., López, M. L., Knorth, E. J., & Grietens, H. (2018). Meaningful participation for children in the Dutch child protection system: A critical analysis of relevant provisions in policy documents. *Child Abuse & Neglect*, *79*, 279–292. https://doi.org/10.1016/j.chiabu.2018.02.016

Bunting, L., Montgomery, L., Mooney, S., MacDonald, M., Coulter, S., Hayes, D., & Davidson, G. (2019). Trauma-informed child welfare systems—A rapid evidence review. *International Journal of Environmental Research and Public Health*, *16*(13), 2365. https://doi.org/10.3390/ijerph16132365

Cashmore, J., Kong, P., & McLaine, M. (2023). Children's participation in care and protection decision-making matters. *Laws*, *12*(3), 49. https://doi.org/10.3390/laws12030049

Children Act, UK Public General Acts, c. 41 (1989). https://www.legislation.gov.uk/ukpga/1989/41/contents

Dillon, J., Greenop, D., & Hills, M. (2016). Participation in child protection: A small-scale qualitative study. *Qualitative Social Work*, *15*(1), 70–85. https://doi.org/10.1177/1473325015578946

Falch-Eriksen, A., Toros, K., Sindi, I., & Lehtme, R. (2021). Children expressing their views in child protection casework: Current research and their rights going forward. *Child & Family Social Work*, *26*(3), 485–497. https://doi.org/10.1111/cfs.12831

Gal, T. (2015). From social exclusion to child-inclusive policies: Toward an ecological model of child participation. In T. Gal & B. Duramy (Eds.), *International perspectives and empirical findings on child participation: From social exclusion to child-inclusive policies* (pp. 451–463). Oxford University Press.

Hansen, H. A., Westerhof, L., & Gerdts-Andresen, T. (2024). From frozen words to dialogue: Turning around involuntary relationships in social work practice. *Nordic Social Work Research*. Advance online publication. https://doi.org/10.1080/2156857X.2024.2395938

Honneth, A. (1995). *The struggle for recognition: The moral grammar of social conflicts*. Polity Press.
Houston, S. (2015). When I look, I am seen, so I exist to change: Supplementing Honneth's recognition model for social work. *Social Work & Society*, *13*(2). https://ejournals.bib.uni-wuppertal.de/index.php/sws/article/view/437
Houston, S., & Montgomery, L. (2017). Reflecting critically on contemporary social pathologies: Social work and the "good life." *Critical and Radical Social Work*, *5*(2), 181–196. https://doi.org/10.1332/204986016X14811848967494
Husby, I. S. D., Slettebø, T., & Juul, R. (2018). Partnerships with children in child welfare: The importance of trust and pedagogical support. *Child & Family Social Work*, *23*(3), 443–450. https://doi.org/10.1111/cfs.12435
Kauhanen, I., & Kaukko, M. (2020). Recognition in the lives of unaccompanied children and youth: A review of the key European literature. *Child & Family Social Work*, *25*(4), 875–883. https://doi.org/10.1111/cfs.12772
Keddell, E. (2023). Recognising the embedded child in child protection: Children's participation, inequalities and cultural capital. *Children and Youth Services Review*, *147*, 106815. https://doi.org/10.1016/j.childyouth.2023.106815
Kennan, D., Brady, B., & Forkan, C. (2018). Supporting children's participation in decision making: A systematic literature review exploring the effectiveness of participatory processes. *The British Journal of Social Work*, *48*(7), 1985–2002. https://doi.org/10.1093/bjsw/bcx142
Kosher, H., & Ben-Arieh, A. (2020). Children's participation: A new role for children in the field of child maltreatment. *Child Abuse & Neglect*, *110*, 104429. https://doi.org/10.1016/j.chiabu.2020.104429
Lindahl, R. (2021). Individualising or categorising recognition? Conceptual discussions concerning the relationship between foster children and their child welfare workers. *European Journal of Social Work*, *24*(4), 566–577. https://doi.org/10.1080/13691457.2019.1696755
Lundy, L. (2007). "Voice" is not enough: Conceptualising Article 12 of the United Nations Convention on the Rights of the Child. *British Educational Research Journal*, *33*(6), 927–942. https://doi.org/10.1080/01411920701657033
Lundy, L., & McEvoy, L. (2011). Children's rights and research processes: Assisting children to (in)formed views. *Childhood*, *19*(1), 129–144. https://doi.org/10.1177/0907568211409078
Marshall, G., Winter, K., & Turney, D. (2020). Honneth and positive identity formation in residential care. *Child & Family Social Work*, *25*(4), 733–741. https://doi.org/10.1111/cfs.12749
McCafferty, P. (2017). Implementing Article 12 of the United Nations Convention on the Rights of the Child in child protection decision making: A critical analysis of the challenges and opportunities for social work. *Child Care in Practice*, *23*(4), 327–341. https://doi.org/10.1080/13575279.2016.1264368
McCafferty, P. (2024). Children's participation in child welfare decision making: Recognising dichotomies, conceptualising critically informed solutions. *Child Care in Practice*, *30*(2), 112–129. https://doi.org/10.1080/13575279.2021.1896990
McCafferty, P., Duffy, J., & Hayes, D. (2021). Permanency decisions in child welfare: A qualitative study. *The British Journal of Social Work*, *51*(6), 2134–2154. https://doi.org/10.1093/bjsw/bcab095
McCafferty, P., & Mercado García, E. (2024). Children's participation in child welfare: A systematic review of systematic reviews. *The British Journal of Social Work*, *54*(3), pp. 1092–1108.
McMellon, C., & Tisdall, E. K. M. (2020). Children and young people's participation rights: Looking backwards and moving forwards. *The International Journal of Children's Rights*, *28*(1), 157–182. https://doi.org/10.1093/bjsw/bcad167
Mitchell, M. (2021). The value of recognition theory to family group conferencing and child-care and protection. *British Journal of Social Work*, *51*(6), 2191–2209. https://doi.org/10.1093/bjsw/bcaa207

Mitchell, M. (2022). "Because I'm a kid…": The struggle for recognition of children and young people involved in child and family social work. *Child & Family Social Work*, *27*(3), 526–534. https://doi.org/10.1111/cfs.12905

Niemi, P. (2021). Recognition and the other in social work. *The British Journal of Social Work*, *51*(7), 2802–2818. https://doi.org/10.1093/bjsw/bcaa023

Nunes, R. R. (2021). Participation in child protection: Empowering children in placement processes. *The International Journal of Human Rights*, *26*(3), 420–436. https://doi.org/10.1080/13642987.2021.1931137

Patmisari, E., McLaren, H., & Jones, M. (2024). Reconsidering recognition in the lives of children and young people in care: Insights from the Mockingbird Family in South Australia. *Social Sciences*, *13*(2), 81. https://doi.org/10.3390/socsci13020081

Rossiter, A. (2014). Axel Honneth's theory of recognition and its potential for aligning social work with social justice. *Critical and Radical Social Work*, *2*(1), 93–108. https://doi.org/10.1332/204986014X13912564145762

Schofield, G., Moldestad, B., Höjer, I., Ward, E., Skilbred, D., Young, J., & Havik, T. (2011). Managing loss and a threatened identity: Experiences of parents of children growing up in foster care, the perspectives of their social workers and implications for practice. *British Journal of Social Work*, *41*(1), 74–92. https://doi.org/10.1093/bjsw/bcq073

Shuttleworth, P. D. (2023). Recognition of family life by children living in kinship care arrangements in England. *The British Journal of Social Work*, *53*(1), 157–176. https://doi.org/10.1093/bjsw/bcac114

Skauge, B., Storhaug, A. S., & Marthinsen, E. (2021). The what, why and how of child participation—A review of the conceptualization of "child participation" in child welfare. *Social Sciences*, *10*(2), 54. https://doi.org/10.3390/socsci10020054

Thomas, N. (2012). Love, rights and solidarity: Studying children's participation using Honneth's theory of recognition. *Childhood*, *19*(4), 453–466. https://doi.org/10.1177/0907568211434604

Toros, K. (2021). A systematic review of children's participation in child protection decision-making: Tokenistic presence or not? *Children and Society*, *35*(3), 395–411. https://doi.org/10.1111/chso.12418

Toros, K., DiNitto, D. M., & Tiko, A. (2018). Family engagement in the child welfare system: A scoping review. *Children and Youth Services Review*, *88*, 598–607. https://doi.org/10.1016/j.childyouth.2018.03.011

United Nations. (1989). *Convention on the rights of the child*. https://www.ohchr.org/en/instruments-mechanisms/instruments/convention-rights-child

van Bijleveld, G. G., Dedding, C. W., & Bunders-Aelen, J. F. (2015). Children's and young people's participation within child welfare and child protection services: A state-of-the-art review. *Child & Family Social Work*, *20*(2), 129–138. https://doi.org/10.1111/cfs.12082

Warming, H. (2015). The life of children in care in Denmark: A struggle over recognition. *Childhood*, *22*(2), 248–262. https://doi.org/10.1177/0907568214522838

Wilson, S., Hean, S., Abebe, T., & Heaslip, V. (2020). Children's experiences with child protection services: A synthesis of qualitative evidence. *Children and Youth Services Review*, *113*, 104974. https://doi.org/10.1016/j.childyouth.2020.104974

Winnicott, D. W. (1965). *The maturational processes and the facilitating environment: Studies in the theory of emotional development*. Hogarth Press.

Woodman, E., Roche, S., & McArthur, M. (2022). Children's participation in child protection—How do practitioners understand children's participation in practice? *Child & Family Social Work*, *28*(1), 125–135. https://doi.org/10.1111/cfs.12947

# 2 Bourdieu's Application to Children's Rights in Social Work with Children and Young People

## Common Sense, Clarity, and a Feel for the Game

*Jo Dillon*

### Introduction

In child protection social work, children and their circumstances are unique, often lacking in clarity and requiring a subjective view. For social workers, the dominant discourse is safeguarding, and in certain circumstances, identifying, predicting, and analysing risk of harm may be straightforward. Once established, social workers can offer appropriate support, money, and access to services for the child and family. Although social workers regularly assign risk of harm as the dominant discourse, the deeper layers and lived experiences of children and families create alternative, competing discourses from a service user perspective, leading to a false clarity. With children and their parents often excluded from iterative participatory processes, their progression in the field of child protection is curtailed and their experiences and opinions unheard. Lack of clarity is evident in what children and families do not know about their child protection planning.

Using Bourdieu's (1990) concepts of social space (field) and *illusio*, this chapter explores how common sense and clarity practice for social workers and related actors may be new and confusing to children and parents with no previous experience of social work. For children who may already have a feel for the game (illusio), the "rhetoric of participation does not sit easily within statutory child protection services, particularly when the child is an involuntary high-risk client" (Dillon et al., 2016, p. 75). This chapter, therefore, suggests creative ways in which children can gain clarity and meaningfully participate in their child protection planning.

### Methods

This chapter builds on the findings of a 3-year longitudinal qualitative study designed to explore how children and parents meaningfully participate in their family's child protection planning and how social workers and participation workers routinely embed participation into practice (Dillon, 2019, 2021). Creative methods were employed alongside semistructured interviews with children (aged 8–12 years) and parents, all of whom had child protection plans

DOI: 10.4324/9781003582410-4

in place at that time. Qualitative interviews were also conducted with child protection social workers, alongside a focus group of participation workers (or advocates). All participants were involved with three local authorities in the United Kingdom.

The work of Bourdieu spans a wide spectrum of topics, including art, education, class, deprivation, the state, and housing (Bourdieu & Wacquant, 1992). Although rejecting the notion of him as a theorist, Bourdieu encouraged his work to be used as a tool to make sense of situations and problems (Webb et al., 2002). Covering two epistemological strands—the logic of practice and reflexivity—Bourdieu's concepts can be used to think more deeply about social work practice rather than to identify problems, which is often overlooked in a time of fast-paced, risk-focused child protection social work.

## The Field of Child Protection

The global literature on participation in child and family social work has highlighted the conflict between encouraging and embedding children's meaningful participation in child protection processes, urging they be sheltered from the stark reality of abuse (Sanders & Mace, 2006). Balancing children's rights alongside the requirements for adults to safeguard has introduced children as social actors able to respond to their environments (Cossar et al., 2016) and whose strengths and experiences of child protection are both a resource and meaningful contribution (Richards-Schuster & Pritzker, 2015). However, their placement in the field of child protection needs further scrutiny to understand how social workers can better bestow children with the capital needed to be an agent, or player, in this space.

Social space, or field, is constructed by the placement of agents in accordance with the level of capital that they hold—e.g., cultural capital (what they know) and economic capital (the wealth they hold). The location of each agent in the field is such that "the closer they are to one another ... the more they have in common; and the more remote they are from one another, the less they have in common. Spatial differences on paper are equivalent to social distances" (Bourdieu, 1998, p. 6). In the United Kingdom, the field of child protection social work involves common actors and agencies tasked with the challenges of safeguarding and sharing power in a social space where service user presence is involuntary. All actors have a reason for their position in this social space, the statutory nature of the child protection investigation requiring agencies come together to "bring their agency perspective, expertise ... to challenge and contribute to decisions about actual or likely significant harm" (Department for Education, 2023, p. 95). In child and family social work, leading practitioners come from local authority (e.g., children's services, education, housing services, family support, drug and alcohol services, and legal teams), National Health Service (e.g., specialist child abuse paediatricians, school nurses, services for children with disabilities, doctors), the police, and voluntary sector services.

All actors and agencies are strategically positioned in the field of child protection, associated relationally and connected primarily through difference (Bourdieu, 1998; Dillon et al., 2021). Agents appearing closer in this social space is representative of commonalities, connections, and capital (Bourdieu, 1989), with the field using high or low positioning to signify influence and power. The local authority, therefore, occupies the most dominant position in the field, possessing a mass of cultural and economic capital combined with duties (and power) enshrined in law (Dillon et al., 2021). Its authority to pursue (Child Protection investigations) (Children Act, 1989) without parental consent reinforces that the progression of the child and family in the field of child protection is curtailed due to the balance of power being tipped towards the state (Ney et al., 2013). In the field of child protection, the child and family often languish at the bottom, the most isolated and dominated actors in this social space who are also constructed as the least knowledgeable (Emirbayer & Williams, 2005).

## Navigating the Field

Distribution and movement in the field of child protection is wholly dependent on the type and structure of capital held by each actor or agency (Bourdieu, 1989). Actors gain privilege as they accrue resources or knowledge (Emirbayer & Williams, 2005); therefore, children and parents who fail to demonstrate an understanding of and a response to safeguarding concerns will have less opportunity to progress in this field than those who do. Ensuring that children and their parents have opportunities to participate meaningfully in child protection proceedings can add weight to their level and structure of capital; service users becoming more aware of both their human and legal rights and how they can challenge decisions made on their behalf. Yet research continues to highlight barriers to child participation, such as diminishing practitioner skills and knowledge (Dillon, 2021), a conflation of rights versus maturity (McCafferty, 2017), and children (and parents) lacking clarity regarding their (mostly involuntary) presence in the field (Dillon et al., 2016).

### *Illusio: A Feel for the High-Stakes Game*

The concept of illusio, derived from the Latin word "ludus," was used by Bourdieu and Wacquant (1992) to compare a social field to that of a game. The involved actors, or agents, are seriously invested in the illusio, with its high stakes and "playworthiness" being mutually accepted for all involved (Emirbayer & Williams, 2005). For any parent working with statutory child welfare services globally, there is a non-negotiable expectation that the safety of their child is paramount. In United Kingdom-based child and family social work, there is also an underlying acknowledgement that if harm is not reduced, the child will be removed from their parents' care (Dillon et al., 2021). With such high stakes from the outset, the field of child protection rapidly exposes children and parents (often new players of the game; Bourdieu & Wacquant, 1992) to social work jargon and an invisible rule book supposedly detailing expected behaviours and etiquette without an adequate level of prior explanation. The absence of United Kingdom-based statutory guidance for participation, coupled with scant participatory instructions scattered throughout documents like *Working Together to Safeguard Children* (Department for Education, 2023), results in children and their parents being unequal game players; they remain uninformed, lack capital, and are unable to progress in the field. Collaboration and play by all actors in the illusio of child protection is crucial; social work assessments often involve commentary on, criticism of, or praise of the level of engagement (or non-engagement) between parents and the multiagency team. However, there are differing levels of interest amongst the players of the game. Whereas some families may take serious investment in the illusio for granted, others will have no concept of the rules, game etiquette, or their presence in this field. This indifferent, rather than disinterested, person "does not see why they are playing," having neither the principles of vision nor division necessary to make distinctions and is neither moved nor affected by the context of the field (Bourdieu, 1998, p. 77). The high-stakes game that is common sense to the social worker lacks clarity and context for other players.

### *The Child Protection Case Conference*

In the social field of United Kingdom-based child protection, other smaller fields emerge—for example, the child protection case conference. Lead practitioners attending a case conference are often familiar to one another, having worked together with other children or been based in the same location; these commonalities create friendships and connections. In contrast, parents may have established limited relationships with one or two conference attendees—for example, family support workers or school pastoral managers—but are unfamiliar with the conference chair, school nurse, or police representatives. With research continuing to evidence that children's participation in child protection is influenced by the quality of their relationship with their social worker (Dillon et al., 2016; Kennan et al., 2018), this relationship may not extend to the lead child protection practitioners, and relative strangers end up making significant decisions on the child's behalf (Dillon, 2021). Therefore, in the field of the child protection case conference, the child has the fewest connections and commonalities and the least amount of power and clarity.

Despite professionals' duty to inform (Muench et al., 2017) and the clear remit of the role of child protection chairperson as detailed in the United Kingdom's statutory guidance document *Working Together to Safeguard Children* (Department for Education, 2023), children often rely on their parents for information (Dillon, 2021). Objective structures "independent of the consciousness and will of agents" (Bourdieu, 1989, p. 14) are reproduced: People are not creating the system; instead, the system is creating them (Webb et al., 2002). Although agency is assumed, the child and family have clear, restrictive boundaries in place. The outcome of the case conference denotes rigid commands for change, allowing children and parents to share their opinions meaningfully yet unable to leave the confines of the process (or structure) without permission. Although striving to be inclusive, case conferences can restrain child participation due to the capital held by practitioners and the non-explicit rules of the illusio (Bourdieu, 1989). Missed opportunities for social workers to build on their connections with children using bespoke resources and unique communication methods leads to repetitive questioning and duplicated work (Cossar et al., 2016; Dillon, 2021; Richardson Foster et al., 2021) and can ultimately contribute to poor relationships and mistrust between social workers and children.

Flemmen (2013) interpreted Bourdieu's structure of social space as continuous; there are no breaks or boundaries. However, in the field of the child protection case conference, the child, their parents, and the advocate are not allowed to participate in decision-making; the local authority and accompanying lead practitioners retain this power, thus creating a boundary. Indeed, in this study's focus group, participation workers discussed an initial child protection case conference during which no evidence of significant harm was presented, yet all attending lead practitioners still voted for the instigation of a child protection plan. As a result, children (and their parents) remain unheard and practitioners fail to assign weight to their opinions, perpetuating a negative cycle of practice until the child's voice disappears entirely (McCafferty, 2017). The dominant discourse of safeguarding permits this poor social work practice, emphasising the power (and capital) of the practitioner and placing them as the expert in the field of child protection. Parent 1, for example, when asked who has the most power in the triad of social worker, parent, and child quickly identified the practitioner as expert:

> The social worker. Then it's the social worker and then it's the social worker. Me and my kids are just nowhere. The social worker will say something, and the social worker will get what they want. We get nothing. Don't even get listened to.

**Case Study: Navigating the Field of Child Protection**

In traditional United Kingdom-based child protection case conferences, children and their parents must leave the room while the police share confidential intelligence (including historical contexts, convictions, or connections to others) with the lead practitioners. Practitioners follow the rules and etiquette of the case conference (common-sense practice) and use this intelligence to inform their decision-making, yet the context (and clarity) of this is absent for the child and their parents.

This research study highlighted further complexity when participation workers (staff that are employed to facilitate the participation of children and families specifically) revealed that they also remain in the room while this confidential information is shared. Already holding a more significant amount of

**Box 2.1 Reflective Questions for Social Workers: Role of Participation Workers**

Take time to consider:

What is the role of a participation worker (or advocate) in child and family social work?
Does this role sit comfortably in a position of power (or increased capital)?
How can this power be more evenly shared in the situation highlighted here?

cultural capital due to their knowledge and experiences of child protection processes and their employment by the local authority, participation workers now know information that the child and family may not, increasing their capital further. Not only does this create a potential conflict of interest, but it also exacerbates the imbalance of power because given the participation workers' limited authority their presence can only serve to benefit the decision-makers.

Although participation workers and social workers gather and give weight to children's opinions on actions taken and services provided (often referred to as "wishes and feelings"; Children Act, 1989, s.17, s.47), the role and purpose of each practitioner is different, as highlighted by a social worker and participant worker: "We're not really decision-makers. We are repeating what people are telling us but using good assessment skills to get that information and good engagement skills" (Participation Worker 1). "That [participation] worker is there solely to echo the voice of the child, and I think that's very important in the whole process" (Social Worker 1).

The participation worker, therefore, illuminates the children's opinions (wishes and feelings) throughout proceedings, while the social worker designs an appropriate response, or action. The participation workers in this study spoke passionately about trying to address the imbalance of power in case conferences, focusing on the redistribution of capital to vulnerable young people through advocacy and creative direct work (Feldman et al., 2016). This led, however, to cries of "conference coaching" being thrown from lead practitioners towards participation workers, whose goal was simply to explain etiquette and provide clarity as a means of empowering and enabling children and parents to "play the game." This example of good practice is eloquently summarised by McGhee and Waterhouse (2017), who stated that "in child protection, social workers are intermediaries akin to that described by Levi-Strauss as between the 'powers above and humanity below'" (p. 1662).

A truly independent advocacy service is non-judgemental, unbiased, and transparent, with information shared with the participation workers on a need-to-know basis only. However, in this study, social workers and participation workers debated the practice implications of the independent advocacy offered in their local authority. For example, the participation workers described themselves as independent, yet they were employed by the local authority, were based in local authority offices, and wore matching local authority lanyards with ID badges. Ironically, despite their power to remain in a case conference and hear confidential information, they are not allowed to participate in any decision-making and have no authority or power to decide whether a child becomes the subject of a child protection plan. Adhering to the values of advocacy, participation workers could choose to leave the case conference during confidential police intelligence sharing. This brings the distance from information among participation workers, children, and parents closer together, reflecting their status more as equals in the case conference field.

## The "Dangling" of Power

In the United Kingdom, statutory guidance for child and family social work recommends that "where possible, children should be seen alone" (Department for Education, 2023, p. 53). The initial visit to the child is often undertaken without any previous knowledge of, or relationship with, the child, which is clearly an odd situation. This sudden intrusion into family life by "stranger" social workers can provoke negative reactions from children, ranging from resignation to anger (Dillon et al., 2016). In this study, Social Worker 2 reflected on their practice, stating, "I try and remember as well, it's weird that a stranger walks into your house and takes you off on your own and talks to you." The imbalance of power in child and family social work is also evident in child protection enquiries that commence with an involuntary investigation by social workers and police, often without the knowledge of the parent or the child. Although this duty to intervene in private and family life is enshrined in law (Children Act, 1989, s.47), it would be rare for lead practitioners to spend time reflecting on this power dynamic following an intense investigation of potential harm, especially when concerns are unsubstantiated. Smith et al.'s (2017) research noted the precedence given to evidence collection over relationship building with children during full criminal investigations because the police retain responsibility for the investigation (Ministry for Justice, 2022). Although trained social workers can conduct investigative interviews with children, there is minimal time to build a relationship, or rapport, with children if they are not known to the local authority. With many investigative interviews leading to decisions of no further action, the experience of reliving an emotional or chaotic situation may be traumatic for the child (Smith et al., 2017)—and is often never again addressed by the social worker due to the closure of the case.

Participating social workers in this research study who had the longest and most varied experience (Social Workers 1, 2, and 3) identified the parent as the most powerful actor in the field of child protection. The more newly qualified social workers (Social Workers 4 and 5) identified themselves as having the most power. Social Worker 5 said that the power imbalance between social worker and child or parent can be lessened by only asserting power when necessary, although it cannot be evidenced that this dangling of power adds any weight or volume to child or parent capital:

> There's always an imbalance of power. But it's how you try not to use that on a constant basis. It's about picking the time, the right time, to say, "Hang on a minute, you know, ... your child is on a child protection plan. The local authority has got concerns, and you need to do this." And not giving them options.
>
> (Social Worker 5)

The dangling of power between actors and agencies in the field of child protection can be illustrated through Bourdieu's linguistic *habitus* (Aguilar & Sen, 2009, p. 432). Differences in articulation, accents, and even the use of silence at appropriate parts of the process can influence and elevate the actor's positioning in the field (Aguilar & Sen, 2009), along with the ability to understand social work jargon. Power is ascribed to language when used in certain ways by certain people (Webb et al., 2002). The overuse of acronyms in social work such as LAC (looked-after children) and CIN (child in need) can frustrate both service users and practitioners, particularly when the acronym has derogatory connotations (e.g., LAC = lack, CIN = sin). Buzzwords or phrases such as "wishes and feelings," "direct work," and "child's voice" become conflated, confused, and used interchangeably (Dillon et al., 2022). Bourdieu (1990) described language as "a system of objective relations which makes possible both the production and the decoding of discourse" (p. 30)—acceptable (and common sense) for those rich in capital in the field of child protection but oppressive (and lacking clarity) to those with little capital. Among children and parents embroiled in child protection social work, there remains an acceptance of this dominance, with dominated people complying because it's just the way it is (Bourdieu, 1999). For example, this research study's findings indicate that practitioners noted the struggle for parents to understand formal language used in child protection documentation. The default position in child and family social work is often an expectation for children and families to learn the new language, as opposed to the profession amending it: "If you want a parent to stop hitting their child, write on the plan, 'You must not hit your child!' It does not need to say 'discombobulation' and all that crap" (Participation Worker 1).

Participation Worker 1 also recalled their work with a parent who was negatively documented in reports as an "aggressive mother," even though the parent simply had a very loud speaking voice. Bodies and voices, therefore, are instruments of cultural capital (Garrett, 2007a).

Bourdieu's (1999) research into social welfare and deprivation revealed a *doxa* among dominated groups: People were unaware of their oppression or imbalance of power yet knowledgeable about the struggles that their families faced daily. Doxa permeates everyday language and thought processes, often via the media. People begin to repeat slogans, statements, or sentiments as facts or internalised truths until they become real and accepted. The most feared yet often unspoken doxa of child protection is the implicit knowledge that social workers "take children away." Although a child protection plan provides appropriate levels of support for children and families, many still view social work intervention as a precursor to removing children.

> And that overrides every other thing before you start any piece of work; that is always in a parent's head. "I've got social workers; therefore, they're going to take my kids." So, there is an implied power just from that.
>
> (Social Worker 4)

Although the media (and increasingly social media) often blames social workers for their role in removing children from their parents' care, there is little understanding that the power of social workers in the United Kingdom is delegated from the Local Authority Social Services Act as a means of discharging its social work function (HM Government, 1970). Bourdieu (1991) succinctly summarised statutory power:

> If I, Pierre Bourdieu, a single and isolated individual, speak only for myself, say "you must do this or that, overthrow the government or refuse Pershing missiles," who will follow me? But if I am placed in statutory conditions such that I may appear as speaking "in the name of the masses" ... that changes everything.
>
> (p. 212)

The continued negative reporting in the media regarding social work intervention (headlines describing social workers as "baby snatchers" or accusations regarding "adoption to order") means child removal becomes a societally accepted subtext (Fram, 2004). This implied threat questions the validity and accrual of child or parent capital in the field of child protection. If the parents' decision to accrue capital is solely based on playing the game as a coerced player, the rules and game etiquette must have clarity.

To add further complexity, participation in the illusio of child protection needs to happen within timescales laid down by both statutory guidance (Department for Education, 2023) and the child protection chairperson. More than a decade ago, Munro (2011) acknowledged that parents need time to make changes to their parenting and recommended specific timescales for assessment, yet the threshold of child protection indicates that if significant risk of harm is present, change must happen now (or else). The rules of the child protection illusio create a visual of a chessboard clock being hit and reset after each player makes a move, and child participation is expected to fall in line with these timescales. Children, however, have agency (Cossar et al., 2016), meaning they can choose what to do and how to do it, despite the limitations placed on the rights of the child by the field of child protection (Dillon et al., 2022).

It is not only the field of child protection that affects the illusio. Poor social worker renumeration, high staff turnover, local authority budget cuts, and high caseloads heavily affect the services provided to vulnerable people (Ravalier et al., 2023). Austerity measures have forced local authorities to downsize in office space, with "hot-desking" becoming a hotly debated topic (Ravalier, 2019). In addition to influencing social workers' mental health and professional identity, it lessens opportunities for workers to chew over practice dilemmas with their colleagues. In Bourdieusian terms, "spatial distance then acts to affirm social distance" (Smith et al., 2017, p. 982). As space decreases, so does the workforce, and it becomes difficult for local authorities to protect caseloads for newly qualified social workers as recommended by the Department for Education. A survey by Community Care (Stevenson, 2018) involved interviews with 640 new social workers, 82% of whom were promised a protected caseload by their employers, yet 49% did not experiencing this outcome. A subsequent survey in 2022 reported that almost 25% of 62 participant social workers said their caseloads were completely unmanageable (Preston, 2022). In this research study (Dillon, 2019), social workers from one local authority used words such as "coping" and "flustered" when referring to their caseloads, with some indicating that their local authority's model of working across all thresholds (from duty and referral through adoption) was not working for them. Social Worker 4, for example, had 12 more children on their caseload as a newly qualified social worker than they were promised at their interview, resulting in political and social pressures in both a professional and personal context (Donovan et al., 2017). This is a concerning outcome when research has concluded that newly qualified social workers are less confident in speaking to children than their more experienced peers (Woodman et al., 2018). Garrett's (2007b) Bourdieusian depiction of the left hand (social work practice) versus the right hand (budget and finance restrictions) makes clear an internal tension, despite the inability to view the left hand's intentions as "unambiguously benign because this would mask the regulatory intent and practice of some of these interventions" (p. 371).

## Sharing the Power and Increasing Volume of Capital

In research by Križ and Roundtree-Swain (2017), findings showed that practitioners in the field of child protection were more likely to respect the opinion of children who engaged and showed respect for the workers. This is concerning. Although workers should indeed celebrate their positive and participatory relationships with children, social work should respect the right to self-determination (i.e., for the child not to participate, if they so choose) and focus on identifying the strengths in every relationship. In recognition of the Lundy (2007) model and findings from this research study, the adoption of Dillon et al.'s (2022, p. 9) participatory principles is a great starting point to embedding meaningful participation in child and family social work. For example:

- Children have the right to be included and consulted on any decisions that affect them, with their responses shaping subsequent actions.
- Every child has the right to a creative life and the ability to express their wishes and feelings in the manner they choose.
- Practitioners should recognise that all children are unique and have different preferences, qualities, and attributes. As such, every child will need an individual, bespoke approach to participation that does not rely on homogenous and standardised ways of working.
- Children have the right to redress and reflection.
- Practice should endeavour to build children's capital (the set of resources available to them—for example, power, knowledge, inclusion, safety, confidence, and agency).

**Case Study: Achieving Clarity for Children**

This chapter has thus far considered the positioning of actors and agencies in the field of child protection, along with the challenges for children and their parents in navigating this space. The illusio of child protection further complicates the navigation, with common-sense practice for lead practitioners lacking clarity for children and families. Drawing on the examples of participatory principles (Dillon et al., 2022), consider how small, common-sense tweaks to social work practice can add clarity, particularly for children.

In this research study, one child did not know the name of their social worker and only two children had the ability and resources to contact their social worker without their parents needing to be involved. None of the five children interviewed from one local authority had contact details for their advocate, despite the fact they were receiving advocacy. The research study produced no examples of child-friendly child protection plans or core group minutes shared with young children at any stage of the child protection process. All participating children except for one lacked clarity and understanding about their safety goals, as defined for them by their child protection core group and parents.

**Box 2.2 Reflective Questions for Social Workers: Principles of Child Participation**

Pause and reflect on these findings for a short while, reminding yourself of the principles of child participation.

How can children seek clarity or give their opinion on actions being taken or services provided if they are not connected to their social worker or do not have access to decisions made on their behalf?

If social workers are visiting only at times prearranged by them (e.g., statutory visits), how can children exercise their right to redress and reflection?

In a profession with competing demands, high caseloads, and consistent practitioner turnover, how can social workers create a bespoke approach to participation that does not rely on homogenous ways of working?

As adults, we have the right to reflect on decisions we make and change our minds. Yet if the children in this study changed their opinions on decisions made for them between visits, how could they contact their social worker or advocate? Are social workers providing opportunities for children to communicate at a time that suits the children, rather than the workers? If not, the children's cultural capital remains low, wholly dependent on their ability to remember their questions, opinions, and feelings at the time of the next (often unannounced) social work visit.

This study's findings evidence that children who lacked clarity and understanding of their child protection planning and decision-making felt angry and upset. Two children had intense feelings of anger towards practitioners due to not knowing why their routines were changing. Without knowing the safety goals and support planned for their families, children will struggle to connect to their plans and will be unable to link changes to their routine with actions designed for safety. The gathering of wishes and feelings requires action and repetition—seeking children's opinions, assigning weight to them, and acting and feeding back. They are part of an iterative process which needs to be revisited consistently as children's opinions change as circumstances change. The child's plan can then be updated.

Verbal conversations are great, if that is how the child chooses to communicate. However, with verbal conversations, it is harder to check back with the child. Having something—a story, poem, picture, photo, object, or video—enables the worker to say, "OK, so you were feeling this way about [the thing] when we last spoke. What has changed? Shall we update this [thing]?" This rechecking is important; children need redress and reflection, too (Dillon et al., 2022) and checking in again connects the child to the plan designed to keep them safe. Use of creative methods that enable children to record or communicate their opinions and feelings between visits can be a good foundation for "stranger" social work visits—e.g., when social workers go on annual leave or are sick or at another child's case conference. Having something that is iteratively and consistently used during relationship building avoids the stranger social worker from resorting to using a generic, black-and-white A4 printed template (e.g., "The Three Houses"; Bunn, 2013) for the sake of doing direct work. Creative work done with children on child protection plans should remain with the child and could provide a starting point for communication if social workers change (in this study, Rebecca had three social workers in an 18-month period); if the child moves to another local authority; or if plans change to align with child in need (Children Act, 1989, s.17) or early help guidelines. Along with ensuring the positive attribution of capital to the child and alleviating opportunities for self-blame (Winter, 2010), a creative pack of coproduced items can be utilised in all four sections of the revolutionising participation model: information sharing, wishes and feelings, relationship building, and decision-making (Dillon, 2021).

## Conclusion

For every actor entering a social field, Bourdieu (1998) stated that a commitment to and passion for the field, and the game (illusio), is a prerequisite. However, nothing stops the players from revolutionising the game and achieving better outcomes for all involved.

They may want to overturn the relations of force in the field, but for that very reason, they might grant recognition to the stakes; they are not indifferent. Wanting to undertake a revolution in a field is to accord the essential of what the field tacitly demands—namely, that it is important that the game played is sufficiently important for one to want to undertake a revolution in it (Bourdieu, 1998, p. 78).

Children and their parents who lack clarity on the presence and purpose of social workers in their lives are unequal (and involuntary) players in the illusio. Although the common-sense rules of the game are understood and exercised by lead practitioners (experienced in child protection investigations), the low level of capital held by children often leaves them languishing at the bottom of the field of child protection, devoid of the knowledge and actions needed to progress. More robust statutory guidance, in which clear expectations of practice and interpretations of legislation are succinctly explained, will better equip social workers who are already balancing the rights of the child (United Nations, 1989) with safety. Social workers must be careful to exercise their duties in the manner laid out in the Children Act (1989) rather than adopting a potentially skewed translation of legislation that may miss the elements of participation that the law originally intended (Dillon, 2021).

With the dangled threat of child removal being ever present, the etiquette of the illusio must be transparent, understood, and collaboratively pursued. Although the local authority will retain its ultimate power and responsibility for safeguarding, small tweaks to social work practice can enrich the capital held by children and enable them and their parents to be more equal players in the illusio. Participation in child and family social work must become clear, routine, and common sense, never viewed as "just more paperwork" in what was once a creative and innovative job. Bourdieu (1999) urged social workers to project hope and confidence, to fight for the oppressed and against administration and bureaucracy; without this fight, the dichotomy between participation and protection will continue to widen. With social workers expected to follow the policy directive, the buzzwords of participatory practice must not become "self-mystifying fictions that technocracy uses to give itself a bit of soul" (Bourdieu, 1999, p. 190).

## References

Aguilar, J. P., & Sen, S. (2009). Comparing conceptualizations of social capital. *Journal of Community Practice*, *17*(4), 424–443. https://doi.org/10.1080/10705420903299979

Bourdieu, P. (1989). *Social space and symbolic power*. Blackwell.

Bourdieu, P. (1990). *The logic of practice*. Polity Press.

Bourdieu, P. (1991). *The political ontology of Martin Heidegger*. Polity Press.

Bourdieu, P. (1998). *Practical reason: On the theory of action*. Polity Press.

Bourdieu, P. (1999). *The weight of the world: Social suffering in contemporary society*. Polity Press.

Bourdieu, P., & Wacquant, L. (1992). *An invitation to reflexive sociology*. University of Chicago Press.

Bunn, A. (2013). Three Houses tool. In *Signs of Safety in England: An NSPCC commissioned report on the Signs of Safety model in child protection* (pp. 30–31). NSPCC.
Children Act, UK Public General Acts, c. 41 (1989). https://www.legislation.gov.uk/ukpga/1989/41/contents
Cossar, J., Brandon, M., & Jordan, P. (2016). "You've got to trust her and she's got to trust you": Children's views on participation in the child protection system. *Child & Family Social Work*, *21*(1), 103–112. https://doi.org/10.1111/cfs.12115
Department for Education. (2023). *Working together to safeguard children*. HM Government.
Dillon, J. (2019). "Revolutionizing" participation in child protection proceedings [Doctoral thesis, Liverpool John Moores University]. https://researchonline.ljmu.ac.uk/id/eprint/10646/
Dillon, J. (2021). "Wishes and feelings": Misunderstandings and missed opportunities for participation in child protection proceedings. *Child & Family Social Work*, *26*(4), 664–676. https://doi.org/10.1111/cfs.12847
Dillon, J., Evans, F., & Kippen, R. (2022). *Enabling and embedding creative participation in child and family social work*. Dartington Trust. https://www.researchinpractice.org.uk/media/vd0idafe/enabling_and_embedding_pt_web.pdf
Dillon, J., Evans, F., & Wroe, L. (2021). COVID-19: Changing fields of social work practice with children and young people. *Critical and Radical Social Work*, *9*(2), 289–296. https://doi.org/10.1332/204986021X16109919842882
Dillon, J., Greenop, D., & Hills, M. (2016). Participation in child protection: A small-scale qualitative study. *Qualitative Social Work*, *15*(1), 70–85. https://doi.org/10.1177/1473325015578946
Donovan, J., Rose, D., & Connolly, M. (2017). A crisis of identity: Social work theorising at a time of change. *The British Journal of Social Work*, *47*(8), 22912307. https://doi.org/10.1093/bjsw/bcw180
Emirbayer, M., & Williams, E. M. (2005). *Bourdieu and social work*. The University of Chicago Press.
Feldman, G., Strier, R., & Schmid, H. (2016). The performative magic of advocacy organisations: The redistribution of symbolic capital. *The British Journal of Social Work*, *46*(6), 1759–1775. https://doi.org/10.1093/bjsw/bcv088
Flemmen, M. (2013). Putting Bourdieu to work for class analysis: Reflections on some recent contributions. *The British Journal of Sociology*, *64*(2), 325–343. https://doi.org/10.1111/1468-4446.12020
Fram, M. (2004). Research for progressive change: Bourdieu and social work. *Social Service Review*, *78*(4), 553–576. https://doi.org/10.1086/424544
Garrett, P. M. (2007a). Making social work more Bourdieusian: Why the social professions should critically engage with the work of Pierre Bourdieu. *European Journal of Social Work*, *10*(2), 225–243. https://doi.org/10.1080/13691450701318010
Garrett, P. M. (2007b). The relevance of Bourdieu for social work. *Journal of Social Work*, *7*(3), 355–379. https://doi.org/10.1177/1468017307084076
HM Government. (1970). *Local Authority Social Services Act*. Crown.
Kennan, D., Brady, B., & Forkan, C. (2018). Supporting children's participation in decision making: A systematic literature review exploring the effectiveness of participatory processes. *The British Journal of Social Work*, *48*(7), 1985–2002. https://doi.org/10.1093/bjsw/bcx142
Križ, K., & Roundtree-Swain, D. (2017). We are merchandise on a conveyer belt: How young adults in the public child protection system perceive their participation in decisions about their care. *Children and Youth Services Review*, *78*, 32–40. https://doi.org/10.1016/j.childyouth.2017.05.001
Lundy, L. (2007). "Voice" is not enough: Conceptualising Article 12 of the United Nations Convention on the Rights of the Child. *British Educational Research Journal*, *33*(6), 927–942. https://doi.org/10.1080/01411920701657033

McCafferty, P. (2017). Implementing Article 12 of the United Nations Convention on the Rights of the Child in child protection decision-making: A critical analysis of the challenges and opportunities for social work. *Child Care in Practice*, *23*(4), 327–341. https://doi.org/10.1080/13575279.2016.1264368

McGhee, J., & Waterhouse, L. (2017). The lady and the pram: Women in child protection. *The British Journal of Social Work*, *47*(6), 1652–1668. https://doi.org/10.1093/bjsw/bcx100

Ministry for Justice. (2022). *Achieving best evidence in criminal proceedings*. Crown.

Muench, K., Diaz, C., & Wright, R. (2017). Children and parent participation in child protection conferences: A study in one English local authority. *Child Care in Practice*, *23*(1), 49–63. https://doi.org/10.1080/13575279.2015.1126227

Munro, E. (2011). *The Munro review of child protection: A child-centred system*. Department for Education.

Ney, T., Stoltz, J. A., & Maloney, M. (2013). Voice, power and discourse: Experiences of participants in family group conferences in the context of child protection. *Journal of Social Work*, *13*(2), 184–202. https://doi.org/10.1177/1468017311410514

Preston, R. (2022). "I feel out of my depth": NQSWs report "unmanageable" caseloads and lack of support. *Community Care*. https://www.communitycare.co.uk/2022/04/04/i-feel-out-of-my-depth-nqsws-report-unmanageable-caseloads-and-lack-of-support

Ravalier, J. (2019). Psycho-social working conditions and stress in UK social workers. *The British Journal of Social Work*, *49*(2), 371–390. https://doi.org/10.1093/bjsw/bcy023

Ravalier, J., Allen, R., & McGowan, J. (2023). Social worker working conditions and psychological health: A longitudinal study. *The British Journal of Social Work*, *53*(8), 3818–3837. https://doi.org/10.1093/bjsw/bcad144

Richards-Schuster, K., & Pritzker, S. (2015). Strengthening youth participation in civic engagement: Applying the Convention on the Rights of the Child to social work practice. *Children and Youth Services Review*, *57*, 90–97. https://doi.org/10.1016/j.childyouth.2015.07.013

Richardson Foster, H., Barter, C., Stanley, N., & Churchill, H. (2021). How child-focused are child protection conferences? *Child Abuse Review*, *30*(5), 458–472. https://doi.org/10.1002/car.2710

Sanders, R., & Mace, S. (2006). Agency policy and the participation of children and young people in the child protection process. *Child Abuse Review*, *15*(2), 89–109. https://doi.org/10.1002/car.927

Smith, M., Cree, V. E., MacRae, R., Sharp, D., Wallace, E., & O'Halloran, S. (2017). Social suffering: Changing organisational culture in children and families social work through critical reflection groups—insights from Bourdieu. *The British Journal of Social Work*, *47*(4), 973–988. https://doi.org/10.1093/bjsw/bcw087

Stevenson, L. (2018). 49% of ASYE social workers promised a protected caseload don't have one, a survey finds. *Community Care*. http://www.communitycare.co.uk/2018/06/13/49-of-asye-social-workerspromised-a-protected-caseload-dont-have-one-survey-finds

United Nations. (1989). *Convention on the rights of the child*. https://www.ohchr.org/en/instruments-mechanisms/instruments/convention-rights-child

Webb, J., Schirato, T., & Danaher, G. (2002). *Understanding Bourdieu*. Sage.

Winter, K. (2010). The perspectives of young children in care about their circumstances and implications for social work practice. *Child & Family Social Work*, *15*(2), 186–195. https://doi.org/10.1111/j.1365-2206.2009.00658.x

Woodman, E., Roche, S., McArthur, M., & Moore, T. (2018). Child protection practitioners: Including children in decision making. *Child & Family Social Work*, *23*(3), 475–484. https://doi.org/10.1111/cfs.12439

# 3 Empowering Agency

## The Role of Childhood Sociology in Child Welfare and Protection Systems

*Paul McCafferty*

### Introduction

The sociology of childhood has redefined how social work approaches children, challenging traditional views that often consider children solely as passive recipients of adult intervention or adults in waiting. Instead, this perspective recognises children as active social agents with inherent value, unique insights, and significant roles in shaping their lives and environments. For social work, this shift promotes an approach that respects children's voices, agency, and rights, essential to fostering inclusive and equitable practices that place children's well-being at the centre of social work interventions.

Theories in the sociology of childhood support this child-centred approach by emphasising childhood as a distinct and meaningful life stage. By viewing children as competent and active contributors to their social contexts, these theories advocate policies and practices in social work that prioritise children's perspectives, especially in decision-making processes that affect their welfare. This framework calls on social workers to move beyond protectionist models and adopt practices that respect children's rights, agency, and voices, aligning closely with the field's ethical commitment to inclusivity, empowerment, and equity.

In this chapter, I explore the theoretical foundations that position children as independent social actors in social work practice. These perspectives are critical in shaping a social work approach that balances protective oversight with the acknowledgement of children's agency, empowering professionals to build supportive environments where children's voices are integral to decision-making. Through these theories, social workers can develop more responsive, holistic practices that not only safeguard but also genuinely involve children in their care, enhancing both the effectiveness and ethical grounding of social work in child welfare and protection contexts.

### Reframing Childhood: Theoretical Foundations for Recognising Children as Active Social Agents

The sociology of childhood has emerged as a transformative framework, challenging traditional perspectives that often regard children merely as passive recipients of adult influences or adults in the making. This field fundamentally

DOI: 10.4324/9781003582410-5

repositions children as active social agents, endowed with agency, distinct social value, and unique roles in society. By recognising children as dynamic contributors to social, cultural, and familial contexts, the sociology of childhood seeks to understand and support children's rights, agency, and equitable participation across societal domains, particularly in fields like social work and child protection.

At the core of this approach are key theories that illuminate how children interact with, reshape, and influence the world around them. These theories shift the focus from viewing childhood as a transitional phase towards recognising it as a meaningful, present stage of life, with children actively shaping their environments. This shift calls for child-centred policies and practices that respect children's views, experiences, and agency in matters directly affecting them.

Each following theory provides unique insights into the nature of childhood and children's roles as social actors. These theories not only contribute to a deeper understanding of childhood but also offer practical frameworks for integrating children's voices and perspectives into professional practices, fostering inclusivity and equity in decision-making processes. These theories are pivotal for child protection and social work because they advocate practices that prioritise children's well-being, respect their contributions, and address the structural barriers that may inhibit their participation—and thus, they are worth exploring individually.

#### *Interpretive Reproduction*

William Corsaro's (2005) concept of interpretive reproduction challenges the traditional view of children as mere absorbers of adult culture. Instead, Corsaro argued that children actively interpret, reshape, and reproduce cultural norms in their peer interactions, creating unique social worlds and peer cultures. This theory underscores the importance of understanding children in their social contexts, where they are seen as active participants who can construct their norms and values rather than passively receive them from adults. As Corsaro (2005) noted, children collectively produce unique peer cultures, rather than simply internalising adult culture. This perspective is invaluable in social work and child protection because it emphasises the need to consider children's social environments and interactions when developing support systems.

#### *New Sociology of Childhood*

Alison James and Alan Prout (2015b) introduced the new sociology of childhood, which posits that children are not merely passive recipients of socialisation but active constructors of their lives. This approach opposes developmental models that depict children solely as adults in progress, instead advocating that children be viewed as social actors with inherent value. James and Prout's theory emphasises that children's perspectives should be incorporated into decisions affecting their lives, promoting a child-centred approach that recognises and respects children's voices and agency. In social work, this theory supports practices that seek to include children in discussions about their welfare and well-being. As James and Prout (2015b) stated, the "*new*" sociology of childhood insists that children are and must be seen as active in the construction of their own social lives, the lives of those around them, and of the societies in which they live.

***Structural Perspective on Childhood***

Jens Qvortrup et al. (1994) introduced a structural perspective that positions childhood as a permanent social category with unique societal value, rather than simply a developmental phase leading to adulthood. This theory advocates viewing children collectively as a societal group with specific needs and rights, shaped by socioeconomic and cultural contexts. Qvortrup emphasised that policies should account for children's social experiences and recognise childhood as a structural element of society. In child protection, this approach promotes equitable practices that address social inequalities and ensures that children are included in policymaking as a distinct and valued group.

***Children's Agency and Power Dynamics***

Berry Mayall's (2002) work on children's agency examined the power dynamics in adult–child relationships, arguing that children exercise agency even in hierarchical structures. Mayall called for a shift from hierarchical to collaborative adult–child relationships, advocating mutual respect and shared decision-making. This perspective highlights the importance of transferring some decision-making power to children, recognising them as capable agents. Mayall's focus on agency is particularly relevant in child protection, where professionals are encouraged to involve children meaningfully in decisions about their care and challenge power imbalances that may hinder children's voices. Mayall (2002) asserted that "power is always exercised in interactions with children, who in turn resist, evade, and shape power relations" (p. 21).

***Ecological Systems Theory***

Urie Bronfenbrenner's (1979) ecological systems theory, though not exclusive to the sociology of childhood, is a widely applied framework that posits that children's development is shaped by multiple environmental layers—family, school, community, and society. Bronfenbrenner emphasised that each layer affects children's well-being and participation, advocating a holistic approach to understanding childhood. In child protection, this theory supports examining the interconnected systems influencing a child's life, thereby promoting practices that consider family dynamics, social contexts, and community support structures in child welfare decisions.

***Social Capital Theory***

Pierre Bourdieu's (1989) concept of social capital involves how access to resources, relationships, and social networks affects children's opportunities and agency. In childhood sociology, this theory highlights how social capital, or lack thereof, can influence children's ability to participate meaningfully in society. Bourdieu's theory encourages professionals to consider how factors such as family background, education, and community connections shape children's agency and social mobility. Social capital theory, thus, underscores the importance of addressing inequalities that affect children's capacity to access resources, opportunities, and social participation.

***Lundy's Model of Participation***

Laura Lundy's (2007) model of participation provides a practical framework based on the sociology of childhood for ensuring children's voices are integrated into decision-making processes. Lundy emphasised four components: space (providing children with safe opportunities for expression), voice (ensuring children can communicate freely), audience (guaranteeing their views are heard), and influence (ensuring their views have an impact on outcomes). Lundy's model is widely applicable in social work and child protection, reinforcing children's roles as active agents by ensuring they are not only heard but also meaningfully included in decisions affecting their lives.

Together, these theories challenge traditional views of childhood, advocating a child-centred approach that recognises children's capabilities, perspectives, and contributions as independent social actors. These perspectives collectively inform a comprehensive foundation for child-centred practices, promoting respect for children's rights, equitable participation, and agency. In social work and child protection, these theories guide professionals towards inclusive practices that prioritise children's voices, address structural inequalities, and enhance child-centred support across multiple societal domains. The next natural step is to align these theories with the United Nations Convention on the Rights of the Child (UNCRC; United Nations, 1989), creating a cohesive framework that centres on children's rights and active participation in social work. This alignment allows for the practical application of childhood sociology in child protection, strengthening the focus on children as key stakeholders. By integrating UNCRC principles, social work can enhance its commitment to equity, inclusivity, and child-centred practices. Ultimately, this approach empowers children by embedding their rights and voices into social work decision-making processes that affect their lives.

## Aligning UNCRC Principles with the Sociology of Childhood in Social Work: Empowering Children as Active Agents in Child Protection

The principles of the UNCRC align closely with the sociology of childhood, which recognises children as active, rights-bearing participants in society. This transformation in social work and child protection goes beyond conventional adult-focused perspectives, recognising children as valuable social actors in the here and now (James & Prout, 2015a, 2015b; Mayall, 2002). The core principles of the UNCRC—non-discrimination, prioritising the best interests of the child, ensuring their survival and development, and respecting their views—serve as a foundation for integrating children's agency, perspectives, and well-being into child protection practices. These principles underscore the importance of treating children as active participants in decisions that affect their lives, aligning with childhood sociology's emphasis on recognising children as competent social actors. By upholding these principles, social workers are encouraged to develop practices that not only honour children's voices but also promote equity, inclusivity, and a focus on their holistic well-being. This approach supports a child-centred model in which children's unique needs and rights are central, fostering an environment that empowers them in the protective frameworks of social work. I examine each in turn; however, see Box 3.1 for a summary of the principles, their alignment with the sociology of childhood, and the implications for social work.

The principle of non-discrimination (Article 2) ensures that all children have equal rights without disadvantages based on race, gender, socioeconomic background, or other factors. This principle mirrors the sociology of childhood's view of children as a distinct social category with equal societal value (Qvortrup et al., 1994). Social work in child protection is encouraged to uphold this principle by dismantling systemic inequalities and ensuring that children from diverse backgrounds are afforded equal access to resources, representation, and opportunities for participation (Berrick et al., 2015; Horgan et al., 2017). By adopting an inclusive, child-centred approach, social workers can create equitable pathways to protection that reflect the diversity of children's experiences. As Qvortrup et al. (1994) emphasised, "Children must be seen as a permanent and structural category in society, one that is integral to social policy and worthy of focused consideration" (p. 4).

**Box 3.1 Reflective Questions for Social Workers: Integrating UNCRC Principles with the Sociology of Childhood in Child Protection**

How can I ensure that children from diverse backgrounds and experiences have equitable opportunities to express their views, and how am I addressing any systemic inequalities that might limit their participation?

In what ways am I incorporating children's interpretations and perspectives into my decision-making processes, and how can I balance their input with considerations for their safety and well-being?

How can I apply frameworks like Laura Lundy's model of participation to create safe spaces where children feel empowered to share their views, and how can I ensure these views influence the outcomes that affect their lives?

The best interests of the child principle (Article 3) is foundational in child protection. Instead of viewing children as passive recipients of adult decisions, this principle aligns with childhood sociology by emphasising children's voices, experiences, and perspectives as central to their well-being. Social workers guided by this principle incorporate children's unique insights into decisions affecting them, acknowledging their ability to contribute meaningfully to discussions about their lives. Corsaro's (2005) concept of interpretive reproduction highlights how children actively interpret and make sense of their worlds, reinforcing the importance of trusting children's contributions. By shifting from a protectionist model to a participatory one, social work more accurately aligns with the child's agency and welfare. This approach reflects Corsaro's (2005) assertion that children collectively produce unique peer cultures, rather than simply internalising adult culture.

The right to life, survival, and development (Article 6) includes not only physical needs but also social, emotional, and cognitive development, aligning with the sociology of childhood's holistic view of well-being. Social workers must consider not only children's immediate safety but also their broader developmental needs. Childhood sociologists emphasise that children should be valued in the present, not solely as future adults. Bronfenbrenner's (1979) ecological systems theory complements this principle by illustrating how family, school, and community influence children's development. Supporting children's growth in these areas allows social workers to ensure they have access to resources that enable both current and future participation and well-being.

Respect for the views of the child (Article 12) is perhaps the most direct connection between the UNCRC and the sociology of childhood. This principle emphasises children's right to express their views on matters affecting them—a key consideration in child protection, where children's voices significantly influence their well-being and sense of agency. Alison James and Alan Prout (2015b) advocated moving beyond a traditional socialisation model, which sees children as moulded by adults, to a model that views children as capable of shaping their own environments. Laura Lundy's (2007) model of participation highlights space, voice, audience, and influence and offers a practical framework for integrating children's perspectives into decision-making, ensuring that children's views are actively considered in matters concerning their lives.

Overall, aligning UNCRC principles with sociological insights empowers social work in child protection to build practices that respect children as active agents, promote equity, and prioritise holistic well-being (Gu, 2022). A thorough understanding of the sociology of childhood, combined with the application of key theories and frameworks, is therefore essential for child welfare professionals seeking to foster genuine participation. The work of theorists such as William Corsaro, Alison James, Alan Prout, Jens Qvortrup, and Berry Mayall, along with frameworks like Bourdieu's concept of social capital, Bronfenbrenner's ecological systems theory, and participatory models like Laura Lundy's approach, enriches approaches to integrating children's voices and rights in child welfare systems. This foundation equips social workers with insights and tools to implement real-world guidance for honouring children's agency and advancing child-centred, equitable practices in child protection (see Table 3.1).

For example, Corsaro's interpretive reproduction theory, which shows that children shape their social worlds, and James and Prout's view of children as active constructors of their lives allow social workers to gain a deeper appreciation of children's unique forms of participation and expression. Qvortrup's recognition of childhood as a distinct social category reinforces the need to address structural inequalities, whereas Mayall's focus on shifting power

*Table 3.1* Aligning UNCRC Principles with the Sociology of Childhood in Social Work and the Implications for Social Work Practice

| *UNCRC Principle* | *Sociology of Childhood Alignment* | *Social Work Implications* |
|---|---|---|
| Non-discrimination (Article 2) | Emphasises equal rights for all children without discrimination based on race, gender, socioeconomic background, or other factors. Recognises children as a distinct social category with equal societal value (Qvortrup et al., 1994). | Dismantle systemic inequalities, ensuring equitable access to resources, representation, and participation for children from diverse backgrounds. |
| Best interests of the child (Article 3) | Prioritises children's voices, experiences, and perspectives as central to their well-being. Highlights children's ability to actively contribute, reflecting interpretive reproduction (Corsaro, 2005). | Encourage participatory models in decision-making that incorporate children's unique insights and experiences, moving away from purely protectionist models. |
| Right to life, survival, and development (Article 6) | Encompasses physical, social, emotional, and cognitive development. Advocates valuing children in the present, not only for future adulthood (Bronfenbrenner, 1979). | Address broader developmental needs and provide access to resources that support well-being in the present and future, considering influences from family, school, and community. |
| Respect for the views of the child (Article 12) | Supports children's right to express their views on matters that affect them. Views children as capable of shaping their environments, encouraging meaningful inclusion in decision-making (James & Prout, 2015a; Lundy, 2007). | Create frameworks to include children's views meaningfully in decision-making processes, which will ensure that children's voices actively influence outcomes affecting their lives. |

dynamics underlines the importance of respecting children's agency in adult–child relationships. Equally, in applying Bronfenbrenner's ecological model, a social worker might assess the influence of a child's extended family, school environment, and community services, identifying both protective and risk factors that shape the child's development. This approach helps in creating a comprehensive support plan tailored to each child's unique situation (Skauge et al., 2021). Together, these theoretical insights and legal principles encourage social work practices that value children as active agents, support equitable engagement, and advance holistic development in child protection contexts.

### Case Study: Applying the Sociology of Childhood to Social Work Practice: Sarah's Family Reunification Conference

In a family reunification case conference, Sarah, a 10-year-old, shares her feelings of fear and apprehension about returning to her previous home. This expression is crucial, because it provides insight into her emotional experiences and concerns that might otherwise have been overlooked. By applying Article 3 (best interests of the child) and Article 12 (child's right to express views) of the UNCRC, social workers ensure that Sarah's voice is not only heard but actively incorporated into the decision-making process.

In this case, the principles of the sociology of childhood were instrumental. Rather than viewing Sarah simply as a passive recipient of adult decisions, social workers saw her as an active social agent whose insights, shaped by her lived experiences, added critical value to the conference's discussions. This aligns closely with James and Prout's (2015a, 2015b) view of children as active constructors of their social worlds, emphasising that children's unique perspectives are valuable and necessary for fully understanding their situations. Sarah's ability to articulate her fears demonstrated that, even at a young age, children can provide informed and meaningful input, supporting the sociology of childhood's argument that children are not merely adults in the making but social actors in their own right.

Social workers in Sarah's case also applied Laura Lundy's (2007) model of participation, ensuring that Sarah had space to express herself, a voice that was heard, an audience that respected her views, and influence on the outcome. Her perspective informed the team's assessment of the potential risks associated with returning home, guiding them to approach the reunification process more cautiously. Corsaro's (2005) concept of interpretive reproduction further underscores this approach by showing that children like Sarah actively make sense of and respond to their environments, rather than simply reflecting adult expectations.

By acknowledging Sarah's perspective, the social workers fostered a more child-centred decision-making process. This approach reinforces the sociological understanding that children's voices are not merely supplemental but essential to understanding their best interests fully. In practical terms, Sarah's input led to additional assessments and support considerations that might have been

> **Box 3.2 Reflective Questions for Social Workers: Child Representation in Child Protection**
>
> How can I ensure that each child's voice is respected and given due weight, especially when their views differ from the perspectives of adults involved in the case?
>
> In what ways can I recognise and mitigate any biases that may prevent equal participation for children from diverse backgrounds?
>
> How can I balance children's expressed wishes with the duty to prioritise their safety, especially in cases where participation may involve high-risk situations?

missed in a more adult-dominated process, demonstrating how the sociology of childhood informs child protection practices that truly respect and integrate children's agency

### Key Challenges in Aligning UNCRC Principles with the Sociology of Childhood in Social Work

Aligning the UNCRC's principles with the sociology of childhood in social work presents unique challenges. Although both frameworks emphasise children's agency, voice, and rights, social workers often navigate complex ethical and practical dilemmas to balance child protection with the promotion of participation and inclusion.

Balancing agency with protection in child welfare, for example, presents a nuanced challenge for social workers. Recognising children as active social agents redefines traditional protectionist views, creating a balancing act between respecting children's voices and ensuring their safety. In high-risk situations, this balance is delicate—although an overemphasis on protection may stifle children's participation, prioritising too much agency could expose them to risk (Henze-Pedersen & Bengtsson, 2024). Successfully integrating children's perspectives while safeguarding their well-being requires skilled judgement and ethical sensitivity. Digital tools, such as photovoice and video diaries, have shown promise in enabling children to express their perspectives safely and meaningfully, especially for those who might find verbal communication challenging. Integrating such tools supports a participatory approach and can help social workers access children's insights in a non-intrusive way (Cuevas-Parra, 2022). This approach aligns closely with Article 3 of the UNCRC, which rightly prioritises the child's best interests, encouraging social workers to adopt practices that harmonise protection with participatory, rights-based approaches (Featherstone et al., 2014; Percy-Smith et al., 2023).

Beyond balancing agency and protection, social workers confront systemic inequities that hinder children's participation. According to the principle of non-discrimination in Article 2 of the UNCRC, dismantling structural barriers that limit access for children from diverse backgrounds is crucial (Horgan et al., 2017; Qvortrup et al., 2009). Social workers must address inequalities stemming from race, socioeconomic status, gender, and disability to foster inclusivity. Achieving this requires advocacy, reallocation of resources, and sometimes significant shifts in policy and practice (Berrick et al., 2015). Implementing social work practices that prioritise these goals, however, is essential to establish equity in children's access to participation and resources.

Creating meaningful opportunities for children's participation also involves applying frameworks such as Lundy's (2007) model, which emphasises space, voice, audience, and influence. Providing an empowering environment where children feel safe and respected enough to share their views remains challenging, particularly when communicating across varied ages and developmental stages (Winter, 2011). Social workers must develop skills in fostering inclusive settings, using age-appropriate communication techniques and respecting each child's unique expressions (Barnes, 2012). Through these frameworks, social workers can uphold Article 12 of the UNCRC, reinforcing children's right to express their views freely on matters affecting them (Lundy & McEvoy, 2012).

Navigating adult–child power dynamics is an ongoing challenge in social work, where authority traditionally rests with adults (Tisdall & Cuevas-Parra, 2021). This imbalance can marginalise children's agency and perspectives (Cuevas-Parra, 2022). To counter this marginalisation, social workers are encouraged to adopt collaborative approaches that regard children's views as equally valuable, especially in decisions directly affecting their lives (Sudarsan et al., 2022). Training in child-centred, collaborative practices helps social workers shift towards shared decision-making, in acknowledging children as autonomous social actors, a core tenet of the sociology of childhood (Mayall, 2002). Embracing these approaches supports partnership-based practices in social work (Munro, 2011).

Translating theoretical knowledge into practical applications remains a fundamental aspect of child-centred social work. Theories like Corsaro's (2005) interpretive reproduction, Qvortrup et al.'s (1994) structural perspective, and Bronfenbrenner's (1979) ecological systems model provide insights but require nuanced adaptation in child welfare's real-world constraints. Continued professional development and reflective practice enable social workers to integrate these theories into their daily roles, fostering a holistic understanding of children's needs. This theoretical integration aligns with Article 6 of the UNCRC, which advocates the right of children to survival and holistic development, urging practices that account for the complex social factors shaping each child's life (Skauge et al., 2021).

In essence then, aligning the principles of the UNCRC with the sociology of childhood in social work introduces a transformative yet complex and challenging framework for practice. Both perspectives underscore children's rights, agency, and voices, challenging traditional adult-centred protection approaches. Social workers must navigate a delicate balance between safeguarding children and promoting their participation, address systemic inequities that restrict inclusive engagement, and create empowering environments for children to express their views freely. This is not easy when social workers are constrained by limited resources, high caseloads, and institutional pressures that often prioritise risk management over participatory practices (McCafferty, 2017). These challenges make it difficult to embrace a rights-based approach fully because social workers must juggle the demands of protecting children while advocating their agency, all in systems that may not always support inclusive or child-centred approaches.

This approach also requires social workers to navigate adult–child power dynamics, champion equitable decision-making, and adapt theories from childhood sociology into practical, actionable strategies within the limits of child welfare systems. This task is complicated by the rigid policies and time pressures that often define child welfare, limiting opportunities for meaningful, reflective engagement with children and reducing the flexibility needed to address each child's unique needs (McCafferty & Mercado García, 2024). Within these constraints, social workers strive to empower children, yet the shift away from traditional, adult-centred decision-making remains challenging.

Integrating UNCRC principles with the sociology of childhood, however, can provide an essential framework for social work, transforming it into a practice that not only safeguards children but also recognises and values their agency and participation. This holistic approach aligns with social work's mission to uphold justice, equity, and child-centred care, ultimately establishing a responsive, inclusive system that champions the best interests of every child. Through balancing protection with empowerment, addressing systemic inequities, fostering genuine participation, and promoting collaborative decision-making, social work can create environments where children's voices, rights, and well-being are truly prioritised. This paradigm shift towards child-centred, participatory practice embodies a commitment to a future where children are seen and valued as essential contributors to their lives and society.

## Case Study: Balancing Children's Agency and Protection in Child Protection Social Work

### *Case Background*

A social worker, Clara, is assigned to support a 12-year-old girl named Mia, who has experienced a volatile home environment with ongoing parental conflict and suspected neglect. Mia's case has reached the attention of child protection due to her school's concerns about her withdrawal and reluctance to return home. Recognising Mia as an active social agent with valuable insights into her situation, Clara aims to involve her meaningfully in the assessment process while ensuring her safety.

***Key Challenges***

*1 Balancing Agency with Protection*

Clara aims to respect Mia's voice and agency by allowing her to share her perspective on her home life, but she is mindful of the risks involved in fully following Mia's wishes if her safety is compromised. Mia has expressed a strong desire to stay with her mother, who despite her intentions has not been providing Mia with adequate care due to ongoing challenges. This creates a tension for Clara because fully honouring Mia's preference could expose her to continued neglect. In line with the UNCRC's Article 3, which prioritises the child's best interests, Clara must balance Mia's right to participate in decisions about her life with the need to ensure her safety (McCafferty et al., 2021).

*2 Overcoming Systemic Inequities*

Clara faces the additional challenge of systemic barriers that may limit Mia's participation. Mia comes from a lower socioeconomic background, which has historically influenced her limited access to resources. Clara understands that non-discrimination (UNCRC Article 2) requires dismantling these inequities and addressing potential biases that may limit Mia's opportunities to participate meaningfully in her own case (Horgan et al., 2017; Qvortrup et al., 2009). Clara advocates additional resources for Mia, such as counselling and school support, which could help Mia articulate her needs and develop a sense of agency.

*3 Creating Meaningful Participation Opportunities*

Clara is committed to providing Mia with a safe space where she can express her views without feeling pressured. To foster this, she implements Lundy's (2007) model by ensuring Mia has the space, voice, audience, and influence she needs to participate effectively. Clara uses age-appropriate language, asks open-ended questions, and invites Mia to draw or write down her feelings, allowing Mia to express herself in a comfortable, non-verbal way when needed (Winter, 2011). However, creating this empowering environment is challenging because Mia's past experiences have made her reluctant to trust adults. Clara's persistence in this approach reinforces the UNCRC's Article 12, which emphasises the child's right to express their views freely.

*4 Navigating Adult–Child Power Dynamics*

Clara is aware that traditional adult–child power dynamics can marginalise Mia's voice. To counteract this, she promotes a partnership approach, encouraging Mia to share her views as equal to those of adults involved in the case. Clara includes Mia in family discussions about her care and fosters a collaborative atmosphere by seeking Mia's opinions on her care options, thus enabling Mia to feel a sense of ownership over her future (Stoecklin & Fattore, 2018).

5 *Integrating Theoretical Knowledge into Practical Contexts*

Clara applies theories from the sociology of childhood to better understand Mia's experiences. For instance, Corsaro's (2005) interpretive reproduction concept helps Clara recognise that Mia's interpretations of her home life are shaped by her unique social interactions, which need to be respected. Clara also draws on Bronfenbrenner's (1979) ecological systems theory, which emphasises the influence of family, school, and community on children's lives. This holistic understanding of Mia's situation supports Clara's efforts to integrate a range of support systems to provide Mia with a sense of stability.

***Challenges and Solutions***

*Challenge:* Balancing Mia's expressed wishes with her safety.

*Solution:* Clara engaged in ongoing discussions with Mia, carefully explaining her safety concerns in an age-appropriate manner. She provided Mia with choices regarding aspects of her care, empowering her while remaining cautious about her well-being.

*Challenge:* Systemic inequities limiting Mia's access to resources.

*Solution:* Clara advocated services to support Mia's mental health and educational needs, securing a counsellor who could provide additional emotional support. Clara also worked with Mia's school to offer tutoring, ensuring Mia had equitable opportunities to thrive.

*Challenge:* Creating trust and empowering Mia to share her thoughts freely.

*Solution:* Clara gradually built trust by maintaining transparency and following Lundy's (2007) framework. She used creative communication tools and frequently checked in with Mia to ensure she felt comfortable expressing herself.

**Box 3.3 Reflective Questions for Social Workers: Protecting and Empowering Children**

How can I strike a balance between respecting a child's expressed wishes and ensuring their safety in high-risk situations?

What strategies can I use to recognise and mitigate the systemic biases that may limit a child's access to participation and resources?

How can I build trust and create a participatory environment that encourages children to share their views freely, especially when they have experienced trauma or distrust towards adults?

### Towards Best Practices in Aligning UNCRC Principles with the Sociology of Childhood in Social Work

Aligning the UNCRC's principles with the sociology of childhood in social work calls for child-centred, participatory, and ethically-grounded practices that honour children as active social agents. Moving beyond protection-focused approaches, these best practices advocate a balanced, equitable framework that respects children's voices and prioritises their holistic well-being.

Empowering children's voices and agency is fundamental to this shift. Social workers can use frameworks such as Laura Lundy's (2007) model of participation, which emphasises space, voice, audience, and influence, to ensure children feel safe and respected when sharing their views. Establishing an environment where children can communicate freely and without fear is essential to meaningful participation. Through age-appropriate language and active listening, social workers create open dialogues, which are foundational to Article 12 of the UNCRC, ensuring individual children's perspectives are taken seriously in decisions that affect them (McCafferty, 2017; Roesch-Marsh et al., 2017).

Although valuing children's input is crucial, social workers must also balance this participation with their duty to protect (Kosher et al., 2017). The UNCRC's best interests of the child principle (Article 3) guides social workers to make informed, ethically sensitive decisions that consider children's agency and safety simultaneously. Listening to children's perspectives, assessing the risks involved, and making well-rounded judgements are all vital in balancing agency with protection (McCafferty & Taylor, 2020). Social workers benefit from using structured risk assessment tools (Killick & Taylor, 2020) and following ethical guidelines to prevent situations where children may be inadvertently placed at risk by decisions they have influenced (Kettle, 2018).

Promoting inclusivity and addressing systemic inequalities is equally important for aligning social work practices with the sociology of childhood. The UNCRC's principle of non-discrimination (Article 2) reinforces that all children, regardless of their background, should have equal opportunities for participation and protection. Social workers are encouraged to adopt culturally responsive approaches that accommodate diverse needs and advocate policy and structural changes that reduce barriers to inclusion (Bennett & Morse, 2023). By addressing these systemic inequalities, social workers create a more equitable environment where children from various racial, socioeconomic, and ability backgrounds can engage meaningfully in decisions that affect their lives (Laird & Williams, 2023).

A collaborative partnership between adults and children further strengthens this inclusive, child-centred approach (Husby et al., 2018). Social work has historically been marked by adult–child power imbalances, but recognising children as social actors encourages more balanced, respectful relationships (Abebe, 2019). Social workers can benefit from training that emphasises collaborative, child-centred approaches that promote shared decision-making processes that value children's perspectives as equal to those of adults. By fostering partnership-oriented relationships, social workers can better adhere to the sociology of childhood's call to recognise children as equal social participants and agents in their lives.

Integrating theoretical insights from the sociology of childhood into practice allows social workers to approach child protection with a nuanced understanding of children's social contexts and experiences. Concepts such as Corsaro's (2005) interpretive reproduction, which views children as creators of their social worlds, and Bronfenbrenner's (1979) ecological systems theory, which considers the interconnected layers influencing a child's life, provide essential frameworks for understanding children's unique needs. Professional development opportunities, such as workshops and reflective practice, can help social workers translate these theoretical insights into effective, child-centred strategies that honour children's rights and agency.

Finally, continuous reflection and ethical sensitivity are essential to maintaining high standards in social work. Reflective practice encourages social workers to evaluate their biases critically, assess the power dynamics present in their interactions with children, and refine their approaches. Regular reflection not only enhances individual growth but also fosters an ethical, rights-focused culture in the field (Ferguson, 2018). By committing to reflective practices, social workers can improve their ability to integrate the UNCRC principles and the sociology of childhood into everyday practice, upholding children's rights, promoting their agency, and enhancing the effectiveness of child protection interventions (Ferguson, 2018).

Through these interconnected practices, social workers are equipped to create an empowering framework in child protection that aligns with both the UNCRC principles and the sociology of childhood. This framework respects and prioritises children's voices, promotes equity and inclusion, and ultimately fosters a supportive environment in which children's unique perspectives are not only valued but also instrumental in shaping their lives.

## Conclusion

The sociology of childhood, in tandem with legal frameworks such as the UNCRC and national legislation, offers transformative insights that deepen the ethical foundation and effectiveness of child welfare and protection practices. By viewing children as active social agents with rights, perspectives, and capacities, this sociological approach moves beyond traditional models that often position children as passive recipients of care (James & Prout, 2015a, 2015b). Instead, it acknowledges children's agency, fostering environments that prioritise meaningful participation, equity, and respect for children's contributions. This shift aligns directly with child welfare's core values because it brings children's voices to the forefront of decisions that affect their lives. The application of theoretical models—like Lundy's model of participation, Corsaro's interpretive reproduction, and Bronfenbrenner's ecological systems theory—provides social workers with practical frameworks to integrate children's insights into welfare systems.

The UNCRC principles, particularly Articles 2 (non-discrimination), 3 (best interests of the child), 6 (right to life and development), and 12 (respect for the views of the child), underscore the importance of children's participation and well-being as non-negotiable aspects of child protection. When social workers engage these principles with a sociological lens, they are empowered to dismantle systemic inequities, balance protection with agency, and create inclusive, supportive practices. Recognising children as capable social actors not only supports ethical standards but also leads to more effective and sustainable welfare outcomes because decisions shaped by children's perspectives are more likely to meet their needs holistically.

## Final Reflection for Practitioners

For social work practitioners, a reflective approach is vital in ensuring the successful integration of these insights. Reflecting on sociological perspectives and participatory practices encourages social workers to evaluate continuously how they interact with children and to consider both their immediate needs and long-term development. Practitioners are invited to consider questions such as: How am I valuing each child's unique perspective? How can I address any systemic barriers that may limit their participation?

By adopting this reflective stance, social workers can deepen their commitment to children's rights and enhance their practice, embedding children's agency at the heart of child welfare and protection settings. This approach not only respects children's rights but also elevates their experiences, fostering an environment where each child feels empowered, heard, and supported. As social work continues to evolve, the integration of sociology of childhood insights remains essential, guiding practitioners to honour children's voices and perspectives in ways that contribute to a more equitable, responsive, and child-centred welfare system.

## References

Abebe, T. (2019). Reconceptualising children's agency as continuum and interdependence. *Social Sciences*, *8*(3), 81. https://doi.org/10.3390/socsci8030081

Barnes, M. (2012). *Care in everyday life: An ethic of care in practice*. Policy Press.

Bennett, B., & Morse, C. (2023). The continuous improvement cultural responsiveness tools (CICRT): Creating more culturally responsive social workers. *Australian Social Work*, *76*(3), 315–329. https://doi.org/10.1080/0312407X.2023.2186255

Berrick, J. D., Dickens, J., Pösö, T., & Skivenes, M. (2015). Children's involvement in care order decision-making: A cross-country analysis. *Child Abuse & Neglect*, *49*, 128–141. https://doi.org/10.1016/j.chiabu.2015.07.001

Bourdieu, P. (1989). *Social space and symbolic power*. Blackwell.

Bronfenbrenner, U. (1979). *The ecology of human development: Experiments by nature and design*. Harvard University Press.

Corsaro, W. A. (2005). *The sociology of childhood* (2nd edn.). Pine Forge Press/Sage.

Cuevas-Parra, P. (2022). Multi-dimensional lens to Article 12 of the UNCRC: A model to enhance children's participation. *Children's Geographies*, *21*(3), 363–377. https://doi.org/10.1080/14733285.2022.2071598

Featherstone, B., White, S., & Morris, K. (2014). Towards a just culture: Designing humane social work organisations. In *Re-imagining child protection: Towards humane social work with families* (pp. 75–94). Policy Press.

Ferguson, H. (2018). How social workers reflect in action and when and why they don't: The possibilities and limits to reflective practice in social work. *Social Work Education, 37*(4), 415–427. https://doi.org/10.1080/02615479.2017.1413083

Gu, X. (2022). Introduction: The case for a value turn in childhood sociology. *Current Sociology, 70*(4), 478–495. https://doi.org/10.1177/00113921211006102

Henze-Pedersen, S., & Bengtsson, T. T. (2024). Developing a model for child participation in child welfare services. *Child & Family Social Work, 29*(4), 1086–1095. https://doi.org/10.1111/cfs.13150

Horgan, D., Forde, C., Martin, S., & Parkes, A. (2017). Children's participation: Moving from the performative to the social. *Children's Geographies, 15*(3), 274–288.

Husby, I. S. D., Slettebø, T., & Juul, R. (2018). Partnerships with children in child welfare: The importance of trust and pedagogical support. *Child & Family Social Work, 23*(3), 443–450. https://doi.org/10.1111/cfs.12435

James, A., & Prout, A. (2015a). *Constructing and reconstructing childhood: Contemporary issues in the sociological study of childhood* (3rd edn.). Routledge.

James, A., & Prout, A. (2015b). *The new sociology of childhood.* Routledge.

Kettle, M. (2018). A balancing act: A grounded theory study of the professional judgement of child protection social workers. *Journal of Social Work Practice, 32*(2), 219–231. https://doi.org/10.1080/02650533.2018.1438997

Killick, C., & Taylor, B. J. (2020). *Assessment, risk and decision making in social work: An introduction.* Learning Matters.

Kosher, H., Ben-Arieh, A., & Hendelsman, Y. (2017). *Children's rights and social work.* Springer.

Laird, S., & Williams, C. (2023). An applied model of cultural competence in child protection practice. *Journal of Social Work, 23*(4), 721–740. https://doi.org/10.1177/14680173231162551

Lundy, L. (2007). "Voice" is not enough: Conceptualising Article 12 of the United Nations Convention on the Rights of the Child. *British Educational Research Journal, 33*(6), 927–942. https://doi.org/10.1080/01411920701657033

Lundy, L., & McEvoy, L. (2012). Children's rights and research processes: Assisting children to (in)formed views. *Childhood, 19*(1), 129–144. https://doi.org/10.1177/0907568211409078

Mayall, B. (2002). *Towards a sociology for childhood: Thinking from children's lives.* Open University Press.

McCafferty, P. (2017). Implementing Article 12 of the United Nations Convention on the Rights of the Child in child protection decision-making: A critical analysis of the challenges and opportunities for social work. *Child Care in Practice, 23*(4), 327–341. https://doi.org/10.1080/13575279.2016.1264368

McCafferty, P., Duffy, J., & Hayes, D. (2021). Permanency decisions in child welfare: A qualitative study. *The British Journal of Social Work, 51*(6), 2134–2154. https://doi.org/10.1093/bjsw/bcab095

McCafferty, P., & Mercado García, E. (2024). Children's participation in child welfare: A systematic review of systematic reviews. *The British Journal of Social Work, 54*(3), 1092–1108. https://doi.org/10.1093/bjsw/bcad167

McCafferty, P., & Taylor, B. J. (2020). Risk, decision-making and assessment in child welfare. *Child Care in Practice, 26*(2), 107–110. https://doi.org/10.1080/13575279.2019.1703369

Munro, E. (2011). *The Munro review of child protection: Final report—A child-centred system.* Department for Education.

Percy-Smith, B., Thomas, N. P., O'Kane, C., & Imoh, A. T. D. (Eds.). (2023). *A handbook of children and young people's participation: Conversations for transformational change*. Taylor & Francis.

Qvortrup, J., Bardy, M., Sgritta, G., & Wintersberger, H. (1994). *Childhood matters: Social theory, practice and politics*. Avebury.

Qvortrup, J., Corsaro, W. A., & Honig, M. S. (2009). *The Palgrave handbook of childhood studies*. Palgrave Macmillan.

Roesch-Marsh, A., Gillies, A., & Green, D. (2017). Nurturing the virtuous circle: Looked after children's participation in reviews, a cyclical and relational process. *Child & Family Social Work*, *22*(2), 904–913. https://doi.org/10.1111/cfs.12310

Skauge, B., Storhaug, A. S., & Marthinsen, E. (2021). The what, why and how of child participation: A review of the conceptualization of "child participation" in child welfare. *Social Sciences*, *10*(2), 54. https://doi.org/10.3390/socsci10020054

Stoecklin, D., & Fattore, T. (2018). Children's multidimensional agency: Insights into the structuration of choice. *Childhood*, *25*(1), 47–62. https://doi.org/10.1177/0907568217743557

Sudarsan, I., Hoare, K., Sheridan, N., & Roberts, J. (2022). Giving voice to children in research: The power of child-centered constructivist grounded theory methodology. *Research in Nursing & Health*, *45*(4), 488–497. https://doi.org/10.1002/nur.22231

Tisdall, E. K. M., & Cuevas-Parra, P. (2021). Beyond the familiar challenges for children and young people's participation rights: The potential of activism. *The International Journal of Human Rights*, *26*(5), 792–810. https://doi.org/10.1080/13642987.2021.1968377

United Nations. (1989). *Convention on the rights of the child*. https://www.ohchr.org/en/instruments-mechanisms/instruments/convention-rights-child

Winter, K. (2011). *Building relationships and communicating with young children: A practical guide for social workers*. Routledge.

## Section II

# Children's Rights to Protection from Harm

# 4 Protecting Children by Supporting Families

*Davy Hayes*

## Introduction

Article 19 of the United Nations Convention on the Rights of the Child (UNCRC; United Nations, 1989) outlines the state's duty to take measures to ensure children are protected from "all forms of physical or mental violence, injury or abuse, neglect or negligent treatment or exploitation, including sexual abuse" while in the care of parents, guardians, or others (Section 19.1). In Section 19.2, the types of protective measures the state is required to provide are outlined, including the provision of "necessary support for the child and for *those who have the care of the child*" (emphasis added). Article 19, therefore, reflects the dual mandate of social workers in the United Kingdom for both protecting children at risk of immediate harm and promoting the overall development and well-being of children in need by providing services and support to the family. This dual mandate is reflected in the UNCRC, with Article 3 outlining that the child's best interests must take precedence in all decisions affecting children, and Article 18 emphasising that the state must support parents by providing support services for children and helping parents raise their children. These responsibilities can sometimes be in conflict, creating tension for social workers as they attempt to both protect children from harm from their caregivers while simultaneously support the family by offering services. Trotter (2022) argued that one way of dealing with this tension is for social workers and their agencies to focus on one responsibility almost to the exclusion of the other.

Several years ago, during a post-qualifying course, the case study and questions outlined in Box 4.1 were discussed with course participants in the context of considering the nature of risk in social work with children and families. The responses surprised me and raised similar concerns as those outlined by Featherstone et al. (2014, p. 2) when they heard the phrase, "I'm only here for the child." The social workers present, all of whom had been qualified for 2 years or more, were adamant that Ben was at risk of further abuse; that his mother, by her own admission, was culpable; and that a child protection response was required. Course participants generally expressed a feeling that there was insufficient evidence to remove Ben from his mother's care. Although

DOI: 10.4324/9781003582410-7

he no longer had visible bruising on his face, they said his name should be placed on the Child Protection Register (a confidential list of children who have been identified as being at significant risk of harm and subject to a child protection plan) and the family should be closely monitored by social services. Asked what support the social worker could offer to Ben's mother, the participants stated forcefully that it was their role to ensure the protection of the child, not to offer help and support to the mother. Their argument, however, seemed to lack any acknowledgement of support to parents or caregivers identified in Article 19.2 as a protective measure the state is required to provide or the emphasis on family support in legislation in United Kingdom jurisdictions: the Children Act 1989 (England and Wales), the Children (Scotland) Act 1995, and the Children (Northern Ireland) Order 1995.

### Case Study I

The responses of the participants in my post-qualifying course to the case study outlined in Box 4.1 seemed to reflect what has been described as a child protection orientation to work with children and families. This has been contrasted with a family support or family service orientation (Berridge, 1997; Parton & Berridge, 2011). Article 19 of the UNCRC encapsulates these two approaches, reflecting the dual mandate of social workers in the United Kingdom. This chapter begins by outlining these two orientations before going

**Box 4.1 Child Protection or a Child in Need?**

A community psychiatric nurse contacts social services to make a referral about Mrs. Jones. She is a 34-year-old woman who suffers from depression, and the nurse reports that he has been visiting her since the birth of her 3-year-old son, Ben. During a visit yesterday, the nurse reports that Mrs. Jones told him that she had hit Ben across the face 2 weeks ago because he had been crying. She stated that she had "lost control" and slapped him, leaving a bruise on his face. The nurse states that there were no marks visible on Ben's face yesterday and that he interacted well with his mother while in the home. Mrs. Jones said her husband is away from home for long periods with work, and there are three other children present in the home: Billy, 11; Joanne, 9; and Jess, who just had her first birthday.

Is Ben a child at risk who requires protection from his mother? What are the reasons for your answer?

Should Ben and his siblings be considered children in need who would benefit from family support services to enable them to remain living at home? What are the reasons for your answer?

What support could the social worker allocated to this case offer to Mrs. Jones?

on to argue that in the United Kingdom the child protection orientation dominates practice and is overly focused on narrow concerns about harm and abuse rather than broader concerns about children's overall well-being and development. As outlined below, this may affect other rights under the UNCRC. The chapter contributes to the ongoing debate about the need for child protection and family support to be integrated more effectively to provide enhanced protection for children and uphold their rights.

### *Child Protection and Family Support*

The history of childcare law, policy, and practice in the United Kingdom evidences a competition between these two orientations, often portrayed as a swinging pendulum with one, then the other gaining prominence at various times. Other commentators, however, have suggested that a more appropriate metaphor may be a "sustained tug of war" (Tunstill, 1996, p. 152) or continual "push–pull" between the two (Colton et al., 2001, p. 9). Fox-Harding (1997) noted that the two orientations represent relatively extreme positions on a dimension of views and that it may be possible to identify intermediate positions between them. She highlighted, however, that both are underpinned by fundamentally different values and assumptions regarding the family, origins of childcare problems, and the proper role of the state vis-à-vis the family, as summarised in Table 4.1.

*Table 4.1* A Summary of the Values and Assumptions Underpinning the Child Protection and Family Support Orientations

| | *Child Protection* | *Family Support* |
|---|---|---|
| View of the family | Emphasis on good care rather than biological bonds<br>Child seen as distinct entity from their natural family<br>Child is paramount and seen as essentially dependent and vulnerable<br>Child's right to good quality care and protection from abuse emphasised<br>Parental rights given low priority; parental duty to provide adequate care emphasised | Emphasis on the benefits of biological parent–child bonds<br>Biological or natural family provides the optimum context for the child's growth, upbringing, and development<br>Attention paid to the concept of parental rights and parents, especially working-class parents, seen as vulnerable and powerless in relation to statutory agencies |
| Origins of childcare problems | Individualistic: personal inadequacy and culpability<br>Cyclical nature of poor parenting: Adults who have not experienced good psychological parenting or good care have a poor chance of becoming effective parents | Structural: social divisions<br>Parenting problems are, to a much greater extent, due to external material conditions, such as poverty, environmental stress, and inadequate provision of services and social divisions such as class, gender, and ethnicity |

(*Continued*)

*Table 4.1* (Continued)

| | *Child Protection* | *Family Support* |
|---|---|---|
| Role of the state | Wide and authoritarian<br>Intervention by compulsion in families at low level of concern for child's welfare<br>Intervention is individualised and focused on particular families and children rather than concerned with widespread family support<br>Need for state intervention to protect children from poor parental care<br>When parental care is poor, help to family experiencing problems may be appropriate, but emphasis on removal of child to different home when parental care is poor or abusive<br>If speedy rehabilitation with natural parents seems unlikely, contact should be severed to provide child with certainty and permanence | Wide but less authoritarian<br>Concerned with providing for welfare of children across broad front through various supportive services offered on voluntary basis<br>State intervention aimed at preserving, supporting, and strengthening family unit<br>When parenting is inadequate, support should be offered and intervention should strive to keep child with family<br>Child should only be removed from family as last resort and substantial effort should be put into maintaining links for child with family, and ultimately rehabilitation |

Adapted from Fox-Harding (1997).

The differing underpinning values and assumptions also lead to different emphases in childcare practice (see Table 4.2). A child protection orientation is primarily concerned with the recognition of harm, abuse, and neglect and the protection of children, usually from their parents or caregivers. It is, therefore, built around investigatory and legal concerns and the need to gather and assess forensic evidence, with the relationship between social workers and parents often becoming adversarial in nature. In relation to the UNCRC, a child protection orientation reflects Article 19 (protection from violence, abuse, and neglect) and Article 20 (special protection and assistance for children unable to live with their family, including the provision of alternative care). A family support orientation, by contrast, is more concerned with understanding events or situations thought of as being harmful to children in the wider social context of the difficulties experienced by families. It is, therefore, focused on the assessment of family difficulties and provision of therapeutic and practical services to ameliorate these issues, leading to a working relationship between parents and social workers. A family support orientation, in terms of children's rights, is evident in Article 5 (respect for the rights and responsibilities of parents to provide guidance and direction to their children), Article 9 (the child's right not to be separated from their parents against their will), Article 18 (support for children and parents), and Article 27 (the child's right to an adequate standard of living and help for families who cannot afford to provide this standard).

*Table 4.2* Practice Implications of the Child Protection and Family Support Orientations

| *Child Protection* | *Child Welfare* |
|---|---|
| Recognition of child abuse or neglect | Social context of event or situation |
| Investigation | Assessment |
| Forensic and legal concerns | Provision of therapy and services |
| Adversarial relationships | Partnership relationships |
| North American | European |

Adapted from Spratt (2001) and Khoo et al. (2002).

Although the United Kingdom has frequently been described as exemplifying a child protection orientation, Thoburn (2023) pointed out that child protection services have always been delivered in the context of a broader child welfare and family support approach to families experiencing difficulties. This emphasises Fox-Harding's (1997) observation that there may be intermediate positions between the two orientations, but the extent of dominance of one over the other at any point is the important consideration. In the United Kingdom, a risk-averse approach to practice has developed, and consequently there are high thresholds for family support services, with social workers devoting most of their time and resources to "heavy-end child protection cases" (Thoburn, 2023, p. 136).

The development of this risk-averse approach to social work practice with children and families can be traced back to child abuse inquiries and reviews in the 1970s and 1980s, most notably the 1974 inquiry into the death of Maria Colwell (Butler & Drakeford, 2011). Purcell (2020) argued that the reforms introduced after the Colwell inquiry "changed the face of social work practice irrevocably" (p. 6), leading to a strong focus on child protection. This contrasted with the period from the mid-1940s to the mid-1970s, which Parton (2002) described as being characterised by "a positive and supportive approach to the family … so that the state and the family could work in partnership to ensure that children were provided with the appropriate conditions in which to develop" (p. 14).

The strong focus on child protection heralded by the Colwell inquiry was further bolstered by inquiries in the 1970s and 1980s. Ayre (2001) argued that these events contributed to a climate of fear, mistrust, and blame, with social workers being fearful of being criticised by the media and blamed for a child abuse tragedy. Such fears were not unjustified, given the significant personal and professional consequences for workers who found themselves in such a position (Aldridge, 1999; Valentine, 1994). The public became increasingly mistrustful of social workers, with Jack (1997) noting that:

> Where once social workers were perceived by families as potential sources of assistance with their problems, they now … constitute a further threat to the family's survival, to be avoided if at all possible. … An atmosphere

> of mutual suspicion and mistrust has been created in which the social worker's fear of "getting it wrong" creates a defensive orientation to practice. Preventive approaches have been squeezed out by the increasingly restrictive procedural requirements and the draining away of resources to child protection systems.
>
> (p. 664)

## Balancing Child Protection and Family Support

The difficulties associated with social work practice being narrowly focused on the identification and assessment of individual children suspected of being at risk of abuse have been acknowledged since the late 1980s. Both professionals and policy makers became increasingly concerned that an imbalance had developed between the professional resources devoted to the "blue light" child protection services and services aimed more at prevention and family support (Butler & Hickman, 2011).

The child protection orientation has been particularly difficult to shift despite several reforms that attempted to balance child protection and family support in practice (Biehal, 2019). The legislation in the four United Kingdom nations mentioned earlier, for example, promoted a balance in practice between protecting children at risk of significant harm and providing family support services to children in need and their families. Early evidence following the implementation of the Children Act 1989 in England and Wales, however, indicated that there were difficulties achieving this balance in practice (Aldgate & Tunstill, 1995; Audit Commission, 1994; Colton et al., 1995; Department of Health, 1994, 1996) and that in the context of scarce resources local authorities continued to focus on identifying and providing services for high-risk families at the expense of promoting the welfare of a broader group of children through the provision of family support. As predicted by Parton (1991), therefore, the central concern of social workers has continued to be the identification and management of child protection risks.

In 1995, the publication of a summary of research studies into the routine operation of the child protection system (Department of Health, 1995) recommended a refocusing of policy and practice to prioritise providing support to families with children in need rather than focusing narrowly on investigating alleged incidents of abuse. Parton (1996) summarised the findings of these studies as follows:

> Many investigations are undertaken, many families are visited and case conferences called but … in the end, little support is offered to the family. Not only do the parents become alienated, angry and bewildered, but the children are not helped. Perhaps most crucially, valuable time and resources are wasted, particularly on investigations, with little apparent benefit.
>
> (p. 5)

Some commentators expressed concern that such an approach may compromise the needs of the most severely abused children (Littlechild, 1998) and the refocusing of services in this way would prove to be problematic, as confirmed by several research studies (Department of Health, 2001; Platt, 2006). Hayes and Spratt (2009, 2014), for example, noted that even when referrals were refocused families continued to receive a largely investigatory response from social workers that resulted in little help being offered and case closure once it had been established there were no immediate risks to the children in the family.

The United Kingdom government's response to the Victoria Climbie inquiry (Laming, 2003) also sought to "go beyond protecting children from risk to promoting children's welfare" (Featherstone et al., 2014, p. 8). The aim was to develop preventive services for families with low levels of concern so that all children would be helped to reach their potential. This approach was formalised in the Children Act 2004 in England and in policy across the four United Kingdom nations (Stafford et al., 2012; Vincent, 2010), although some commentators were sceptical and concerned that it may divert attention away from children at serious risk (Munro & Calder, 2005). This model was also called into question following the death of Peter Connelly in 2007 (Jones, 2014; Shoesmith, 2016), and the system reverted to a narrow focus on child protection (Purcell, 2020).

## A Perpetual Problem

Concerns about the dominance of the child protection orientation in social work practice in the United Kingdom have continued unabated since the late 1980s, and as noted this approach has been particularly resistant to reform efforts. Bunting et al. (2018), for example, compared trends in national statistics relating to the operation of child protection systems across the four countries of the United Kingdom, arguing that all are continuing to be increasingly oriented towards child protection, indicated by increasing rates of child protection investigations, children subject to child protection planning, and care proceedings. These issues are not confined to the United Kingdom but apparent across Anglophone countries (United States of America, Canada, Australia, and New Zealand), with increasing numbers of families being investigated for suspected abuse and neglect (Bilson et al., 2015; Featherstone et al., 2018; Lonne et al., 2009; Trocmé et al., 2014).

L. Devine and Parker (2016) analysed data on child protection and safeguarding referrals and assessment outcomes dating back to 1991 and 1992 in England and concluded that a large number of families requiring support services are needlessly being assessed for risk and that this causes resource issues for social workers, contributes to social workers' fears of the consequences of missing a serious case of abuse, and may prevent families from seeking help from social workers and potentially damage those who do. These findings are depressingly similar to those reported some 20 years earlier in research studies (Department of Health, 1995) and summarised by Parton (1996).

Clapton (2020) argued that social work with children and families "helps neither children nor the families in which they live" and that it has become "a narrow, unhelpful and reactive form of child protection" (p. 75). Echoing concerns expressed by Featherstone et al. (2014), he concluded:

> "Child protection" is now the main, if not the only, reason for local authority social workers to be involved with families, to the extent that supporting families is not even seen as part of the role of social workers. … Social workers regularly counterpose the welfare of families with that of children, and interventions are badged as "for the children."
>
> (Clapton, 2020, p. 89)

In response to these continuing concerns, attempts to promote a reorientation of social work practice towards supporting children and families rather than identifying risk of harm and abuse have continued.

In Northern Ireland, for example, there has been growing recognition that the child welfare system is under severe pressure and cannot provide the level of help needed by children and families. The impact of high workloads, bureaucracy, and staff vacancies and turnover on the ability of social workers to meet demand and a focus on child protection at the expense of family support have been highlighted in several reports (Department of Health Northern Ireland, 2022; Northern Ireland Association of Social Workers, 2012, 2016). High levels of staff vacancies, for example, have led to large numbers of unallocated cases, with more than 4,000 children and their families waiting for assessment and services (Reimagine Children's Collective, 2023).

These increasing demands and pressures culminated in the Department of Health Northern Ireland commissioning a review of children's social care services (Jones, 2023). The review concluded that child social work in Northern Ireland has become skewed and heavily focused on child protection and needs to be refocused towards family support. The report argued that this should happen in a structure that provides greater focus on children's social care and proposed that a single, region-wide organisation be created for statutory child and family social care services. This central recommendation has not been implemented at the time of writing, leading the report author to conclude that children's social care reform is being "lost in the long grass" (British Association of Social Workers, 2025, para. 1). This has led to considerable frustration among young people in care and their families regarding care experiences (Voice of Young People in Care, 2025):

> They feel there's a power imbalance, that the system is difficult to navigate. They feel that if a situation gets too complex that the default action is to take the kids away. … They all say that while they acknowledge social workers have to consider what is best for the kids, there are also times when they feel families could have received more help. For instance, there

> are cases of kids being taken on the grounds of being "at risk of emotional abuse" or "at risk of neglect." Many of the families I spoke to argue, rightly or wrongly, that perhaps a family who could get more support to overcome these challenges could be spared the trauma of separation.
>
> (Jordan, 2025)

The government also commissioned a review of children's services in England (MacAlister, 2022), which concluded that children's services had become unduly skewed away from family support and prevention and become overly focused on "crisis intervention, with outcomes for children that continue to be unacceptably poor" (p. 8). The government, however, did not provide the substantial investment in family support services that the review requested, which was notably only about 20% of what directors of children's services had deemed necessary to bring about the required reorientation in social work practice (Willow, 2023). It seems, therefore, very unlikely that the level of funding earmarked for implementing the review's recommendations will be sufficient to effect the changes required. The proposals from the review have also been critiqued by some commentators as likely to fail, given the scale of change proposed, and may have the unintended consequences of increasing the number of child protection cases and undermining family support (Community Care, 2025; Samuel, 2025).

A system that prioritises child protection over family support, investigates families for suspected abuse, fails to deliver help to children and their parents and caregivers, and alienates families from seeking help from social workers is highly problematic. It is even more concerning that these issues are well known yet the current dominance of the child protection orientation to social work practice is stubbornly entrenched and resistant to reform efforts. The problems with this orientation are exacerbated when we consider which families are on the receiving end of social work intervention: overwhelmingly those experiencing poverty and disadvantage.

## The Problem of Poverty and Disadvantage

The case study outlined in Box 4.2 is based on an article by Kellagher (2023) in which he warns of the dangers of mistaking child poverty for child neglect instead of seeing it as systemic government neglect. This is an interesting observation, given the responsibilities of the state under Article 27 of the UNCRC to recognise the right of every child to a standard of living adequate for their development. While recognising that parents and caregivers have the primary responsibility in this regard, Article 27 indicates that the state should "take appropriate measures to assist parents and others responsible for the child to implement this right and shall in case of need provide material assistance and support programmes, particularly with regard to nutrition, clothing and housing" (Section 3).

**Box 4.2 Seeing the System, Not Just the Parent: Poverty and Child Protection Decision-Making**

Jenny Magee is a 24-year-old single parent who has two children (Sam, 5, and Dean, 2). She sought social services after being discharged from hospital, having been admitted due to malnutrition because she had been missing meals so she could afford to feed Sam and Dean. The children received care from their maternal grandmother while Jenny was in the hospital. On the first visit to the home, the social worker noted that there was no heating, inadequate bedding, and very little food in the cupboards. The social worker observed that although there were very few toys in the house, the children appeared to be happy and content, and Jenny was very attentive to them.

Reflecting on this scenario, do you think Sam and Dean are experiencing neglect or poverty? What are the reasons for your answer?
Who is culpable in this situation? Is Jenny neglecting her children, or is the scenario reflective of systemic government neglect?
Should social workers have a role in tackling poverty? If so, how could they do this in relation to this case study at the personal, cultural, and structural levels?

**Case Study II**

Statistics regarding poverty in the United Kingdom are sobering; B. Devine (2025) reported that, accounting for housing costs, 21% of people in the United Kingdom were in relative poverty and 18% were in absolute poverty in 2023 and 2024. Some groups are more likely to be in poverty after housing costs:

- Working-age adults (43%) and children (62%) living in a family where nobody is employed
- People in social rented (40%) and private rented (37%) accommodation
- Children in families with three or more children (44%)
- People in families with a family member who has a disability (28%)
- People in Bangladeshi (53%) and Pakistani (47%) households

Bilson and Martin (2017), based on a freedom of information request, collected data from 75% of all English children's social services departments about children born in the 2009 and 2010 financial year. From this data, they observed that 1 in 9 children born that year was suspected of being abused and 1 in 19 was formally investigated. The authors argued that such a high level of intervention could only be justified if it is "demonstrably reducing harm and promoting well-being of children—an outcome which is contested" (Bilson & Martin, 2017, p. 793). They observed that many of these children lived in families experiencing high levels of poverty and, in recognition of this, called for a move away from the emphasis on individualised and investigative approaches towards more work with children and families.

As Featherstone et al. (2014) noted, most children who come under the investigative gaze of social workers, including those who are removed from their families, are "overwhelmingly economically and socially deprived" (p. 4). The UNCRC, however, applies to every child without discrimination (Article 2), and intervention that is overly focused on poor and disadvantaged families breaches principles of social justice and the enjoyment of equal rights by all children.

In a response to a call for evidence from the review of children's social care services in England, a group of academics (Hood et al., 2021) provided the following commentary:

> A system whose statutory underpinning emphasises the duty to support children to live and thrive in their birth families and home communities has become out of kilter, preoccupied with, and overwhelmed by, the regulatory activities of surveillance, investigation and protection. Recent studies have found: a steep social gradient in referrals to CSC [children's social care] and in subsequent interventions ... over-representation of some minority ethnic groups in the child protection ... and care systems ... disproportionate targeting of low-income neighbourhoods in otherwise affluent local authorities ... [and] professional practice that often does not assess or address families' material circumstances.
>
> (p. 2)

Bywaters and The Child Welfare Inequalities Project Team (2020) reported large-scale inequalities in child welfare, noting that the chances of children being looked after by the state or being subject to child protection plans or registers were profoundly unequal both within and among the four countries in the United Kingdom. The authors noted that children in the most deprived 10% of small neighbourhoods were more than 10 times more likely to be in foster or residential care or on protection plans than children in the least deprived 10%. They concluded that this "is unfair. It is contrary to principles of social justice and human rights enshrined in the Convention on the Rights of the Child. It has lifelong and life-threatening consequences for children" (Bywaters & The Child Welfare Inequalities Project Team, 2020, p. 5).

When we read stories in the social work trade press that cases of child neglect are on the rise but the reasons given are the rising cost of living and a reduction in support for parents (Professional Social Work, 2024) or that children are being removed from their families due to unsafe or inappropriate housing conditions, including maintenance issues, mould, damp, insect or vermin infestations, or cramped conditions (Social Workers Union, 2025), perhaps we should reflect on how fair and just these situations are and who is culpable—individual families or the government.

## Conclusion

The dual mandate of social workers in the United Kingdom for both protecting children at risk of immediate harm and promoting the overall development and well-being of children in need by providing services and support to the family is skewed towards the former with too little emphasis on the latter. Although it is unquestionable that some children require immediate protection and removal from very damaging situations, child protection responses should be limited to "the relatively small number of cases where damage to children is evident and serious" (Hood et al., 2021, p. 3), with much more emphasis on supporting children and families experiencing poverty and disadvantage rather than subjecting them to a child protection investigation. Rather than seeing child protection and family support as alternatives, they need to be viewed more as overlapping and complementary activities, as outlined in the notions of protective support and supportive protection described by McGregor and Devaney (2020).

The notion that social workers are only there for the child also needs to be challenged, especially if this is an argument for not supporting parents. As Lord Laming (2003) argued in the Victoria Climbie inquiry report, "It is not possible to separate the protection of children from wider support to families. Indeed, often the best protection for a child is achieved by the timely intervention of family support services" (p. 6). Echoing this point, the UNCRC General Comment 13 "emphasizes in the strongest terms that child protection must begin with proactive prevention. … Preventive measures offer the greatest return in the long term" (para. 4.6). Also, as noted by Featherstone et al. (2014, p. 3), social workers need to reflect on the ethical desirability of focusing on "rescuing children … [and] leaving their parents behind in a society riven by inequalities" (p. 3).

As a society, we also need to reflect on what we mean by child protection and move from a narrow focus on abuse and neglect towards a broader focus on harm experienced by children due to poverty and inequality and provision of services to families to ameliorate these issues. "Child protection has rarely meant protection from poverty and the effects of poverty such as malnutrition, homelessness, poor educational achievement and bad health, nor is it protection from bullying, from racism or from risk of road accidents" (Clapton, 2020, p. 91).

Despite acknowledgement that the current system is problematic and needs to be reoriented towards family support, the current dominance of the child protection orientation has proven resistant to reform efforts since the late 1980s. It remains to be seen if such a shift can be achieved, both in the minds of social workers, who may fear the dangers associated with the blame culture if they miss child protection risks (Ayre, 2001), and in the purse strings of the government to release sufficient funding for the development of family support services. Such a shift, however, is imperative because the current system interferes with children's full enjoyment of their rights under the UNCRC and social work practice, and effectively balancing child protection and family support would provide a clear mechanism to address this issue.

## References

Aldgate, J., & Tunstill, J. (1995). *Making sense of Section 17: Implementing services for children in need within the 1989 Children Act*. Her Majesty's Stationery Office.
Aldridge, M. (1999). Poor relations: State social work and the press in the UK. In B. Franklin (Ed.), *Social policy, the media and misrepresentation* (pp. 89–103). Routledge.
Audit Commission. (1994). *Seen but not heard: Co-ordinating child health and social services for children in need*. Her Majesty's Stationery Office.
Ayre, P. (2001). Child protection and the media: Lessons from the last three decades. *British Journal of Social Work*, *31*(6), 887–901. https://doi.org/10.1093/bjsw/31.6.887
Berridge, D. (1997). England: Child abuse reports, responses, and reforms. In N. Gilbert (Ed.), *Combatting child abuse: International perspectives and trends* (pp. 72–101). Oxford University Press.
Biehal, N. (2019). Balancing prevention and protection: Child protection in England. In L. Merkel-Holguin, J. Fluke, & R. Krugman (Eds.), *National systems of child protection: Understanding the international variability and context for developing policy and practice* (pp. 51–73). Springer.
Bilson, A., Cant, R., Harries, M., & Thorpe, D. (2015). A longitudinal study of children reported to the child protection department in Western Australia. *British Journal of Social Work*, *45*(3), 771–791. https://doi.org/10.1093/bjsw/bct164
Bilson, A., & Martin, K. (2017). Referrals and child protection in England: One in five children referred to children's services and one in nineteen investigated before the age of five. *British Journal of Social Work*, *47*(3), 793–811. https://doi.org/10.1093/bjsw/bcw054
British Association of Social Workers. (2025). *Children's social care reform is being kicked into the long grass*. https://basw.co.uk/about-social-work/psw-magazine/articles/childrens-social-care-reform-being-kicked-long-grass
Bunting, L., McCartan, C., McGhee, J., Bywaters, P., Daniel, B., Featherstone, B., & Slater, T. (2018). Trends in child protection across the UK: A comparative analysis. *British Journal of Social Work*, *48*(5), 1154–1175. https://doi.org/10.1093/bjsw/bcx102
Butler, I., & Drakeford, M. (2011). *Social work on trial: The Colwell inquiry and the state of welfare*. Policy Press.
Butler, I., & Hickman, C. (2011). *Social work with children and families: Getting into practice* (3rd edn.). Jessica Kingsley.
Bywaters, P., & The Child Welfare Inequalities Project Team. (2020). *The Child Welfare Inequalities Project: Final report*. Nuffield Foundation.
Clapton, G. (2020). Child protection anxieties and the formation of UK child welfare and protection practices. In L. Tsaliki & D. Chronaki (Eds.), *Discourses of anxiety over childhood and youth across cultures* (pp. 75–98). Palgrave MacMillan.
Colton, M., Drury, C., & Williams, M. (1995). *Children in need: Family support under the Children Act 1989*. Avebury.
Colton, M., Sanders, R., & Williams, M. (2001). *An introduction to working with children: A guide for social workers*. Palgrave.
Community Care. (2025). *Ray Jones: A critique of the DfE's children's social work reforms*. https://www.communitycare.co.uk/2025/05/23/ray-jones-a-critique-of-the-dfes-childrens-social-work-reforms/
Department of Health. (1994). *The Children Act report 1993*. Her Majesty's Stationery Office.
Department of Health. (1995). *Child protection: Messages from research*. Her Majesty's Stationery Office.
Department of Health. (1996). *The Children Act report 1994*. Her Majesty's Stationery Office.
Department of Health. (2001). *The Children Act now: Messages from research*. Her Majesty's Stationery Office.

Department of Health Northern Ireland. (2022). *Social work workforce review Northern Ireland 2022.*
Devine, B. (2025). *Poverty in the UK: Statistics.* House of Commons Library.
Devine, L., & Parker, S. (2016). *Making the case for rethinking child protection strategy: Findings from a large-scale study in England.* University of Edinburgh. https://blogs.sps.ed.ac.uk/revisitingchildprotection/index.html%3Fp=187.html
Featherstone, B., Gupta, A., Morris, K., & Warner, J. (2018). Let's stop feeding the risk monster: Towards a social model of child protection. *Families, Relationships and Societies*, *7*(1), 7–22. https://doi.org/10.1332/204674316X14552878034622
Featherstone, B., White, S., & Morris, K. (2014). *Re-imagining child protection: Towards humane social work with families.* Policy Press.
Fox-Harding, L. (1997). *Perspectives in child care policy* (2nd edn.). Longman.
Hayes, D., & Spratt, T. (2009). Child welfare interventions: Patterns of social work practice. *British Journal of Social Work*, *39*(8), 1575–1597. https://doi.org/10.1093/bjsw/bcn098
Hayes, D., & Spratt, T. (2014). Child welfare as child protection then and now: What social workers did and continue to do. *British Journal of Social Work*, *44*(3), 615–635. https://doi.org/10.1093/bjsw/bcs161
Hood, R., Featherstone, B., Bywaters, P., Gupta, A., Bilson, A., Morris, K., & Webb, C. (2021). *Evidence for system reform needed to address the socio-economic drivers of demand and reduce inequalities in child welfare provision.* https://apsw.org.uk/wp-content/uploads/2021/05/Submission-1.pdf
Jack, G. (1997). Discourses of child protection and child welfare. *British Journal of Social Work*, *27*(5), 659–678. https://doi.org/10.1093/oxfordjournals.bjsw.a011259
Jones, R. (2014). *The story of Baby P: Setting the record straight.* Policy Press.
Jones, R. (2023). *The Northern Ireland review of children's social care services report.* Department of Health Northern Ireland.
Jordan, C. (2025). Families' dismay as number of children in care in Northern Ireland rises. *UTV/ITV News.* https://www.itv.com/news/utv/2025-10-01/a-system-in-crisis-inside-nis-social-care-system
Kellagher, P. (2023, September/October). Shocking case highlights need for us to give voice to poverty. *Professional Social Work*, 13.
Khoo, E., Hyvonen, U., & Nygren, L. (2002). Child welfare or child protection: Uncovering Swedish and Canadian orientations to social intervention in child maltreatment. *Qualitative Social Work*, *1*(4), 451–471. https://doi.org/10.1177/1473325002001004
Laming, H. (2003). *The Victoria Climbie inquiry report.* Her Majesty's Stationery Office.
Littlechild, B. (1998). Does family support ensure the protection of children? Messages from child protection research. *Child Abuse Review*, *7*(2), 116–128. https://doi.org/10.1002/(SICI)1099-0852(199803/04)7:2%3C116::AID-CAR348%3E3.0.CO;2-V
Lonne, B., Parton, N., Thomson, J., & Harries, M. (2009). *Reforming child protection.* Routledge.
MacAlister, J. (2022). *The independent review of children's social care: Final report.* Department for Education.
McGregor, C., & Devaney, C. (2020). Protective support and supportive protection for families "in the middle": Learning from the Irish context. *Child and Family Social Work*, *25*(2), 277–285. https://doi.org/10.1111/cfs.12683
Munro, E., & Calder, M. (2005). Where has child protection gone? *The Political Quarterly*, *76*(3), 439–445. https://doi.org/10.1111/j.1467-923X.2005.00703.x
Northern Ireland Association of Social Workers. (2012). *Social work not paperwork: Cutting bureaucracy in childcare social work.* https://basw.co.uk/sites/default/files/resources/basw_123352-5_0.pdf
Northern Ireland Association of Social Workers. (2016). *Above and beyond: At what cost?* https://basw.co.uk/policy-and-practice/resources/above-and-beyond-what-cost
Parton, N. (1991). *Governing the family: Child care, child protection and the state.* Palgrave.

Parton, N. (1996). Child protection, family support and social work: A critical appraisal of the Department of Health research studies in child protection. *Child and Family Social Work*, *1*(1), 3–11. https://doi.org/10.1111/j.1365-2206.1996.tb00002.x

Parton, N. (2002). Protecting children: A socio-historical analysis. In K. Wilson & A. James (Eds.), *The child protection handbook* (2nd edn.), pp. 11–28). Bailliere Tindall.

Parton, N., & Berridge, D. (2011). Child protection in England. In N. Gilbert, N. Parton, & M. Skivenes (Eds.), *Child protection systems: International trends and orientations* (pp. 60–85). Oxford University Press.

Platt, D. (2006). Threshold decisions: How social workers prioritise referrals of child concern. *Child Abuse Review*, *15*(1), 4–18. https://doi.org/10.1002/car.929

Professional Social Work. (2024, September/October). Child neglect on the rise. *Professional Social Work*, 6.

Purcell, C. (2020). *The politics of children's services reform: Re-examining two decades of policy change*. Policy Press.

Reimagine Children's Collective. (2023). *Reimagining children's social care services in Northern Ireland*. https://www.barnardos.org.uk/sites/default/files/2023-11/Reimaging%20Children%27s%20Social%20Care.pdf

Samuel, M. (2025). Munro: Children's social care reforms "very likely to fail" due to scale of change and lack of testing. *Community Care*. https://www.communitycare.co.uk/2025/07/03/munro-childrens-social-care-reforms-very-likely-to-fail-due-to-scale-of-change-and-lack-of-testing/

Shoesmith, S. (2016). *Learning from Baby P: The politics of blame, fear and denial*. Jessica Kingsley.

Social Workers Union. (2025). *Social workers report housing crisis for children*. https://swu-union.org.uk/2025/04/social-workers-report-housing-crisis-for-children

Spratt, T. (2001). The influence of child protection orientation on child welfare practice. *British Journal of Social Work*, *31*(6), 933–954. https://doi.org/10.1093/bjsw/31.6.933

Stafford, A., Vincent, S., Parton, N., & Smith, C. (2012). *Child protection systems in the United Kingdom: A comparative analysis*. Jessica Kingsley.

Thoburn, J. (2023). Child welfare and child protection services in England. In J. D. Berrick, N. Gilbert, & M. Skivenes (Eds.), *The Oxford handbook of child protection systems* (pp. 135–155). Oxford University Press.

Trocmé, N., Kyte, A., Sinha, V., & Fallon, B. (2014). Urgent protection versus chronic need: Clarifying the dual mandate of child welfare services across Canada. *Social Sciences*, *3*(3), 483–498. https://doi.org/10.3390/socsci3030483

Trotter, C. (2022). *Working with involuntary clients: A guide to practice* (4th edn.). Routledge.

Tunstill, J. (1996). Family support: Past, present and future challenges. *Child and Family Social Work*, *1*(3), 151–158. https://doi.org/10.1111/j.1365-2206.1996.tb00021.x

United Nations. (1989). *Convention on the rights of the child*. https://www.ohchr.org/en/instruments-mechanisms/instruments/convention-rights-child

Valentine, M. (1994). The social worker as bad object. *British Journal of Social Work*, *24*(1), 71–86. https://doi.org/10.1093/oxfordjournals.bjsw.a056041

Vincent, S. (2010). An overview of safeguarding and protecting children across the UK. In A. Stafford, S. Vincent, & N. Parton (Eds.), *Child protection reform across the United Kingdom* (pp. 1–11). Dunedin Academic Press.

Voice of Young People in Care. (2025). *Show us you care: A call to action from care experienced young people*. https://www.voypic.org/wp-content/uploads/2025/10/Show-Us-You-Care-Call-to-Action-FINAL.pdf%20

Willow, C. (2023). Where now? Children's rights in England into the 2020s. In R. Sen & C. Kerr (Eds.), *The future of children's care: Critical perspectives on children's services reform* (pp. 14–37). Policy Press.

# 5 Balancing Protective Legislation and Children's Rights*

*Ravit Alfandari and Shiran Reichenberg*

## Introduction

A global commitment to ensure children's right to protection from maltreatment was reinforced by the United Nations Convention on the Rights of the Child (UNCRC; United Nations, 1989). The UNCRC placed on member states the responsibility of establishing measures to react to all forms of maltreatment and exploitation, to decrease their occurrence and prevent their recurrence.

Article 19 of the UNCRC (United Nations, 1989) reads as follows:

1. State parties shall take all appropriate legislative, administrative, social and educational measures to protect the child from all forms of physical or mental violence, injury or abuse, neglect or negligent treatment, maltreatment or exploitation, including sexual abuse, while in care of parent(s), legal guardian(s) or any other persons who have care of the child.
2. Such protective measures should, as appropriate, include effective procedures for the establishment of social programmes to provide necessary support for the child and for those who have the care of the child, as well as for other forms of prevention and for identification, reporting, referral, investigation, treatment and follow-up of instances of child maltreatment described heretofore, and, as appropriate, for judicial involvement.

Although the significance of Article 19 in forming a unified international obligation to preserve the safety of children is undisputable, leaving it to the states to construct their national protective responses is arguably problematic (Berrick et al., 2023, 2024). One line of critique relates to operational definitions of eligibility criteria, including fundamental dimensions such as who is considered a child and what risks they require protection against, these being variable and depending on social and cultural ideological traditions and circumstances (Berrick et al., 2024). For example, regarding definitions of

* Research for this chapter was supported by Israel Science Foundation Grant No. 1569/23.

DOI: 10.4324/9781003582410-8

maltreatment, violence, and abuse, practices like corporal punishment or child marriage are often cited yet may not be categorised as forms of abuse in some countries and cultures (Berrick et al., 2024).

In this regard, Israel, the focus of this chapter, is an interesting case due to its diverse population demonstrating a range of cultural norms and religious values, including Arab, ultra-Orthodox Jewish, and immigrant societies from the former Soviet Union and Ethiopia.

Another line of critique relates to the UNCRC not providing answers regarding the appropriate balance between protecting children and regarding them as autonomous individuals with rights to shape their future. This leads to tensions when establishing procedural and systemic responses to secure children's protection against maltreatment while actualising their other fundamental rights recognised in the convention (Mitchell et al., 2023). Considerable attention has been given to the realisation of children's right to participation (i.e., Article 12) as a source of conflict, with implementation of the right to be protected from harm an issue frequently discussed in the context of child protection decision-making practices (Alfandari, 2016; McCafferty, 2017; Mitchell et al., 2023). Dedicated chapters in Section III of this book offer further discussion on this topic.

This chapter discusses Section 2 of Article 19—i.e., the arrangements taken by states to secure the protection of children against all forms of maltreatment or exploitation "while in care of parent(s), legal guardian(s) or any other persons who have care of the child," as specified in Section 1 of Article 19. Particularly, it focuses on legislative responses established by governments to safeguard children's right to be protected from harm, with Israel serving as a case study. The strong relationship between the law and social work practice in Israel (Doron, 2012) has significantly shaped supportive services established to prevent and treat child maltreatment. In child protection cases, social workers hold legal duties in criminal investigations of maltreatment; they are required to collaborate with courts or quasi-judicial bodies, creating a legalistic approach to their work (Rosenfeld & Kedem, 1998).

The core underlying argument at the heart of this chapter is that legislation to support the objective of Article 19 requires a deliberate balance among (a) the state's authority to intervene in a family's life to protect children from harm, (b) safeguarding parents' or caregivers' parental rights to privacy and family integrity, and (c) recognition of children as autonomous individuals accorded with unique individual rights separate from their parents (Berrick et al., 2022, 2023). The analysis demonstrates how this inherent tension among the interests of the state, parents, and children is expressed through legislative developments established to secure the protection of children. Three key legislative responses are examined in this chapter, dealing with child maltreatment mandatory reporting (Penal Code Amendment No. 26, 1989), the provision of daycare services for children at risk of maltreatment (Young Children at Risk (Eligibility for Day Care) Law, 2000; hereafter referred to as the Toddlers at Risk Law), and out-of-home foster care arrangements (Children Foster Care Law, 2016).

This original analysis evokes Gilbert et al.' (2011) well-known typology of child welfare system orientations in relatively high-income Western nations (i.e., child risk, family service, and child-centric approaches) as a conceptual framework. The typology is used to reflect on how the government's legal actions involve deliberate choices as to how the pressures on the interests of stakeholders (i.e., the state, parents, and children) should be balanced and regulated. Such systemic contexts influence social workers' practices in terms of the threshold set for activating state responses such as child maltreatment assessment and services delivery (Berrick et al., 2022; Turney et al., 2024).

The chapter is structured into four parts, starting with an outline of the conceptual framework, followed by a short description of the Israeli context from a global perspective. The core section addresses protective legislation arrangements to secure children's right to protection from parental harm, starting from an outline of international perspectives and moving to an analysis of three key legislative responses in Israel. The chapter ends with a conclusion.

## Conceptual Framework: Child Welfare System Typology

As mentioned, Gilbert et al.' (2011) typology of child welfare system orientations in industrialised Western countries serves as a lens to examine the Israeli government's responsibility for safeguarding children from harm as expressed in legislative responses. Gilbert et al. (2011) characterised three primary orientations to child welfare systems. The first is a child risk approach, focusing on assessment of indicators of likely harm and employing a relative high threshold for intervention. Thus, the state interferes in the private sphere of family life mainly to evaluate the serious risk of harm and provides services when the likelihood of future harm is estimated as high. The child protection systems in the United Kingdom and California are examples of such a risk-focused approach (Alfandari et al., 2023; Berrick et al., 2022).

The second orientation, a family service approach, emphasises the provision of a wide range of universal primary and secondary preventive support services for families prior to the onset of risk or at its early stage. Such need-focused systems apply a low threshold for supportive interventions with the aim of empowering parents and strengthening the family's protective capacities to prevent the possibilities of intrusive interventions like out-of-home placement. Most Nordic countries are examples of this approach (Gilbert, 2011).

The third style is a child-oriented approach that presents a profound commitment to children's rights. Children are treated as individuals with their own rights, independent of the family. Accordingly, the child's interests are a priority and should govern parents' rights, including when intervening to protect children from maltreatment. Child protection systems in some Nordic countries are exemplars of such a child-centric orientation, being highly responsive to children's rights and unique needs while according them the power and agency to which they are entitled (Berrick et al., 2022).

## The Israeli Context

The UNCRC, ratified by the government of Israel in 1991, is not part of Israeli law, unlike in countries such as Mexico, Norway, Iceland, Sweden, and Scotland, where it was incorporated into local laws and is part of the judicial system (Berrick et al., 2023). In 1997, the Israel Ministry of Justice (2003) appointed a formal commission (known as the Rotlevi Commission) to scrutinise Israeli law thoroughly and suggest systemic adjustments in light of the UNCRC. Although some of the commission's findings progressed to enacted legislation, most remained as guiding principles for policymakers. Furthermore, the Israeli Supreme Court has established an interpretative presumption that legislation should be interpreted, as much as possible, in accordance with the provisions of the convention (*Abu-Hasan v. State of Israel*, 1999).

Although a detailed description of Israel's institutional professional social services provisions established to safeguard children's right to protection from harm is beyond the scope of this chapter, it is important to position Israel in the international context in this regard. Using Berrick et al.'s (2023) global ranking of 50 counties according to the degree of governmental ability to finance and provide systematically organised and professionally functioning institutionalised services to protect children from harm or risk of harm, Israel is included in the highest category, representing the most fully developed capacity (i.e., institutionalised), together with other high-income, industrialised Western countries.

## Protective Legislation Arrangements for Children

From a global perspective, the varied landscape of children's protective legislation arrangements can be broadly divided into three key categories: (a) countries that have a single coherent law that consolidates all relevant aspects of child protection matters, such as Estonia and South Korea; (b) countries that have laws designed to regulate various areas of child maltreatment (e.g., reporting, assessment, and intervention), such as Israel and the Slovak Republic and; (c) countries that have united legal arrangements regarding child protection with protection of other vulnerable groups in society (e.g., older adults or people with disabilities), such as Denmark and Sweden (Berrick et al., 2023).

Israel's binding legislative framework underlying the national response to children's right to protection is not a matter of systematic, thorough, and well-planned programming; rather, it has been shaped by macro-level influences throughout the years (e.g., public pressure after high-profile cases of children's deaths and mass immigration waves), creating a fragmented and inconsistent legal structure for protective services provision (Doron, 2001, 2012). Various laws, enacted in different periods, reflect shifting and often contradictory social perspectives, different perceptions of rights, and the lack of a unified ideology or consistent direction (Doron, 2001).

The rest of this section is dedicated to the analysis of three key pieces of protective legislation in Israel relating to mandatory reporting of child maltreatment (Penal Code Amendment 26, 1989), provision of child daycare services to families (Toddlers at Risk Law, 2000), and foster care arrangements (Foster Care for Children Law, 2016). The analysis demonstrates shifts over time in systemic child welfare orientations and how they represent different approaches to balancing the relationship among the state, parents, and children by giving greater weight to each stakeholder's rights.

#### *Mandatory Reporting: Child Risk Approach—The Interest of the State*

Mandatory reporting laws for child maltreatment have been long-standing policy in many countries, including Israel, to address the nondisclosure of abuse by individuals well-positioned to identify it, with the primary goal of ensuring that suspected cases are reported to state authorities (Mathews, 2015). Israeli law mandates that any adult can report a "reasonable suspicion" of offenses against children and young people by anyone, including their primary caregivers, to the police or social services (Penal Code Amendment 26, 1989).

When viewed in the context of international child maltreatment reporting laws, such as those in the United States, Australia, Canada, Sweden, and Taiwan, Israel's law is considerably harsher and more comprehensive (Alfandari, 2016; Mathews, 2015; Mathews & Kenny, 2008). This is reflected in several aspects of the legislation. First, the policy is incorporated in the criminal law (penal code), rather than being part of child protection or social services legislation. Second, it designates all citizens as mandatory reporters, not only professionals working closely with children such as teachers and doctors, who have a particular duty to report with harsher sanctions for noncompliance. The law encompasses a wide range of conditions necessitating a report, including any reasonable suspicion of an offense that endangers a child's life or health: sexual offenses, neglect, abandonment, assault, abuse, and human trafficking. It also grants both the police and social workers special legal authority and power to investigate these reports. Last, rather than imposing financial penalties for failing to report, the law stipulates imprisonment of 3 months for a citizen and 6 months for a caregiver or professional (Alfandari, 2016; Mathews, 2015; Mathews & Kenny, 2008).

Israeli reporting law arguably demonstrates a child risk orientation, given its focus on identifying parents who are committing child maltreatment, yet it does not specify any services that must be provided to secure the child's right to protection in cases of substantial harm or risk of harm. Furthermore, findings from qualitative studies in Arab and ultra-Orthodox Jewish societies have highlighted the problematic nature of this precedence of the legal process over the delivery of help, particularly in these communities (Alfandari, Enosh, et al., 2021a; Alfandari, Massarwa, et al., 2021b). For example, a common pattern reported by Arab art therapists is that in the aftermath of reporting child maltreatment suspicions their therapeutic relationship is terminated immediately, and the child does not return to treatment (Alfandari, Massarwa, et al., 2021b).

Through this comprehensive mandatory law, the state takes over the responsibility to protect children from harm caused by their parents and functions as watchdog to ensure children's safety via greater intervention in family life and sanctions (Gilbert, 2011). A good example is a subsequent amendment to the reporting law enacted in 2007 (Penal Code Amendment 94), which obligates parents to report suspicion of sexual abuse between minor siblings. The change was enacted to address the possible dilemma for parents in such situations regarding which of their children to support (Asif, 2009). Such a risk-focused and investigative or forensic approach can generate adversarial state–parent relationships (Gilbert, 2011).

A notably unique aspect of Israeli law is the exceptional authority given to professional forums, appointed by the Minister of Justice, to waive mandatory reporting to the police if such reporting is deemed to interfere with the child's best interests (Penal Code Amendment 26, 1989). Yet the law does not specify crucial aspects of this procedure, including the criteria to waive reporting to the police, leaving considerable room for professional judgement (Nachmani-Rot, 2009). The implications of these policies at practice level are illustrated in the following case study of the Levi family (pseudonyms are used for confidentiality).

Michal, aged 12, is removed from her home to out-of-home placement due to her parents' difficulties in caring for and protecting her. Before removal, Michal's parents divorced. Their family social worker received reports about worrying deterioration in Michal's mental and emotional functioning following this drastic change in her family life. During Michal's stay in the placement, she discloses being sexually abuse by an acquaintance of her father. About 3 months after Michal is removed to placement, her younger sister Noa, aged 10, discloses to her schoolteacher that Michal had sexually abused her. The social worker makes a request to waive mandatory reporting to the police in Noa's case, based on Michal's mental and emotional condition, the fact that she was placed out of the home and supervised while visiting the family, and the parents' cooperation with a designated therapeutic programme for them and their daughters. The social worker's request is granted by the professional forum, at first temporarily and later as a permanent arrangement.

**Box 5.1 Reflective Questions for Social Workers: Balancing the Rights and Safety of Children**

How can I ensure the delivery of help to children in cases of substantial harm or risk of harm caused by their parents under mandatory reporting laws?

How can I balance the rights of all children in the family in reported cases of abuse between minor siblings?

How much weight do I give to social and cultural ideological traditions and circumstances when operating under mandatory reporting laws?

***Toddlers at Risk Law (Right to Daycare): Family Service Approach—The Interest of the Family***

The Toddlers at Risk Law (2000), known as the right to daycare, puts the obligation on the state to provide toddlers up to age 36 months with subsidised daycare services when there is a risk to their appropriate development. The law was designed with a preventive objective: Child daycare services are expected to meet the children's needs and prevent the need for out-of-home placement. It should be noted that in Israel, no state-funded daycare arrangements are available for children until age 3, and paid maternity leave is only 3 months.

Prior to the enactment of the law, several attempts throughout the years by the Israeli parliament (Knesset) sought to promote a legal change that would obligate the state to provide services to vulnerable children and young people. Yet such efforts became tangled in long parliamentary processes due to political conflicts and did not progress into legislation (Weissblei, 2011). The Toddlers at Risk Law (2000) thus represents exceptional legislation that confers specific rights to services for eligible populations—in this case, toddlers at risk—under defined legal conditions.

On the face of it, the law may be regarded as demonstrating a family services orientation, given parents' rights to family life are facilitated by professional social workers who intervene through needs assessment and provision of support services to strengthen the family unit (Gilbert, 2011). Such an approach is expected to promote a partnership between the state and parents, with the state embracing and encouraging parents' responsibility for their children's care and safety. However, this legislation is another example of the child risk approach, marked by greater state intervention justified by taking on the duty of protecting children from harm caused by their parents.

First, the law does not prescribe universal services, and the threshold for support is not as low as would be expected if the policy were oriented towards family services. Eligibility criteria necessitate evidence that the child has been abused, suffered continuous neglect to the point that their developmental needs have not been met, or experienced serious developmental delays due to familial circumstances or that one of the parents demonstrated impaired functioning due to conditions such as substance abuse, mental illness, or serious disability. Thus, in effect, the aim of this state intervention is not prevention as emphasised by a family services orientation, but rather reduction of circumstances of severe harm to the child after maltreatment or harm has been substantiated, a strong indicator of a child risk approach.

Beyond setting gatekeeping mechanisms such as formal decision-making committees and a high threshold for determining who is entitled to child daycare services, the law forms unintended stigmatisation, which paradoxically may deter parents from accessing the very services designed to support them. The law's terminology, specifically the use of the term "at risk," creates a labelling effect that can potentially negatively affect the child's and family's standing in their community (Krumer-Nevo, 2016). Such labelling can result in social isolation or discrimination that runs counter to the law's protective intentions, particularly for Arab and ultra-Orthodox Jewish societies, in which the family's unity and reputation are of primary value (Alfandari, Enosh, et al., 2021a; Alfandari, Massarwa, et al., 2021b). Furthermore, the at-risk label may negatively affect how parents view their capacity to parent their children safely, leading to damaging self-perceptions as inadequate or problematic.

In addition, the law can result in reluctance among parents to engage with social services due to concerns about possible interventions in family life being more invasive, such as child removal. Being labelled at risk in a legal context may discourage families from seeking help, even when they recognise the need for support. The implications of this argument in practice are illustrated by the following example of Dana, a young mother to Tammy, aged 18 months.

Dana, a 24-year-old single mother to a toddler, is recovering from a serious car accident. Dana's mother has been helping her take care of Tammy, given Dana's physical functioning is still impaired and she needs to attend physiotherapy sessions to recover from her injury. However, Dana's mother expects to return to work shortly, meaning Dana will lose her crucial support.

Dana has a long and complex history of state intervention in her family of origin. At age 9, Dana's father left home, leaving her mother overwhelmed and burdened by financial debt. Despite her mother's best efforts, caring for Dana and her two siblings became increasingly difficult, leading her mother to seek help from social services. After a year of intervention responses aimed at supporting the family in the community, Dana was removed from home to an out-of-home placement.

Dana describes how through the process of social workers' involvement with the family, she felt unheard and without control over her life circumstances. Thus, as a young single mother facing health difficulties, Dana is reluctant to approach social services for assistance. She knows that any daycare assistance for her daughter would only be granted under the framework of the Toddler at Risk Law—a prospect that revives her feelings of powerlessness. She is terrified that social workers' involvement could lead to removal of her daughter from the home, and thus she strongly refuses to approach them to actualise her right to daycare services.

**Box 5.2 Reflective Questions for Social Workers: Supporting Parents**

How do I actively encourage parents to use support services for the benefit of their children's care and safety in an empowering, non-judgemental, and respectful way?

How do I currently approach parents' fears of being labelled as putting their child at risk and the possibility of their child being removed from home?

In sum, the Toddlers at Risk Law (2000) is an example of a pseudo-attempt to apply the family service approach, or provide services to empower parental capacity and establish a partnership between the state and parents, given its core embrace of the child risk orientation. In practice, as in the case of Dana, instead of encouraging parents to use the service of subsidised daycare arrangements, it may push parents away from seeking help, with the hidden costs of using this service (being labelled as putting a child at risk, possibility of removal from home, social stigma, etc.) deemed too high.

#### *Foster Care for Children Law: Child-Oriented Approach—The Interest of the Child*

The Foster Care for Children Law (2016) is regarded as an important landmark in Israeli legislation in terms of explicitly incorporating the core ideology of the UNCRC principles. To date, it is the only law that clearly stipulates that the UNCRC's perspective on children's rights should guide social interventions policies, procedures and practices relating to children and young people. The Pupils' Rights Law (2000), which addresses the actualisation of children's rights in the education system, is the only other law that directly references the UNCRC. Article 1 of the Foster Care for Children Law reads as follows:

> The purpose of this law is to enshrine the rights of children in foster care and the obligation of the state to ensure their welfare and rights, in accordance with the Convention on the Rights of the Child. This is done with recognition of their unique vulnerability and their right to special protection and assistance, without detracting from the responsibilities, duties, and rights of their parents to ensure the welfare and rights of their children.

This law is considerably lengthy, featuring nine sections. It was designed comprehensively to cover all aspects of children's life in foster care and kindship care arrangements, from the initial decision to intervene through service termination. It refers to a wide range of children's needs and rights, most of them declared by the UNCRC, including the right to appropriate development (physically, mentally, emotionally, cognitively, and socially) and actualisation of capacities; protection from harm, exploitation, cruelty, and punishment; maintenance of relationships with parents and members of their family of origin; stability of care; participation in decisions regarding their life; cultural continuity and individual and cultural identity; privacy; and education and leisure activities.

Although this law represents an important step forward in terms of giving greater weight to children's rights and anchoring them in legislation when the severity of risk to the child increases, it still does not embrace the ethos of children as individual rights-bearers as characterised by the child-oriented approach. According to Berrick et al. (2023), the child-centric orientation extends the two-party relationship between family and the state to a three- party relationship among the child, parents, and the state. In the context of foster care, the complexity of this relationship is even greater because foster caregivers are also included as stakeholders with unique interests. The law gives considerable attention to the issue of balancing the rights and responsibilities of parents and foster caregivers, with insufficient emphasis on children's rights separate from their parents or caregivers.

Section 5 of the law regarding the status of foster parents offers a detailed account of how emerging conflicts and tensions between parents and foster caregivers should be solved in relation to a wide spectrum of everyday life events, health-related decisions, and court proceedings. Yet regarding possible pressures between the interests and needs of children and parents or foster caregivers, the law remains laconic and ambiguous. Section 1 of the law, addressing "objectives, interpretation, and basic principles," stipulates in Article 4(a) that the child's best interests should be given crucial weight in any actions and decisions and be prioritised over the best interests of other children who are not the focus. Furthermore, Article 4(b) lists certain considerations that should be considered when determining the child's best interests, among them the stance of parents, guardians, and other significant people in the child's life on the issue. Thus, the state put forward an obligation to prioritise the child's interests over those of other children, yet not over those of parents, caregivers, or other adults. In this regard, the law sustains a limiting paternalistic view of children, avoids securing their power and agency as an independent party, and leaves it to professionals to decide when their best interests should be given precedence—that is, while acknowledging the complexity of balancing stakeholders' different interests.

Another argument for the restricted nature of this child-centric approach relates to potential institutionalised discrimination by the law due to the exclusion of children in need of protection, who receive alternative support such as placement in residential care arrangements or services in the community. Thus, the legal framework creates a distinction among children, granting specific rights to those in foster care while leaving others—such as children in residential care—without comparable rights-granting legislation. A very practical example is the mechanism established by the law to actualise children's right to make a complaint about their care in an out-of-home placement. The law outlines, in Section 7 on supervision, audits, and complaints, the foundation of novel procedures and a unique professional unit to address children's complaints about any aspect of their life in placement. However, this ombudsman authority to investigate complaints is not available to children in locked residential placements or receiving protective services in their community. As a result, children with the same need for protection from harm are granted different rights according to state responses prescribed to them by professionals.

It is important to note the recognition of the right to cultural continuity and personal and cultural identity for children in foster care. Article 12 of the law stipulates that the selection of a foster family should strive to maintain continuity and stability in the child's emotional connections, education, ethnic background, religious practices, cultural heritage, and linguistic environment, alongside other unique characteristics. Furthermore, it protects the child's right to preserve their personal and cultural identity during placement, including their name, language, religion, and culture. This provision represents a ground-breaking step towards acknowledging the importance of cultural and ethnic identity in child welfare decisions. This provision is important, yet like in previously discussed articles, the law does not address situations involving conflict between the parents and child. The law does not explicitly indicate whether the child's views or the parents' preferences should take precedence in cases of conflict, as shown in the following example.

Jonathan, aged 10, is one of 12 siblings. His parents, who became more religious shortly after marriage, joined an Orthodox community. Following the birth of the youngest child, Jonathan's mother developed severe depression, which led to her hospitalisation in a mental health institution. After her recovery, his parents divorced, and his mother moved to a distant city, maintaining only sporadic contact with her children. Jonathan's father remarried, had three more children, and he and Jonathan's stepmother upheld their religious beliefs strictly. As Jonathan grows older, he begins to question his faith, which his father and stepmother refuse to accept, insisting he follow their religious practices. Unable to reconcile these pressures, Jonathan eventually runs away. He spends time on the streets, occasionally staying at drop-in centres until social services petitions the court to place him in foster care. Although Jonathan hopes for a secular foster family, his parents insist that he be placed with a religious one. Jonathan is placed in a religious foster family.

This case highlights limitations in the foster care law. Even though the law aims to secure children's rights as laid out in the UNCRC, it also respects parental rights without providing clear guidance in cases of direct conflict. As reflected by Jonathan's situation, the law does not specify that a child's rights and views should take precedence when they conflict with the parents' views, leaving him with limited options for a living environment that respects his individual beliefs.

**Box 5.3 Reflective Questions for Social Workers: Balancing Child and Caregiver Rights**

How can I balance the interests and needs of children and those of parents or foster caregivers?

In what decisions will I give preference to children's views over those of their parents or foster caregivers?

How do I actively seek children's feedback about the services provided to them in all residential care arrangements or services in the community?

## Conclusion

This chapter focused on the legislative responses formulated by states to secure children's right to be protected against maltreatment and exploitation as required by Article 19 of the UNCRC. Israel was used as a case study, with critical reflection on its protective legislation arrangements for children. Israel's protective legislation framework is not a unified inclusive law, but rather a collection of laws dedicated to different aspects of reporting, assessing, and treating child maltreatment, and the UNCRC is not manifested as a binding and integral part of the judicial system.

The analysis focused on three key laws based on Gilbert et al.' (2011) typology of child welfare system orientations, enabling an examination of how the tension among the rights and responsibilities of the state, parents, and children is balanced. Although these laws were selected to demonstrate different orientations—i.e., child risk, family services, and child-oriented—to approaching the obligation to safeguard children from harm, the analysis revealed a strong standing of the state and high thresholds and an investigative model for determining who receives services, which are more consistent with a restricted child protection orientation. Legislation that frames children's rights (i.e., Foster Care for Children Law, 2016) has not fully developed in terms of adopting the child-centric approach. Instead, it bypasses the crucial issue of whose rights, those of children or parents, should be given greater weight in situations of potential harm to a child and is insufficiently inclusive in terms of children receiving varied protection services to the point of constituting inequality. Yet most notably, this legislation is missing a preventive quality designed to avoid or stop serious risk and harm to children.

## References

*Abu-Hasan v. State of Israel*, C. A. 3112/94, 53(1) P. D. 442 (1999).

Alfandari, R. (2016). Evaluation of a national reform in the Israeli child protection system designed to improve children's participation in decision making. *Child and Family Social Work*, *22*(S2), 54–62. https://doi.org/10.1111/cfs.12261

Alfandari, R., Enosh, G., & Rechnitzer, H. (2021a). To split or include? Child sexual abuse mandate reporting in the ultra-Orthodox Jewish community in Israel. *Children and Youth Services Review*, *120*, 105759. https://doi.org/10.1016/j.childyouth.2020.105759

Alfandari, R., Massarwa, Z., & Enosh, G. (2021b). Applying intersectionality theory to understand female Arab art-therapists' experiences with child maltreatment mandatory reporting. *Health & Social Care in the Community*, *29*(6), 1747–1755. https://doi.org/10.1111/hsc.13280

Alfandari, R., Taylor, B. J., Baginsky, M., Campbell, J., Helm, D., Killick, C., McCafferty, P., Mullineux, J., Shears, J., Sicora, A., & Whittaker, A. (2023). Making sense of risk: Social work at the interface of care and control. *Health, Risk & Society*, *25*(1–2), 75–92. https://doi.org/10.1080/13698575.2022.2147904

Asif, A. (2009). Mandatory reporting of offences against minors and helpless: Understandings from multi-ministry discussions and the background of Amendment 94 to the Penal Code [in Hebrew]. *Family in the Law*, *2*, 367–377.

Berrick, J. D., Gilbert, N., & Skivenes, M. (2023). Child protection systems across the world. In *Oxford handbook of child protection systems* (pp. 1–50). Oxford University Press.

Berrick, J. D., Gilbert, N., & Skivenes, M. (2024). Developing a global typology of child protection systems. In E. Fernandez, P. Welbourne, B. Lee, & J. L. Ma (Eds.), *The Routledge handbook of child and family social work research: Knowledge-building, application, and impact* (pp. 273–282). Taylor & Francis.

Berrick, J. D., Skivenes, M., & Roscoe, J. N. (2022). Children's rights and parents' rights: Popular attitudes about when we privilege one over the other. *International Journal of Social Welfare*, *31*(4), 449–462. https://doi.org/10.1111/ijsw.12523

Doron, A. (2001). Social welfare policy in Israel: Developments in the 1980s and 1990s [in Hebrew]. *Israel Affairs*, *7*(4), 153–180.

Doron, I. (2012). Social workers and the law in Israel [in Hebrew]. In M. Hovav, E. Lawental, & J. Katan (Eds.), *Social work in Israel* (pp. 68–89). Hakibbutz Hameuchad.

Gilbert, N. (2011). Changing patterns of response and emerging orientations. In N. Gilbert, N. Parton, & M. Skivenes (Eds.), *Child protection systems: International trends and orientations* (pp. 243–258). Oxford University Press.

Gilbert, N., Parton, N., & Skivenes, M. (2011). *Child protection systems: International trends and orientations*. Oxford University Press.

Israel Ministry of Justice. (2003). *Minister of Justice's commission on fundamental issues concerning children and law and their implementation in legislation*, Chairperson: Judge Savyona Rotlevi [in Hebrew].

Israel. (2000). *Young children at risk (eligibility for day care) law, 5760–2000* [commonly referred to in English as the Toddlers at Risk Law]. State of Israel.

Israel. (2016). *Children foster care law, 5776–2016*. State of Israel.

Krumer-Nevo, M. (2016). Poverty-aware social work: A paradigm for social work practice with people in poverty. *British Journal of Social Work*, *46*(6), 1793–1808. https://doi.org/10.1093/bjsw/bcv118

Mathews, B. (2015). Mandatory reporting laws: Their origin, nature, and development over time. In B. Mathews & D. C. Bross (Eds.), *Mandatory reporting laws and the identification of severe child abuse and neglect* (pp. 3–25). Springer.

Mathews, B., & Kenny, M. C. (2008). Mandatory reporting legislation in the United States, Canada, and Australia: A cross-jurisdictional review of key features, differences, and issues. *Child Maltreatment*, *13*(1), 50–63. https://doi.org/10.1177/1077559507310613

McCafferty, P. (2017). Implementing Article 12 of the United Nations Convention on the Rights of the Child in child protection decision-making: A critical analysis of the challenges and opportunities for social work. *Child Care in Practice*, *23*(4), 327–341. https://doi.org/10.1080/13575279.2016.1264368

Mitchell, M., Lundy, L., & Hill, L. (2023). Children's human rights to "participation" and "protection": Rethinking the relationship using Barnahus as a case example. *Child Abuse Review*, *32*(6), e2820. https://doi.org/10.1002/car.2820

Nachmani-Rot, D. (2009). The conditions under which welfare officers may waive reporting to the police on offences against children [in Hebrew]. *Family in the Law*, *2*, 379–399.

Rosenfeld, J., & Kedem, A. (1998). Betwixt and between the "Generation of the Desert" and the "Children of the Dream": Fifty years of social work in child welfare in Israel. In F. Loewenberg (Ed.), *Meeting the challenges of a changing society: Fifty years of social work in Israel* (pp. 75–98). Magnes Press.

Turney, D., Alfandari, R., Taylor, B. J., Helm, D., Ghanem, C., Killick, C., Lyons, O., O'Leary, D., Ebsen, F., & Bertotti, T. (2024). Threshold decisions in social work: Using theory to support practice. *British Journal of Social Work*, *54*, 2996–3013. https://doi.org/10.1093/bjsw/bcae073

United Nations. (1989). *Convention on the rights of the child*. https://www.ohchr.org/en/instruments-mechanisms/instruments/convention-rights-child

Weissblei, E. (2011). *Wait for out-of-home placements for children and young people [in Hebrew]*. Israel Knesset, Center for Research and Information.

# 6 Adoption with Children's Rights at the Centre

## Safeguarding Children's Welfare, Identity, and Family Relationships

*Mandi MacDonald and Simone McCaughren*

### Introduction: Children's Rights and Adoption from Care

A foundational presumption of the United Nations Convention on the Rights of the Child (UNCRC; United Nations, 1989) is that children have a right to be brought up by their parents, who, in turn, should receive support to fulfil their parental responsibilities. The convention also recognises, however, that some children can be harmed by their parents—for example, through neglect or maltreatment—to the extent that remaining in their parents' care is not in their best interests. When children are placed in alternative care for their protection, such as foster care or residential childcare, the onus remains on the state to provide support to enable children to return to their parents or extended family. For some children, however, a safe return to family is not achievable. These children need special protection and have a right to continuity of alternative care, including through adoption, per the UNCRC (United Nations, 1989, Article 20). Adoption is a permanent legal arrangement in which parental responsibility is transferred to the adoptive parents and the child becomes a full member of their adoptive family. Based on the provisions of the UNCRC, adoption from care is permissible if, and only if, parents are unwilling or unable, even with support, to parent the child and meet their responsibilities. In such cases, Article 21 of the UNCRC places an obligation on states to permit a lawful system of adoption implemented by competent authorities in which the best interests of the child are the paramount consideration.

Although Articles 20 and 21 of the UNCRC speak directly and specifically to the adoption of children, they intersect with other key articles, as noted in Box 6.1. Three broad children's rights themes are highlighted: the best interests of the child, their right to retain their identity and family relations, and their right to participate in decisions affecting their welfare. Adoption operates in the contemporary digital world, and so children's digital rights must also be considered (United Nations Committee on the Rights of the Child, 2021).

DOI: 10.4324/9781003582410-9

**Box 6.1 Articles of the UNCRC Pertinent to Adoption of Children from Care**

Article 3: The child's right to have their best interests taken as the primary consideration in all actions concerning them

Article 7: The right to be cared for by their parents as far as possible, unless this would be significantly harmful to them

Article 8: The right to retain their identity and family relations

Article 9: The right not to be separated from their parents against their will unless necessary for their best interests

Article 12: The right to express their views freely in all matters affecting them, with their views being given due weight in accordance with their age and maturity, also known as their participatory rights

Article 20: The right to benefit from the continuity of alternative care, including adoption, if being cared for by their parents is not possible or not in their best interests

Article 21: The right to have their best interests taken as the paramount consideration in a lawful system of adoption

Some tensions and conflicts exist between these rights provisions (Sloan, 2014). Most notably, although adoption can safeguard a child's best interests, it may conflict with their identity rights and with the right that the child and their parents hold, under Article 8 of the European Convention on Human Rights (Council of Europe, 1988), to have their private and family life respected. When a child is adopted into a new family, they are legally regarded as a child born to the adoptive family, and all legal relations between the child and their family of origin are severed. Although the relationship with their family of origin is legally terminated, some adopted children benefit from ongoing connection and interaction with their birth relatives. This open approach to adoption can meet the child's identity needs while ensuring their protection in the security and care of an adoptive family (Neil et al., 2015).

In exploring the implications of adoption for children's rights, this chapter begins by outlining how adoption, as a safeguarding intervention, might protect the best interests of a child. It goes on to explore how an open approach to adoption, including various forms of post-adoption contact between the adopted child and their birth relatives, might promote the adopted child's right to retain their identity and family relations. This includes a discussion of adopted children's rights in a digital world. The chapter then explores children's participatory rights in adoption.

Although arrangements for making adoptions take various forms in different legislative contexts, this chapter refers to the adoption of children who are placed in out-of-home care to ensure their safety and well-being and who cannot safety return to the care of their family of origin, illustrated with examples from the Republic of Ireland and Northern Ireland, the latter a jurisdiction of the United Kingdom.

**Adoption and the Child's Best Interests**

Child welfare legislation in Northern Ireland and the Republic of Ireland reflects important guiding principles of the UNCRC, which specifies that children have a right not to be separated from their parents against their will unless necessary for their best interests (Article 9) and to be cared for by their parents unless this would be significantly harmful to them (Article 7). When children need out-of-home care to ensure their safety and well-being, working towards a return to parents or extended family should be a preferred goal. Adoption, therefore, is likely to be in a child's best interests only when parental care is significantly harmful, and many children adopted from care have experienced neglect, maltreatment, or significant adversities that place them at risk of poor developmental outcomes. Selwyn and Lewis (2023) presented an overview of research evidence across a range of outcomes and concluded that children adopted from care fare better than children who remain in care. However, the physical, emotional, and psychological consequences of early adversity can be extensive and long-lasting, and effective support for adoptive families is crucial for meeting the needs and achieving the best interests of children adopted from care (McCaughren & Parkes, 2019).

When family preservation or reunification is not achievable, child welfare agencies have a duty to provide alternative family placements that are stable and secure (Article 20) and meet the child's need for a sense of belonging. Adoption is the most legally secure form of alternative care and can enable children to feel integrated into lifelong family relationships (Tefre, 2015). Selwyn and Masson's (2014) analysis of permanent alternative care arrangements in England found adoption to be more stable than other placement options; most adopted children remained with their adoptive parents, who "were committed and tenacious, despite experiencing difficulties during their children's teenage years" (p. 1711) Reflective of these benefits, in 2017, legislation was passed in the Republic of Ireland (Adoption Amendment Act, 2017) that paved the way for children in the care of the state to find permanency through adoption, although to date, this has only been realised for a small proportion of all children in alternative care (Burns & McCaughren, 2021).

Adoption of children in care involves a particularly intrusive role for the state in regulating the breaking and making of legal family ties. Permanent removal of birth parents' rights and responsibilities, even in some cases without their consent, can be justified to safeguard the child's welfare, but it does not sit easily with the right to respect of private and family life. Adoption as a child welfare intervention has been critiqued as a disproportionately harsh response to the needs and rights of parents (Bywaters, 2015; Featherstone et al., 2018). The child's right to safety and permanence is juxtaposed with their parents' right to respect for private and family life. However, rights are embedded in relationships, and the rights of children cannot necessarily be neatly separated from those of their parents and other significant adults in their lives. An open approach to adoption, although primarily intended to serve the child's best interests, can also be seen as a means of reconciling the intersecting and apparently competing rights of parent and child (MacDonald & McLoughlin, 2016).

## Adoption and the Child's Identity Rights

Although adoption offers permanent care to a child, it also permanently changes their family identity. Historically, adoption was considered a clean break from the family of origin, with little thought given to the identity needs of the infant as they grew up into adulthood. Adopted people often knew little or nothing about the identity of their parents or circumstances of their birth. Contemporary adoption recognises, however, that information and understanding about one's origins is a basic human right, and this is now reflected in more open approaches to adoption.

Articles 7 and 8 of the UNCRC outline the rights of children in alternative care to stay in contact with their parents and retain their identity and family relations. Children adopted from care, however, are no longer in care. The United Nations Guidelines on the Alternative Care of Children (United Nations General Assembly, 2010, Section III [30b]) specifies that adoption is considered parental care, with the autonomy this affords, and the provisions for alternative care no longer apply. The general expectation associated with the UNCRC, therefore, is that adopted children's identity rights are respected by letting them know that they are adopted and the identity of their biological parents (Luhamaa & O'Mahony, 2021). Adoptive parents are encouraged to talk openly, honestly, and regularly with their child about their adoption and birth history (Brodzinsky, 2006). Having information and knowing about birth relatives, however, is not the same as interacting with and knowing them directly. Recent commentary has suggested more adopted children should have the opportunity for ongoing meaningful connection and direct engagement with their original family (Neil, 2018).

The UNCRC's emphasis on keeping children with their families means that many adopted children will have lived with their birth parents before entering alternative care and stayed in contact with them throughout their placement—thus arriving in their adoptive placement with some relationships with birth relatives. It is in the best interests of some children to retain these relationships in an open adoption that involves ongoing communication between their birth and adoptive families, often referred to as post-adoption contact. This can be in the form of letters exchanged directly or via an intermediary, online interactions via digital communication technology, or in-person meetings between the child and their birth relatives. Open adoption reflects the diversity and fluid nature of modern family life (Wood et al., 2022) and the capacity of children and their birth parents to remain emotionally and psychologically present to each other despite the legal distance created by adoption (Powell & Afifi, 2005).

Contact agreements tend to be negotiated during adoption proceedings, when the child makes a legal (and social and emotional) transition between their birth and adoptive families. Contact planning should take account of the child's right to family life with both their birth and adoptive parents (Hansen, 2019). Ensuring that contact plans do not undermine the security of the adoptive placement is, again, a matter of ensuring the child's best interests.

Many professionals and prospective adopters are wary of open adoption due to concerns that contact with birth relatives may undermine the stability of the placement (Monk & Macvarish, 2019) and thus contradict the best interests principle. Concerns have been raised about unplanned or poorly managed contact—for example, when adolescents are in contact with birth relatives via social media without their adoptive parents' knowledge or supervision (Children's Commissioner, 2017). However, reviews of research have broadly concurred that carefully assessed, well-managed contact that is tailored to a child's particular needs can be beneficial to adopted children and their families (Smith et al., 2020). In the context of the safety, security, and sense of belonging afforded by adoption, appropriate well-managed contact can help with identity development; contribute to higher self-esteem; provide reassurance on birth relatives' welfare; mitigate a sense of loss; and forge positive long-term connections with birth relatives (Thoburn, 2021). It provides an opportunity to get to know birth relatives, leading to more open conversations in the adoptive family and equipping them with essential information on which to base these identity-informing discussions.

***The Challenges of Open Adoption Practice***

Although potentially beneficial, contact can also be emotionally stressful and exacerbate some children's trauma-related difficulties, resulting in anxiety, distress, and behavioural difficulties that place a strain on adoptive family life (MacDonald, 2021; Wright & Collings, 2019). Levels of contact need to be matched, therefore, with adequate levels of professional support (Featherstone et al., 2018). Achieving a more open approach to adoption requires practice development and resourcing to ensure arrangements are managed and supported in a way that is sensitive to the child's and their parents' prior experiences of adversity and trauma (MacDonald, 2021) to ensure safe and beneficial connections can be maintained.

After adoption, relationships are more likely to be sustained and beneficial with birth relatives who have not been involved in the abuse or neglect of the child (Neil, 2018), support the adoption, show commitment to the child's welfare, and have reasonably settled personal circumstances. Given that a threshold of harm in parental care is a requirement for making an adoption, this range of characteristics may be more likely found among birth grandparents or other extended birth relatives, yet they are significantly less likely than birth parents to be included in plans for face-to-face contact (Neil et al., 2015). This research evidence challenges the biogenetic norms enshrined in the language of the UNCRC, which refers to the child's right to remain in contact with their parents (Article 9).

Successful contact depends on cooperation and communication between the birth and adoptive families, with all parties remaining flexible to consider the child's changing needs and circumstances (Neil et al., 2015). Explicit agreements for contact among the parties (for example, birth mother, adoptive parents, and child) can help ensure that connections between children and their birth relatives are maintained throughout childhood (Faulkner & Madden, 2012). Internationally, the status of such agreements varies (Mashburn, 2015), ranging from informal verbal agreements (as is common practice in the Republic of Ireland) to written contracts that although not legally binding carry a strong expectation of being honoured after the adoption is finalised (as is the case in Northern Ireland). However, unlike situations of parental separation and divorce, where court orders specify the terms of child-to-parent contact, post-adoption contact tends not to have the same statutory protection.

Although court orders mandating contact are possible under Northern Ireland law, they tend not to be made, and subsequent arrangements, therefore, are voluntary and not legally enforceable. Practice in Northern Ireland was outlined succinctly by Justice Keegan (2016) when adjudicating on an application for a contact order brought by a birth mother:

> There has been a steady move towards open adoption. That is seen to be a good progression from the point of view of maintaining identity for adopted children. However, the practice in this jurisdiction has not been to make adoption contact orders … contact arrangements are managed by post-adoption services.
>
> (KEE10042)

The current provision in Republic of Ireland law does not allow for mandated post-adoption contact, bringing into question Ireland's compliance with international standards, particularly its obligations under the UNCRC (Department of Children and Youth Affairs, 2019). The argument has also been made that "in the absence of legal regulation, there may be a consequent lack of resources dedicated to supporting families who are engaging in an open adoption arrangement" (McCaughren & Parkes, 2019, p. 51). Debates, therefore, persist regarding whether the Republic of Ireland should consider putting open adoption on a legal footing. In upholding children's right to identity, it must also be acknowledged that open adoption is not a static event but rather evolves and develops over time. Therefore, whatever the nature of the agreement, retaining the flexibility to review and change arrangements to suit the child's developmentally changing needs is crucial.

Due consideration must be given to children's views on contact and the complex feelings it can generate for them. A key tenet of trauma-informed approaches to post-adoption contact is that children are afforded a genuine sense of choice and control over arrangements as far as possible (MacDonald, 2021), without placing on them undue responsibility for managing or making choices about these birth relationships (Iyer et al., 2020). This requires those involved in making contact arrangements to help children understand their circumstances, formulate and express their feelings and wishes, and ensure their views reach an attentive audience and receive proper regard (Lundy, 2007). Children's views are unlikely to remain fixed, often evolving as they grow and develop, and these changing preferences need to be heard and considered. In adolescence, for example, young people can exercise greater autonomy over increasing or ceasing contact.

For some children, it is not in their best interests to meet or interact directly with their birth family. If families cannot exchange identifying information directly with each other yet want to maintain some level of contact, albeit at a distance, adoption agencies often provide a logistical solution, acting as a conduit for the exchange of cards, letters, photographs, and small gifts. Several challenges have been associated with this form of information exchange, including its emotional toll on parties; the level and consistency of letterbox contact over time; different approaches to managing contact that varies from agency to agency; and the time-consuming nature of facilitating this type of contact for adoption agencies (McCaughren, 2010). The appropriateness of letter exchange for sustaining meaningful connections has been questioned, with proposals made for a more modern approach that takes advantage of digital communication technology (Barnett-Jones & Manning, 2021).

The spectrum of openness varies considerably, and the specific nature of the proposed connection with birth family is a key consideration in determining whether adoption is in an individual child's best interests. A growing body of research and practice development (summarised by MacDonald, 2023) can help determine what arrangements for open adoption might be in a particular child's best interests and how these arrangements might practically and safely be sustained and supported over time.

### *Adoption, Contact, and Children's Digital Rights*

In the contemporary digital world, where social media applications are ubiquitous and drive ever-expanding networks of online relationships, some have suggested that a closed model of adoption is unrealistic (Thoburn, 2021). The fact that many adopted young people look for and find birth information online points to the relevance of children's digital rights and the importance of considering digital platforms as a more modern, flexible, and convenient approach for post-adoption contact (A. Shier, 2024). Digital interactions between adopted children and birth relatives can take place via social networking sites, email, video calls, or text messaging (Greenhow et al., 2015). Although interactions that take place using digital technology are often thought of as virtual, these relationships and emotions are very real for children, and attention needs to be paid to their privacy and protection and to supporting their digital resilience and skills for interacting online (MacDonald, 2023). Any form of post-adoption contact using communication technology must be consistent with the principles of children rights in a digital world outlined by the United Nations Committee on the Rights of the Child (2021).

Although the temptation might be to turn exclusively to digital post-adoption contact, something might be gained for the child by holding onto more tangible forms of communication. Traditionally, birth and adoptive parents used the adoption agency as a conduit for passing on hand-written letters and carefully chosen gifts. There is something very personal about these artefacts, which can be a physical and symbolic marker of both identity and memory. Therefore, thought must be given to how digital platforms can facilitate contact without losing the authenticity of personalised correspondence, which is at risk of being compromised in the virtual space (MacDonald et al., 2023).

"Digital solutions broaden the potential for creating adaptive, flexible, and accessible forms of communication that meet needs over time" (Barnett-Jones & Manning, 2021, p. 8). However, it is important that any discussion of the benefits and opportunities of digital post-adoption contact are weighed against any risks that it might also introduce (Greenhow et al., 2015). Digital technology can make it easier for children and birth relatives to share thoughts and feelings in a less intense, more spontaneous and contemporaneous way. However, the boundaries in online relationships are more diffuse and difficult to regulate (A. Shier, 2024). Adoptive parents have voiced concerns regarding the privacy implications of birth relatives sharing children's photographs or achievements on their social media accounts and the safety implications if identifying information is included (MacDonald et al., 2023). Parents and caregivers should be alerted to the potential impact of online sharing, and children should be equipped to make informed choices about consenting to the use of their images and information. As with in-person contact, given the uniqueness of each child, arrangements for digital contact must be left to families to agree and decide upon, with the child having a voice, choice, and preference.

***Case Study 1: Rian***

This case example illustrates how adoption can protect a child's best interests while upholding their identity rights.

Rian is 5-years-old and was adopted in Northern Ireland at age 3. When he was born, Rian's parents were using alcohol daily and unable to meet his needs or keep him safe. The family was placed together in a residential parenting assessment centre in an effort to enhance his parents' capacity to care for him, in the hope that he might not have to be separated from them. This placement ended when Rian's parents continued to use alcohol heavily, leading to neglect of his needs. To keep him with his extended family, Rian moved in with his maternal grandmother, Maura, who agreed to be his kinship foster caregiver. Maura loved Rian, and he thrived in her care, but due to her chronic ill health, she could not continue caring for a young toddler and asked for him to be moved. Shortly before his third birthday, Rian moved to live with his current family on a fostering basis with a view to adoption. His adoption was finalised once the required legal and procedural processes were completed, along with an adoption order by the court.

Rian is settled and happy in his adoptive family. His birth mother had acknowledged that she drank alcohol heavily throughout pregnancy, and as a result, he shows some developmental delays and attends paediatric services for ongoing assessment.

**Box 6.2 Reflective Questions for Social Workers: Rian's Rights**

Reflecting on the case example, can you identify whether and in what ways Rian's rights (per the UNCRC) have been considered and protected?
What are the benefits and challenges for Rian in continuing to meet up with his grandmother and having access to information and updates about his parents?
What changes in the arrangements for open adoption would you expect might be needed in the future? How might Rian's needs and wishes for contact with his family of origin change as he gets older?
What role does the social worker have in facilitating and mediating the relationship between Rian's birth and adoptive families?
How could Rian's voice be heard in the process, both now at age 5 and in the future?

Before Rian's adoption, the social worker arranged for Maura and his adoptive parents to meet. Together, they agreed that Rian would continue to see Maura three times a year. The social worker from the adoption agency helps arrange these visits. The social worker speaks with Maura and his adoptive parents before the planned visit so that they can share any important news and updates on Rian's current likes and needs. When the weather is fine, the visits take place in a park or at the beach, so that Rian can play, and they can walk Maura's small dog together. The social worker and one of his adoptive parents join Rian on these visits. The next week, the social worker calls Maura and the adoptive parents to hear their thoughts on the visit. Rian can be a little unsettled after the visit with Maura and wakes in the night. His adoptive parents talk to him more at these times about his family and how he came to be adopted, and he settles after a few days.

Rian's parents move often, sometimes leaving the area for long periods. However, they occasionally contact Maura and ask how Rian is doing. She gives them updates, shows photographs of him, and encourages them to share news that she can pass on to Rian and his adoptive parents.

## Adoption and the Child's Participatory Rights and Voice

Scholars have argued that "adoption has a very powerful adult led agenda, which may or may not act in favour of children's best interests" (Ward & Smeeton, 2017, p. 58). Indeed, as stated by McCaughren and McGregor (2018), the adoption process traditionally was solely focused on the suitability and eligibility of prospective adopters, without considering the views of children either in the present or future. Similar to the changed practices of adoption, how children are now perceived in society has also changed. Instead of being viewed as silent actors, they are viewed as competent individuals with independent rights. Some theoretical frameworks that have influenced this shift are based on a legal paradigm emanating from the UNCRC, a sociological paradigm based on children as competent actors and active agents and a democratic paradigm defining the right to participate as a key concept of democratic cultures (Horgan, 2024). In addition, many conceptual frameworks and models of participation can support practitioners in considering the importance of voice of the child in their work (Hart, 1997; Lundy, 2007; H. Shier, 2001).

The provisions of the UNCRC hold that all children, regardless of their circumstances or abilities, must have the chance to have their opinions heard and considered regarding decisions that affect their lives. The UNCRC (Articles 3, 12, and 21) places a legal obligation on "duty bearers" to heed the voice of the child. In Northern Ireland, when coming to a decision about adoption, the court or adoption agency must consider "the child's ascertainable wishes and feelings regarding the decision (considered in the light of the child's age and understanding)" (Adoption and Children Act [Northern Ireland] 2022, Article 1[4][f]). In the Republic of Ireland, this is reflected in domestic law; Article 42A 4.2 of the Irish Constitution (1937) and the Adoption Act (2017) both state that as practicable, when the child concerned is capable of forming their own views, due weight should be given to the views of that child, considering their age and maturity.

It is important to note here this dual criterion of age and maturity, particular that neither should be viewed in isolation (Parkes, 2015). Indeed, the United Nations Committee of the Rights of the Child (2009) stated regarding Article 12—specifically relating to the voice of the child in adoption proceedings—that "children's levels of understanding are not uniformly linked to their biological age." In addition, the committee has provided very clear guidance on how to interpret Article 12 and cautioned against introducing age limits in law and practice that may affect the implementation of this fundamental right (Parkes, 2015, p. 32). This means that all children (even babies) need to be given voice in adoption decisions, and research has discouraged practitioners from taking a narrow interpretation of voice that risks limiting it to the conventional spoken voice only (McCaughren et al., 2022). When it comes to very young children, rather than dismissing their input based on age, the responsibility lies with adults to interpret their voice (Horgan, 2024). Furthermore, Article 12 stipulates that merely listening to the child is not enough; their views must be seriously considered. In addition, Article 12 also states that after the child has decided to be heard, they can also decide how to be heard, "either directly, or through a representative or appropriate body." The committee has recommended that where possible the child must have the opportunity to be directly heard in any proceedings (United Nations Committee on Rights of the Child, 2009).

Given the prominence of children's participatory rights, it might be expected that their voices would be reflected in adoption decisions. Helland et al. (2023) analysed the material of 213 judgments relating to adoption from care from seven European jurisdictions. They examined if and how children's views are obtained and weighted, what children said about the proposed adoption, and how children were described in the judgments. One core finding from the study was that children in adoption proceedings are mostly invisible, and "despite being the central person in these proceedings, very few ... were given a prominent place in the judgment" (Helland et al., 2023, p. 121). Another concerning finding was that age was at times used as a barrier to participation, such that children even as old as 10 were deemed too young to have a voice in the adoption process.

In a 2024 judgment in the Republic of Ireland, a High Court judge made valuable observations in relation to ascertaining the views of a young person with additional needs in an adoption case. Importantly, the judgment first gave weight to the fact that the young person knew the social worker well and communicated with them at ease. It was acknowledged that the child had multiple modes of communication. The judge remarked that the "child is a person who communicates through a combination of verbal language (although she may find such expression difficult), body language, the expression of her feelings and her actions towards and responses to others" (Jackson, 2024, para. 19[2]). Jackson questioned how the views of the young person were to be interpreted and applied, reflecting on the dilemma of whether the young person's voice should go unheard because she did not understand the concept of adoption or could not verbally articulate her wishes. Significantly, the judge referred to the "manner and mode" of expressing such views, acknowledging that this may vary from child to child, and described it as a "subjective test which must be applied relative to the particular abilities and disabilities of the particular child" (Jackson, 2024, para. 22[a]). This judgment provides important direction for practitioners in highlighting the extent to which voice must be both interpreted and applied in the adoption context. It also emphasises the importance of considering the individualities and particularities of each child.

In a system that is arguably weighted towards adults, to ensure the rights of children and their best interests are wholly protected, the voice of the child must be heard. However, the child needs to be engaged with meaningfully and their views effectively considered, rather than being represented in a tokenistic way or approached as a tick-box exercise. To honour both our international and national obligations to children and uphold their rights, they must remain central to the adoption process with careful consideration given to how children of all ages and capacities are engaged.

### *Case Study II: Julia*

Julia is 8-years-old and has lived with her current foster caregivers since she entered care shortly before her first birthday.

Her birth mother, Kristin, is Polish and had a difficult childhood. She struggled to meet the needs of an infant even with extensive social work support, resulting in a significant risk of severe neglect. Julia's birth father is Irish and is named on her birth certificate; however, Kristin lost contact with him shortly after the birth. Although she assumes he still lives in Republic of Ireland, she does not know his current whereabouts.

**Box 6.3 Reflective Questions for Social Workers: Julia's Rights**

Reflecting on the case example, can you identify whether and in what ways Julia's rights (per the UNCRC) have been considered and protected?
How might you support Julia's participation in the important decision about adoption? What information does she need to be able to give an informed view?
If her birth parents do not consent to adoption, what weight should be given to Julia's views in the care planning process?
What implications does adoption have for Julia's identity rights?
How might digital communication technology be used to maintain a relationship between Julia and Kristin? What benefits and challenges does this type of communication raise?

When Julia was placed in foster care at 11 months, Kristin initially wanted no contact with her because she found the situation distressing. However, with encouragement from social workers, she agreed to meet up with Julia and her foster caregivers four times a year. This arrangement was maintained until 1 year ago, when Kristin returned to Poland, where she had grown up in the care of her grandmother. Apart from a younger brother, Kristin has no immediate family in Poland—her grandmother died before Julia was born. She felt, however, that she wanted to rebuild her life in her home country after several years working in the Republic of Ireland.

Julia is very settled in her foster family. She prefers to refer to her foster caregivers as Mum and Dad, particularly in school and social settings. Although she has enjoyed her visits with Kristin, she is adamant that her foster caregivers are her "real" family. Julia's foster caregivers and social worker feel it is important that Julia has the security of adoption, especially now that her mother has no plans to return to the Republic of Ireland.

## Conclusion

Adoption can safeguard children's right to protection from harm but may conflict with their identity rights and the human right to respect for private and family life in both birth and adoptive families. Open adoption might provide balance and integration across the range of rights by securing children's right to protection from harm while also upholding their right to identity and family relationships. If children's identity rights are to align with their best interests and participatory rights, the unique needs of each child should be assessed and prioritised in contact plans. Arrangements should remain flexibly responsive to children's changing needs, and their views should feature prominently. Contact meetings should be carefully managed and well supported in a way that is sensitive to past experiences of trauma, and children's sense of security in their adoptive family must be safeguarded (MacDonald, 2023). Although adoption historically has been a very adult-centred process, practice must now prioritise the voice of the child, even that of very young children and those with additional needs, ensuring that adopted children have the space to formulate and express their views and that a responsive audience takes these views into account.

## References


Barnett-Jones, B., & Manning, C. (2021). *Modernising post-adoption contact: Findings from a recent consultation*. Nuffield Family Justice Observatory.

Brodzinsky, D. (2006). Family structural openness and communication openness as predictors in the adjustment of adopted children. *Adoption Quarterly*, *9*(4), 1–18. https://doi.org/10.1300/J145v09n04_01

Burns, K., & McCaughren, S. (2021). Adoption of children from state care in Ireland: In whose best interests? In T. Pösö, M. Skivenes, & J. Thoburn (Eds.), *Adoption from care: International perspectives on children's rights, family preservation and state intervention* (pp. 177–194). Policy Press. https://doi.org/10.51952/9781447351054.ch004

Bywaters, P. (2015). Cumulative jeopardy? A response to Brown and Ward. *Children and Youth Services Review*, *52*, 68–73. https://doi.org/10.1016/j.childyouth.2015.03.001

Children's Commissioner. (2017). *Growing up digital in care: Submission to the DfE Fostering Stocktake 2017*. https://www.childrenscommissioner.gov.uk/resource/growing-up-digital-in-care/

Council of Europe. (1988). *Protocol to the Convention for the Protection of Human Rights and Fundamental Freedoms (European Convention on Human Rights) as amended by Protocol No. 11*.

Department of Children and Youth Affairs. (2019). *Review and consultation in respect of the potential introduction of open or semi-open adoption in Ireland*. https://aai.gov.ie/images/Final_Report_on_the_Potential_Introduction_of_Open_or_Semi-Open_Adoption_in_Ireland__6_November_2019.pdf

Faulkner, M., & Madden, E. E. (2012). Open adoption and post-adoption birth family contact: A comparison of non-relative foster and private adoptions. *Adoption Quarterly*, *15*(1), 35–56. https://doi.org/10.1080/10926755.2012.661333

Featherstone, B., Gupta, A., & Mills, S. (2018). *The role of the social worker in adoption—ethics and human rights: An enquiry*. British Association of Social Workers.

Greenhow, S., Hackett, S., Jones, C., & Meins, E. (2015). Adoptive family experiences of post-adoption contact in an internet era. *Child and Family Social Work*, *22*(S1), 44–52. https://doi.org/10.1111/cfs.12256

Hansen, S. (2019). Birth relationships after adoption—Is there a role for Article 8? *Child and Family Law Quarterly*, *31*(3), 211–226.

Hart, R. A. (1997). *Children's participation: The theory and practice of involving young citizens in community development and environmental care*. Earthscan.

Helland, H. S., Križ, K., & Skivenes, M. (2023). Gauging the child's presence and voice in adoption proceedings of children from care in seven European countries: Applying a child equality perspective. In N. Lowe & C. Fenton-Glynn (Eds.), *Research handbook on adoption law* (pp. 91–212). Edward Elgar.

Horgan, D. (2024). *A literature review on methodologies for consulting with children aged 0–5 years*. Hub na nÓg and Department of Children Equality, Disability, Integration, and Youth, University College Cork.

Irish Constitution. (1937). *Bunreacht Na hEireann*. https://www.irishstatutebook.ie/eli/cons/en/html

Iyer, P., Boddy, J., Hammelsbeck, R., & Lynch-Huggins, S. (2020). *Contact following placement in care, adoption, or special guardianship: Implications for children and young people's well-being. Evidence review*. Nuffield Family Justice Observatory.

Jackson, N. (2024). Child and Family Agency v's U.D. and M.D. [2024] IEHC 352 delivered 28th May 2024.
Keegan, J. S. (2016). ZH v's Mr and Mrs H and A Health and Social Care Trust 5/6/2016, NIFam 6, KEE10042.
Luhamaa, K., & O'Mahony, C. (2021). International human rights law governing national adoption from care. In T. Pösö, M. Skivenes, & J. Thoburn (Eds.), *Adoption from care: International perspectives on children's rights, family preservation and state intervention* (pp. 177–194). Policy Press.
Lundy, L. (2007). 'Voice' is not enough: Conceptualising Article 12 of the United Nations Convention on the Rights of the Child. *British Educational Research Journal, 33*(6), 927–942. https://doi.org/10.1080/01411920701657033
MacDonald, M. (2021). Supporting face-to-face birth family contact after adoption from care: Learning for trauma-sensitive practice. *The British Journal of Social Work, 51*(3), 1060–1079. https://doi.org/10.1093/bjsw/bcaa121
MacDonald, M. (2023). Post-adoption contact. In N. Lowe & C. Fenton-Glynn (Eds.), *Research handbook on adoption law* (pp. 248–268). Edward Elgar.
MacDonald, M., & McLoughlin, P. (2016). Paramountcy, family rights and contested adoption: Does contact with birth relatives balance the scales? *Child Care in Practice, 22*(4), 401–407. https://doi.org/10.1080/13575279.2016.1208147
MacDonald, M., Wright, A. C., Taylor-Beswick, A., Gillespie, K., & Collings, S. (2023). Digital relationality, rights, resilience: Conceptualising a digital social ecology for children's birth family relationships when in care or adopted. *The British Journal of Social Work, 53*(1), 216–235. https://doi.org/10.1093/bjsw/bcac140
Mashburn, S. (2015). Mediating a family: The use of mediation in the formation and enforcement of post-adoption contact agreements. *Journal of Dispute Resolution, 2*, 383. https://scholarship.law.missouri.edu/jdr/vol2015/iss2/7/
McCaughren, S. (2010). *A study of open adoption in Ireland through the narratives of adoptive parents* [Unpublished doctoral dissertation, University College Cork].
McCaughren, S., & McGregor, C. (2018). Reimagining adoption in Ireland: A viable option for children in care? *Child Care in Practice, 24*(3), 229–244. https://doi.org/10.1080/13575279.2017.1319799
McCaughren, S., & Parkes, A. (2019). Legal analysis of open adoption in Ireland. In *Review and consultation in respect of the potential introduction of open or semi-open adoption in Ireland* (pp. 32–54). Department of Children and Youth Affairs.
McCaughren, S., Holt, S., Parkes, A., & Gregory, S. (2022). *Research report on guidance on contact time for infants and young children in separated families.* One Family, Trinity College Dublin and University College Cork.
Monk, D., & Macvarish, J. (2019). Siblings, contact and the law: An overlooked relationship? *Family Law, 50*, 180–187.
Neil, E. (2018). Rethinking adoption and birth family contact: Is there a role for the law? *Family Law, 2018*, 1178–1182.
Neil, E., Beek, M., & Ward, E. (2015). *Contact after adoption: A longitudinal study of post adoption contact arrangements.* Coram BAAF.
Parkes, A. (2015). *Children and international human rights law: The right of the child to be heard.* Routledge.
Powell, K. A., & Afifi, T. D. (2005). Uncertainty management and adoptees' ambiguous loss of their birth parents. *Journal of Social and Personal Relationships, 22*(1), 129–151. https://doi.org/10.1177/0265407505049325
Selwyn, J., & Lewis, S. (2023). Keeping in touch: Looked after children and young people's views on their contact arrangements. *Adoption & Fostering, 47*(2), 120–137.
Selwyn, J., & Masson, J. (2014). Adoption, special guardianship and residence orders: A comparison of disruption rates. *Family Law, 44*, 1709–1714.

Shier, A. (2024). Adoption reunions: An exploratory study of the "lived experience" of Irish adult intercountry adoptees who have reunions with their birth families in the digital age [Doctoral thesis, University College Cork].

Shier, H. (2001). Pathways to participation: Openings, opportunities and obligations. *Children and Society*, *15*(2), 107–117. https://doi.org/10.1002/chi.617

Sloan, B. (2014). Post-adoption contact reform: Compounding the state-ordered termination of parenthood?. *Cambridge Law Journal*, 73, 378.

Smith, M., González-Pasarín, L., Salas, M. D., & Bernedo, I. M. (2020). Review of benefits and risks for children in open adoption arrangements. *Child and Family Social Work*, *25*(4), 761–774. https://doi.org/10.1111/cfs.12753

Tefre, Ø. S. (2015). The justifications for terminating parental rights and adoption in the United States. *Children and Youth Services Review*, *48*, 87–97. https://doi.org/10.1016/j.childyouth.2014.12.009

Thoburn, J. (2021). The adoptive kinship network: Issues around birth family contact in adoption. In T. Pösö, M. Skivenes, & J. Thoburn (Eds.), *Adoption from care: International perspectives on children's rights, family preservation and state intervention* (pp. 233–248). Policy Press.

United Kingdom. (2017). *The adoption and children act 2002* (Miscellaneous Amendments) Regulations 2017 (SI 2017/…). The Stationery Office.

United Nations. (1989). *United Nations Convention on the Rights of the Child*. https://www.ohchr.org/en/instruments-mechanisms/instruments/convention-rights-child

United Nations Committee on the Rights of the Child. (2021). *General Comment No. 25 on children's rights in relation to the digital environment*. https://digitallibrary.un.org/record/3906061

United Nations Committee on the Rights of the Child, General Comment No 12 (2009): The Right of the Child to be Heard, 51st sess, CRC/C/GC/12 (20 July 2009).

United Nations General Assembly. (2010). *Guidelines for the alternative care of children, Resolution A/RES/64/142*. https://digitallibrary.un.org/record/673583/files/A_RES_64_142-EN.pdf

Ward, J., & Smeeton, J. (2017). The end of non-consensual adoption? Promoting the wellbeing of children in care. *Practice*, *29*(1), 55–73. https://doi.org/10.1080/09503153.2016.1164131

Wood, K., Featherstone, B., & Gupta, A. (2022). Reordering family practices in an unequal and disorderly world: Contemporary adoption and contact in the UK. *Families, Relationships and Societies*, *11*(2), 192–207. https://doi.org/10.1332/204674321X16388097229006

Wright, A. C., & Collings, S. (2019). Permanency with lifelong connections: Casework practices to support positive relationships between carer and birth families. *Developing Practice: The Child, Youth and Family Work Journal*, *53*, 92–109.

# Section III

# Children's Rights to Participate in Decisions That Affect Their Lives

# 7 Navigating the Quandary of Article 12

## A Comprehensive Review of Children's Participation in Child Welfare Agencies

*Esther Mercado García and Paul McCafferty*

### Introduction

#### *Children's Participation in Social Work: Rights, Challenges, and Practice*

Children's participation in social work, especially in decisions affecting their lives, sits at a crucial intersection of rights, policies, and professional practices (Montserrat & Casas, 2018). It is understood as children's right to be heard and influence decisions that concern them (Hart, 1992). Although the recognition of children's rights—particularly through the United Nations Convention on the Rights of the Child (UNCRC; United Nations, 1989)—has progressed significantly, the practical implementation of their participation in social work contexts continues to face deep and complex challenges (McCafferty, 2017).

Article 12 of the UNCRC enshrines children's right to express their views freely on all matters affecting them and to have those views given due weight according to their age and maturity, recognising children as active agents in their lives (Lansdown, 2005, 2010). However, a gap persists between the rhetoric of rights-based principles and their effective implementation in practice (Kišūnaitė & Bui, 2021), due to challenges in interpreting and fulfilling the obligations of Article 12 (McCafferty, 2021). This raises ethical questions about how social work professionals can ensure genuine and meaningful participation, such that children's voices are not overlooked or marginalised (Lundy, 2007).

Given that professionals are often criticised for persistent failures to involve children in decisions that affect them, this chapter explores these issues and offers meaningful solutions that we hope will help bridge the gap between policy and practice. By examining the structural, cultural, and professional barriers to children's participation in child protection, this chapter identifies strategies that empower social workers to uphold Article 12 in meaningful and effective ways. Through practical insights and case studies, we highlight approaches that ensure children's voices are not only heard but also actively shape the decisions that affect their lives.

The chapter builds on our previous work (see McCafferty & Mercado García, 2024), in which we synthesised data from systematic reviews on the participation of children in social welfare systems. Building on that work, in

DOI: 10.4324/9781003582410-11

this chapter, we extend and further develop the analysis of our findings, specifically exploring children's agency and the importance of incorporating their perspectives into interventions, underscoring the role of social workers in facilitating their participation. The chapter is divided into three sections, incorporating practical case studies to illustrate the real-world application of our perspectives on participation. The first part discusses and problematises children's participation in decisions related to their well-being, framed by the UNCRC. The second part examines the marginalisation of children's voices in welfare systems, focusing on the cultural, structural, and contextual barriers linked to child protection that often cause protection to take precedence over participation, potentially excluding children from crucial decisions about their lives. The third part addresses the critical role of relationships, emphasising the competencies and attitudes of professionals. The chapter concludes by raising key issues related to participation challenges and offering recommendations to enhance children's participation in child welfare systems.

### *Problematising Children's Participation in Decisions Related to Their Well-Being*

The UNCRC established a comprehensive framework for states to uphold and protect children's rights. Featuring 54 provisions, the convention safeguards the civil, political, social, economic, and cultural rights of children (Robinson, 2021). Since its adoption, ensuring that these principles are respected, protected, and promoted has remained a central and ongoing concern. The UNCRC recognises children as individuals with inherent rights and as active contributors in their families and communities. The principles guiding interactions with children emphasise justice, equality, and respect for their integrity, identity, dignity, opinions, and privacy.

Operationalising these principles, the UNCRC identified four general principles that underpin the convention: the best interests of the child (Article 3); the right to life, survival, and development (Article 6); non-discrimination (Article 2); and the right of children to express their views freely (Article 12). These principles are fundamental to the effective implementation of the UNCRC (Kišūnaitė & Bui, 2021, p. 8; United Nations Committee on the Rights of the Child, 2003, point 12). Ensuring the effective implementation of these general principles requires recognising that children must have a voice in matters that affect them. Thus, Article 12 of the UNCRC stands as a landmark provision, reflecting an unprecedented commitment to children's participation in a human rights treaty. It acknowledges the child's legal and social status, affirming that although children do not possess the full autonomy of adults, they are nonetheless recognised as rights holders (United Nations Committee on the Rights of the Child, 2009a, p. 5).

Although Article 12 is among the most frequently cited, in our view, it is one of the least understood provisions of the convention. Article 12(1) of the UNCRC grants every child "capable of forming their own views" the right to express those views freely and to have them "given due weight in accordance with the child's age and maturity" (Lundy et al., 2024, p. 3). Recognising that children lack full legal autonomy in decision-making, it asserts that any child capable of forming an opinion must be guaranteed the right to express it and have it taken seriously, with appropriate consideration given to their age and maturity, including in judicial and administrative proceedings. The obligation for states to "assure to the child" the right to express their views is a powerful directive, creating a firm and unequivocal duty to take all necessary steps to realise this right. This involves actively seeking the child's opinions and giving them appropriate weight (Lansdown, 2022, p. 42; United Nations Committee on the Rights of the Child, 2009b, para. 1).

In practice, however, the reality is that children's ability to exercise their rights under Article 12 largely depends on the cooperation of adults, who may lack commitment to its implementation or have vested interests in ignoring it (Lundy, 2007). For us, then, ensuring that children can freely express their views necessitates a cultural shift in which adults acknowledge the importance of listening to and respecting children. Their concerns, perspectives, and ideas must be meaningfully integrated into decision-making processes that affect their lives. Article 12 also explicitly states that age alone should not be used to limit the significance of children's opinions. A child's level of understanding is not uniformly linked to their age. Instead, it is influenced by factors such as access to information, life experiences, social and cultural expectations, and the level of support they receive, all of which contribute to the development of their capacities (Lansdown, 2005, 2010). So, a genuine commitment to children's participation requires moving beyond tokenistic consultation and ensuring that structures are in place to support and empower them actively. This means creating environments where children feel safe, valued, and confident in expressing their views, while also ensuring that adults have the necessary training and awareness to facilitate meaningful engagement. Without this shift, the promise of Article 12 risks remaining an aspirational ideal rather than a lived reality for children in social work contexts.

Facilitating children's participation in decision-making processes also continues to be a significant challenge. To support professionals in gaining a deeper understanding of children's rights and identifying practices that infringe upon these rights, governments must enact legislation, policies, and practices that guarantee children can assert their rights and be taken seriously in all decisions affecting their lives. For us, Lundy's (2007) model provides a framework for professionals to understand better the structure and scope of Article 12. This is particularly important because the two key elements of Article 12—(a) the right to express an opinion and (b) the right to have that opinion duly considered—are not absolute (Lundy, 2007, p. 931).

This model provides a helpful perspective on conceptualising Article 12 of the UNCRC, emphasising four key components of the provision:

- Space: Children must have opportunities to express their views.
- Voice: Children must be supported in expressing their views effectively.
- Audience: Children's views must be listened to actively.
- Influence: Action must be taken in response to their views, as appropriate.

The interplay among these four components is a crucial aspect of the model, highlighting the overlap between: (a) space and voice (both linked to the right to express an opinion) and (b) audience and influence (both linked to the right to have one's opinion duly considered). The model highlights that Article 12 can only be fully understood when viewed in the context of other related provisions of the UNCRC, specifically Article 2 (non-discrimination), Article 3 (best interests of the child), Article 5 (right to appropriate guidance), Article 13 (right to seek, receive, and share information), and Article 19 (protection from abuse and maltreatment;
Lundy, 2007, p. 933).

Robinson (2021) defined voice as encompassing a child's perspectives, opinions, thoughts, and feelings (p. 33) and being connected to four fundamental values: (a) a conception of communication as dialogue; (b) the requirement for participation and democratic inclusivity; (c) recognition of the unequal and problematic nature of power relations; and (d) the potential for change and transformation (Robinson & Taylor, 2007, p. 8). These values should not be treated as separate or isolated; instead, they are interconnected and interdependent. Therefore, all four values must be considered collectively when applying Article 12 in practice (Robinson, 2021, p. 35).

In this regard, Lundy's (2007) model suggests that Article 12 requires, first, ensuring children's right to express their views, and second, guaranteeing that those views are duly considered. The model acknowledges that decision-making processes are rarely static and expects that once children are informed about the extent of their influence the process may restart (Correia et al., 2022, p. 378). Building on this premise, the European Union Strategy on the Rights of the Child echoes the conclusions drawn by children during the 13th European Forum on the Rights of the Child in 2020, emphasising children's right to participate in decisions that affect them. As stated, nothing about children should be decided without them (European Commission, 2021).

## Case Study of Article 12: Empowering Participation and Decision-Making in Child Welfare

### *Background*

Emma, a 9-year-old girl, is placed under the care of child welfare services following the separation from her biological family due to neglect. Emma has always enjoyed artistic activities. She feels very proud of her work as it is a way to express herself and talk about her interests and personal concerns. In previous placements, Emma often felt unheard, which led to feelings of frustration and alienation. Determined to change this, her new social worker, Mr. García, prioritises Emma's active involvement in decisions affecting her life, aligning his approach with Article 12 of the UNCRC, which emphasises the right of children to express their views and have them considered.

***Adapting the Case to Article 12 of the UNCRC***

*1 Building Trust*

Mr. García implements the principles of Article 12 by creating a strong rapport with Emma, ensuring she feels safe and valued as an active participant in her care decisions. Regular one-on-one meetings allow Emma to express her thoughts and emotions openly, fostering a sense of empowerment and mutual respect.

*2 Space and Voice to Participatory Decision-Making*

To ensure Emma's voice is central to the decision-making process, information about potential foster families is presented in a child-friendly and accessible manner, detailing their lifestyle. Mr. García facilitates interactive discussions, helping Emma articulate her preferences and ensuring her views shape placement decisions.

*3 Influence on Tailored Placement Approach*

Emma's participation influences the final placement decision. Her desire for a family that values creativity is central to the matching process. She is placed with a foster family who encourages artistic pursuits, aligning with her expressed interests and values.

*4 Audience and Ongoing Feedback Mechanisms*

To sustain Emma's involvement, Mr. García conducts regular follow-ups to discuss Emma's adjustment to her new environment and address any evolving needs or concerns. The foster parents receive training on the importance of Emma's active participation in family life and involving her in household decisions like planning activities or setting rules.

**Box 7.1 Reflective Questions for Social Workers: Supporting Emma**

How are the child's opinions heard during meetings or interviews and documented in the intervention plan?

What measures do you take to ensure the child feels safe and empowered to express their opinion?

How do you explain decisions to the child when they are not exactly what they requested?

Do you provide clear information about their rights and the available options?

How do you assess whether the decisions have effectively taken the child's opinions into account?

***Outcomes***

Emma's journey exemplifies the transformative power of respecting a child's voice in welfare decisions, as emphasised in Article 12. Through her involvement in meaningful ways, Emma's emotional well-being improves and she successfully integrates into a loving foster family. This case underscores the importance of viewing children as active participants in their care, setting a standard for ethical and effective child-centred practices in social work.

## Marginalisation of Children's Voices in Welfare Systems

As stated, the right of children to participate in matters affecting their lives is upheld by the UNCRC. However, the fragmented implementation of this right is reflected in a conflicting discursive framework (Keddell, 2023). Children's self-determination and right to influence decisions that concern them face the danger of becoming merely a formality (Pösö, 2022). Here, contemporary conceptualisations of children's rights to protection and participation remain disconnected (Collins et al., 2021). This discourse often portrays children as "becomings" rather than "beings," implying that childhood is constrained by adult standards and positioning children as dependent and incapable (Roche, 2019). These persistent and coexisting conceptualisations of children have varying implications for advancing child participation (Fern, 2014). For example, children have the right to be heard and make decisions about their lives, yet welfare services often fail to recognise them as informed agents (Andenæs, 2012; van Bijleveld et al., 2015).

Child participation is not only at the centre of contentious debates about the nature and meaning of childhood (Collins et al., 2021; Vis et al., 2012) but also influenced by perceptions of diversity and cultural factors (Keddell, 2023), social structures (Bywaters et al., 2015), and systemic and organisational barriers (Bartelink et al., 2015; Davies & Wright, 2008). These challenges may arise from the considerable lack of heterogeneity in child protection systems, including variations in legislation, approaches, and working methods (Skauge et al., 2021). Regarding cultural barriers, Antwi-Boasiako et al. (2021) suggested that too many children are under investigation because assessment tools fail to account for cultural differences. Similarly, Mohamud et al. (2021) argued that eligibility standards and decision-making processes in child welfare are based on racialised conceptions of risk.

Regarding disability, Taylor et al. (2016) argued that the threshold for initiating child protection measures is higher for children with disabilities, and their voices are often overshadowed by those of their parents. Similarly, Engwall et al. (2018) demonstrated that children with disabilities are frequently perceived as lacking capacity and competence and are further marginalised by power structures that favour adult perspectives in social services. Hultman et al. (2019) referred to these circumstances as elusive participation—that is, situations involving discrepancies regarding policy and practice, norms and the perception of normality, perspectives and needs, and the assessment of children's abilities.

This dynamic reinforces the idea that children labelled as vulnerable are viewed as more deserving of support than others, thereby diminishing the relational nature of children in their families, cultures, and communities (Keddell, 2018). Moreover, how services are structured and how risk is codified disproportionately affects certain groups (Keddell, 2022). The attribution of social categorisations, often stigmatising and intersecting at a structural level, serves as a criterion for access to or eligibility for services and evaluation of participation (More, 2023).

Child protection often takes precedence over participation. Concerns about protection, along with bureaucratic and authority-driven systems, restrict the context for meaningful participation (Toros et al., 2018). Systems tend to prioritise safeguarding children, often resulting in their exclusion from significant decisions about their lives. Some children have described an overdependence on expert-driven, deficit-based approaches (Arbeiter & Toros, 2017). A clear lack of information and involvement in risk assessment processes prevents children and adolescents from understanding the specific reasons behind their placement in foster care (Balsells et al., 2017). Consequently, many feel they had little to no opportunity to participate meaningfully in the decisions that affected their lives (Bessell, 2011; Burgund & Zegarac, 2016).

The prevailing perception of collaborative meetings is that discussions are predominantly controlled by professionals, with language and discourse patterns identified as key factors limiting children's opportunities to be heard or influence outcomes (Bolin, 2016). Many children report being unclear about the purpose of child protection conferences and feeling that their participation was minimal (Muench et al., 2017). Bureaucratic structures in child welfare systems often hinder meaningful participation because social workers face constraints related to time, resources, and procedural priorities (McCafferty & Mercado García, 2024). Dillon et al. (2016) underscored the stark contrast between professional perspectives and societal expectations, revealing how large-scale social work practices, driven by a division of labour, risk deepening the gap between the realms of protection and participation.

This is why the interplay between systemic inequities and organisational structures exacerbates challenges surrounding child participation. A predominant focus on protection, the perceived vulnerability and incompetence of children, and an overarching emphasis on the best interests principle can significantly weaken their participation. This, in turn, restricts their access to this right and often reduces participation to symbolic gestures rather than meaningful engagement (Keddell, 2023, p. 3).

## Case Study: The Impact of Formalism on the Care of a Young Person with Autism Spectrum Disorder

### *Background*

David is a 12-year-old boy diagnosed with autism spectrum disorder (ASD) but without intellectual disability. He is placed under the care of the child protection system after a series of family issues. David is highly verbal and able to express his thoughts and emotions clearly.

During the care planning process, social workers organise a meeting to hear his opinions. In this meeting, David requests to maintain his daily routine, continue attending his current school, and retain access to his comfort items, especially materials related to his special interest in computer programming. He explains that these elements help him manage his anxiety and maintain a sense of stability.

Despite the initial consultations, David's opinions are not significantly considered. Faced with the bureaucratic procedures of the system, David's needs are deemed secondary to administrative criteria such as the geographical proximity of available families and the urgency of placement.

David is placed with a foster family that has strong economic and educational resources but lives an hour away from his school. This relocation necessitates his transfer to a new educational institution with a less flexible approach to his learning style and needs. Furthermore, specific accommodations for his routine are not provided, nor is he allowed to bring all his personal items to the new home.

Although he initially tries to adapt, David begins experiencing increasing levels of anxiety. He has lost access to the support networks at his previous school and struggles to integrate into the new environment. His foster family does not fully understand his condition and interprets some of his behaviours as disobedience or lack of interest.

David expresses his frustration on several occasions, but his complaints are not perceived as a significant warning sign, but rather as a failure to adapt to the new environment. Over time, his anxiety transforms into avoidant behaviour. He becomes more introverted and withdrawn and stops attending school. This deterioration leads to the breakdown of his placement, forcing the system to intervene again.

***Lessons from the Case***

This case illustrates how a bureaucratic approach that ignores the specific needs of a young person with ASD can exacerbate their vulnerability. Despite David's high abilities, his emotional and social needs required special consideration, which the system failed to prioritise.

Although David clearly expressed his needs, his voice was not effectively incorporated into the final decisions (lack of genuine participation, child competence, and overrepresentation).

Ignoring the factors that helped him maintain stability (such as his routine and personal items) contributed to his dissatisfaction and emotional deterioration (importance of accommodations).

The foster family was not adequately prepared to understand or respond to David's ASD-specific characteristics, amplifying the challenges of the placement despite being functional and economically and educationally well-resourced (lack of awareness, procedural priorities, and eligibility).

This case highlights the need for a more child-centred approach and the individualisation of care plans, especially for young people with conditions like ASD, for whom stability and understanding are crucial for the success of any intervention.

**Box 7.2 Reflective Questions for Social Workers: Supporting David**

How could the system have ensured that David's opinions and needs were meaningfully integrated into the care plan, rather than merely consulting him as a formal procedure?

How could the balance between bureaucratic demands and David's well-being and individual needs have been achieved, rather than prioritising administrative convenience?

What measures could have been taken to make bureaucratic regulations more flexible and ensure that David maintained his social support network and routine, such as staying in his original school?

How could the system have facilitated David's access to his comfort items and special interests, given their importance for his emotional self-regulation?

What preventive strategies could be implemented to avoid the collapse of David's situation?

What structural changes would be necessary in the care system to ensure that individual needs, such as those of a young person with ASD, take precedence over bureaucratic rules?

## Critical Role of Relationships

The recognition of the relational nature of consent is essential to understanding the position of boys and girls in child welfare (Pösö, 2022), and relationships between social workers and children have been in the spotlight (Winter, 2011). Cossar et al. (2016) stressed the importance of a trusting relationship with social workers to enable children and young people to express their thoughts and feelings. However, building trust between social workers and children in the social work system is fraught with challenges (Salkauskiene et al., 2024).

Professional beliefs regarding children's capacity and understanding of what constitutes a competent viewpoint significantly influence the extent to which professionals consider their opinions (Mitchell & Colville, 2022). Without adequate support, children are unable to safely articulate their views (Pösö, 2022). Consequently, the qualities and professional competence of practitioners play a crucial role (Davies & Wright, 2008), with communication skills being particularly essential (Husby et al., 2018).

In professional practice, however, contact with key professionals is limited, leading to a lack of dialogue, insufficient information about the intervention process, and difficulties in building trusting relationships (Toros, 2021). Ferguson (2017) emphasised the superficial and precarious nature of child protection work in daily practice, which is shaped by the emotional intensity of the work and the complexity of interactions. Similarly, Winter (2010) critiqued elements of the relationship, including the lack of a personal and individualised connection with children, minimal evidence of direct engagement by social workers with children, and poor professional competence and attitude. Additionally, factors such as adult-centric perspectives tied to the monoculture of organisations (Corney et al., 2022) further complicate these dynamics. It is important to highlight, however, that the challenges faced by child protection workers in engaging with children are not solely linked to communication and interpersonal skills. They also stem from fundamental aspects of a child protection system that many criticise as being "not child-friendly" (Vis et al., 2012, p. 16).

## Case Study: The Critical Role of the Child–Social Worker Relationship in the Child Welfare System

### *Background*

María, a 10-year-old Guatemalan girl, lives in a highly vulnerable environment. Her family, consisting of her mother and three younger siblings, faces extreme poverty, domestic violence, and a lack of access to basic services. To contribute to her family's sustenance, María sells candy on the streets, which affects her education, emotional development, and overall well-being. Her school absences catch the attention of her teachers, who refer her case to welfare services.

The assigned social worker, Mr. Holand, faces the challenge of intervening in a complex and delicate situation, where building a strong relationship, effective communication, and creating a bond of trust are not only essential elements of this intervention but also directly influence María's willingness to engage actively in the process.

### *Clear and Child-Centred Communication*

Mr. Holand, during his meetings with María, explains that her situation was reported by her schoolteachers, and he clearly outlines the process she will go through. Open communication fosters in María a sense of belonging to the process, making her feel heard and valued. Additionally, she gains greater confidence to express her concerns.

### *Building the Attachment: Encouraging Active Commitment*

The creation of a strong bond between the social worker and María not only establishes trust but also motivates her to engage with the proposed strategies. This bond is built on consistent presence, genuine empathy, and mutual recognition. This connection influences her participation because María feels her contribution is valuable and that she has control over decisions affecting her life. This emotional commitment strengthens her motivation to implement changes, such as re-enrolling in school or collaborating to improve her family's situation with the support of the child welfare system.

**Box 7.3 Reflective Questions for Social Workers: Supporting María**

How can I ensure that the child perceives my presence as a source of support rather than as an authoritative or imposing figure?
What can I improve in my way of interacting to strengthen the relationship with the child?
Am I using age-appropriate and context-sensitive language to ensure that the child truly understands the objectives and steps of the intervention process?
How can I ensure that I maintain a child-centred approach despite my emotions, institutional pressures, or resource limitations?
How can I measure whether the bond I have built with the child has influenced the effectiveness of the intervention process?

### *Outcomes*

The relationship, communication, and bond between the social worker and María are the pillars that enable her active participation in the intervention process. These aspects not only facilitate the identification of solutions but also empower María to become an agent of change in her life. Active participation is not a secondary outcome but the core of success in the social welfare system, demonstrating how human connections can transform lives.

## Implications for Practice Based on These Considerations

### *In Child Welfare Systems*

Ensuring meaningful child participation requires a cultural shift due to the following factors:

- The fragmented implementation of children's right to participation reflects a discursive tension between protection and participation, often reduced to a mere formality and constrained by bureaucracy and the hierarchical structure of child welfare systems. This results in a superficial approach to child welfare and protection work.
- The disconnection between protection and participation, whereby children are not recognised as legitimate actors in decisions regarding their well-being.
- Organisational and structural barriers stemming from a monocultural institutional approach, an adult-centred perspective, and risk assessments that fail to consider cultural diversity.
- The lack of accessible information and meaningful participatory spaces, such that technical language and professional hierarchy dominate the discourse.

***In Professional Relationships***

Child participation requires:

- The establishment of trust-based relationships between children and professionals, allowing children to express their feelings and thoughts in a safe environment.
- A shift in professionals' beliefs regarding children's capacities, fostering genuine participation in decision-making processes.
- Professional competencies and effective communication strategies that ensure children feel understood and secure throughout the process.

***For Child Welfare Systems***

- Strengthen policies and legal frameworks to enhance compliance with Article 12, ensuring that all decisions affecting children include systematic and mandatory consultation procedures. This should guarantee that children receive adequate information about decision-making processes and therefore counteract evasive participation.
- Develop effective mechanisms to ensure children's participation in decision-making. Implement methodologies inspired by Lundy's (2007) model to assess participation and incorporate accessible tools that facilitate their understanding of their rights.
- Incorporate an intersectional approach in child protection, recognising the structural barriers that affect children's participation based on the breadth of diversity.
- Monitor and evaluate the impact of child participation through periodic research that accounts for children's perceptions regarding their level of involvement in decision-making processes.
- Develop continuous training programmes to improve professionals' skills in using tools and techniques that foster participation while increasing sensitivity to children's perspectives.

***For Professionals Involved in Child Welfare Processes***

- Implement dialogue-based models that foster the creation of safe spaces and thus break away from hierarchical and deficit-based approaches.
- Reduce bureaucratisation and promote active listening by allocating more time and resources to direct interactions to facilitate more frequent and meaningful contact.
- Encourage an individualised approach in social interventions that recognises each child's uniqueness while also reviewing and reformulating child consent models.
- Reform eligibility criteria and risk assessment processes to move away from standardised approaches. Adopt evaluations based on children's resilience and capabilities.

## Conclusion

In this chapter, we have problematised and explored the dilemmas arising from the application of Article 12 of the UNCRC in child welfare agencies. For us, promoting children's participation in welfare systems is essential to ensure respect for their rights, particularly the right to be heard in matters that affect their lives. However, several challenges hinder meaningful participation. First, there is a lack of awareness and understanding of children's rights. There is a widespread underestimation of children's capacities (Lansdown, 2010), stemming from the failure to recognise and implement their right to be heard fully (Strømland et al., 2022). Second, cultural conceptions, the adult-centred worldview of social work professionals, age discrimination, denial of opportunities, and ineffective participatory efforts remain significant challenges (Collins, 2017; Strømland et al., 2022). Concerns about protection, along with bureaucratic and authority-driven systems, further restrict this participatory context (Toros et al., 2018). Third, institutional and structural barriers arise from inadequate policies (Lundy, 2007). Fourth, the lack of trained professionals with skills to engage children in a respectful and meaningful way is a major limitation (van Bijleveld et al., 2015). Finally, challenges in representation mean participation can be superficial, in that it shows inclusion without genuinely considering children's opinions (Hart, 1992) or results in overrepresentation driven by doubts about their capabilities due to diversity issues (Toros et al., 2018).

Based on the three main themes discussed in the chapter, the case studies highlighted how real-world practices either support or hinder children's participation. The cases of Emma, David, and María illustrated the challenges in implementing Article 12 of the convention, along with the crossroads of formalism and the need to foster frameworks that balance inequalities between protection and participation. The process of participation involves understanding the importance of children's experiences in the context of their daily lives (Skauge et al., 2021).

This exploration of Article 12 of the UNCRC in child welfare agencies underscores the critical need to foster meaningful participation for children in decisions that affect their lives. Although the right to be heard is a fundamental principle, its implementation remains fraught with challenges, ranging from a lack of awareness and understanding of children's rights to deeply ingrained cultural and structural barriers. The persistence of adult-centric perspectives, institutional constraints, and the shortage of trained professionals further complicate efforts to ensure genuine participation.

The case studies of Emma, David, and María highlight the tensions between formalism and substantive engagement, revealing the complexities of balancing child protection with participatory rights. Their experiences emphasise the importance of moving beyond superficial inclusion to establish frameworks that actively address inequalities and empower children as legitimate stakeholders in their lives.

Ultimately, achieving meaningful participation requires a paradigm shift in how children's voices are valued in welfare systems. This necessitates not only policy and structural reforms but also a cultural transformation in how professionals and institutions perceive children's agency. By fostering a participatory environment that respects children's perspectives, acknowledges their evolving capacities, and addresses systemic barriers, child welfare agencies can truly uphold the spirit of Article 12 and contribute to a more equitable realisation of children's rights.

## References

Andenæs, A. (2012). From "placement" to "a child on the move": Methodological strategies to give children a more central position in Child Welfare Service. *Qualitative Social Work*, *11*(5), 486–501. https://doi.org/10.1177/1473325011408174
Antwi-Boasiako, K., Fallon, B., King, B., Trocmé, N., & Fluke, J. (2021). Examining decision-making tools and child welfare involvement among Black families in Ontario, Canada. *Children and Youth Services Review*, *126*, 106048. https://doi.org/10.1016/j.childyouth.2021.106048
Arbeiter, E., & Toros, K. (2017). Participatory discourse: Engagement in the context of child protection assessment practices from the perspectives of child protection workers, parents and children. *Children and Youth Services Review*, *74*, 17–27. https://doi.org/10.1016/j.childyouth.2017.01.020
Balsells, M. A., Fuentes-Pelaez, N., & Pastor, C. (2017). Listening to the voices of children in decision-making: A challenge for the child protection system in Spain. *Children and Youth Services Review*, *79*, 418–425. https://doi.org/10.1016/j.childyouth.2017.06.055
Bartelink, C., van Yperen, T. A., & ten Berge, I. J. (2015). Deciding on child maltreatment: A literature review on methods that improve decision-making. *Child Abuse & Neglect*, *49*, 142–153. https://doi.org/10.1016/j.chiabu.2015.07.002
Bessell, S. (2011). Participation in decision-making in out-of-home care in Australia: What do young people say? *Children and Youth Services Review*, *33*(4), 496–501. https://doi.org/10.1016/j.childyouth.2010.05.006
Bolin, A. (2016). Children's agency in interprofessional collaborative meetings in child welfare work. *Child & Family Social Work*, *21*(4), 502–511. https://doi.org/10.1111/cfs.12167
Burgund, A., & Zegarac, N. (2016). Perspectives of youth in care in Serbia. *Child and Adolescent Social Work Journal*, *33*(2), 151–161. https://doi.org/10.1007/s10560-015-0413-5
Bywaters, P., Brady, G., Sparks, T., Bos, E., Bunting, L., Daniel, B., Featherstone, B., Morris, K., & Scourfield, J. (2015). Exploring inequities in child welfare and child protection services: Explaining the "inverse intervention law." *Children and Youth Services Review*, *57*, 98–105. https://doi.org/10.1016/j.childyouth.2015.07.017
Collins, T. M. (2017). A child's right to participate: Implications for international child protection. *The International Journal of Human Rights*, *21*(1), 14–46. https://doi.org/10.1080/13642987.2016.1248122
Collins, T. M., Rizzini, I., & Mayhew, A. (2021). Fostering global dialogue: Conceptualisations of children's rights to participation and protection. *Children & Society*, *35*(2), 295–310. https://doi.org/10.1111/chso.12437
Corney, T., Cooper, T., Shier, H., & Williamson, H. (2022). Youth participation: Adultism, human rights and professional youth work. *Children & Society*, *36*(4), 677–690. https://doi.org/10.1111/chso.12526
Correia, N., Aguiar, C., & The Participa Consortium. (2022). Children's right to participate: The Lundy model applied to early childhood education and care. *The International Journal of Children's Rights*, *30*(2), 378–405. https://doi.org/10.1163/15718182-30020010

Cossar, J., Brandon, M., & Jordan, P. (2016). You've got to trust her and she's got to trust you: Children's views on participation in the child protection system. *Child & Family Social Work*, *21*(1), 103–112. https://doi.org/10.1111/cfs.12115
Davies, J., & Wright, J. (2008). Children's voices: A review of the literature pertinent to looked-after children's views of mental health services. *Child and Adolescent Mental Health*, *13*(1), 26–31. https://doi.org/10.1111/j.1475-3588.2007.00458.x
Dillon, J., Greenop, D., & Hills, M. (2016). Participation in child protection: A small-scale qualitative study. *Qualitative Social Work*, *15*(1), 70–85. https://doi.org/10.1177/1473325015578946
Engwall, K., Östberg, F., Andersson, G., Bons, T., & Bringlöv, Å. (2018). Children with disabilities in Swedish child welfare—A differentiating and disabling practice. *European Journal of Social Work*, *22*(6), 1025–1037. https://doi.org/10.1080/13691457.2018.1461073
European Commission. (2021). *The EU strategy on the rights of the child and the European child guarantee*. https://eur-lex.europa.eu/legal-content/EN/TXT/?uri=celex%3A52021DC0142
Ferguson, H. (2017). How children become invisible in child protection work: Findings from research into day-to-day social work practice. *British Journal of Social Work*, *47*(4), 1007–1023. https://doi.org/10.1093/bjsw/bcw065
Fern, E. (2014). "Grown-ups never understand anything by themselves..." *Practice*, *26*(1), 3–22. https://doi.org/10.1080/09503153.2013.867940
Hart, R. (1992). *Children's participation: From tokenism to citizenship*. UNICEF.
Hultman, L., Forinder, U., Öhrvall, A-M., Pergert, K., & Fugl-Meyer, K. (2019). Elusive participation—Social workers' experience of the participation of children with disabilities in LSS assessments. *Scandinavian Journal of Disability Research*, *21*(1), 38–48. https://doi.org/10.16993/sjdr.558
Husby, I. S. D., Slettebø, T., & Juul, R. (2018). Partnerships with children in child welfare: The importance of trust and pedagogical support. *Child & Family Social Work*, *23*(3), 443–450. https://doi.org/10.1111/cfs.12435
Keddell, E. (2018). The vulnerable child in neoliberal contexts: The construction of children in the Aotearoa New Zealand child protection reforms. *Childhood*, *25*(1), 93–108. https://doi.org/10.1177/0907568217727591
Keddell, E. (2022). Mechanisms of inequity: The impact of instrumental biases in the child protection system. *Societies*, *12*(3), 83. https://doi.org/10.3390/soc12030083
Keddell, E. (2023). Recognising the embedded child in child protection: Children's participation, inequalities and cultural capital. *Children and Youth Services Review*, *147*, 106815. https://doi.org/10.1016/j.childyouth.2023.106815
Kišūnaitė, A., & Bui, L. H. (2021). Operationalising children's rights principles: An indicator framework for policy analysis. *Revista Sobre la Infancia y la Adolescencia*, *20*, 1–21. https://doi.org/10.4995/reinad.2020.13291
Lansdown, G. (2005). *The evolving capacities of the child*. UNICEF Innocenti Research Centre and Save the Children.
Lansdown, G. (2010). The realisation of children's participation rights: Critical reflections. In B. Percy-Smith & N. Thomas (Eds.), *A handbook of children and young people's participation: Perspectives from theory and practice* (pp. 11–23). Routledge.
Lansdown, G. (2022). Article 12: The right to be heard. In Z. Vaghri, J. Zermatten, G. Lansdown, & R. Ruggiero (Eds.), *Monitoring state compliance with the UN Convention on the Rights of the Child: An analysis of attributes* (pp. 41–50). Springer.
Lundy, L. (2007). "Voice" is not enough: Conceptualising Article 12 of the United Nations Convention on the Rights of the Child. *British Educational Research Journal*, *33*(6), 927–942. https://doi.org/10.1080/01411920701657033
Lundy, L., Murray, C., Smith, K., & Ward, C. (2024). Young children's right to be heard on the quality of their education: Addressing potential misunderstandings in the context of early childhood education. *British Educational Research Journal*. Advance online publication. https://doi.org/10.1002/berj.3968

McCafferty, P. (2017). Implementing Article 12 of the United Nations Convention on the Rights of the Child in child protection decision making: A critical analysis of the challenges and opportunities for social work. *Child Care in Practice*, *23*(4), 327–341. https://doi.org/10.1080/13575279.2016.1264368

McCafferty, P. (2021). Children's participation in child welfare decision making: Recognising dichotomies, conceptualising critically informed solutions. *Child Care in Practice*, *30*(2), 112–129. https://doi.org/10.1080/13575279.2021.1896990

McCafferty, P., & Mercado García, E. (2024). Children's participation in child welfare: A systematic review of systematic reviews. *The British Journal of Social Work*, *54*(3), 1092–1108. https://doi.org/10.1093/bjsw/bcad167

Mitchell, K. L., & Colville, T. (2022). "Can you hear me?" An exploratory study investigating the representation and impact of children's views in multi-agency meetings. *Children & Society*, *36*(4), 472–493. https://doi.org/10.1111/chso.12506

Mohamud, F., Edwards, T., Antwi-Boasiako, K., William, K., King, J., Igor, E., & King, B. (2021). Racial disparity in the Ontario child welfare system: Conceptualizing policies and practices that drive involvement for Black families. *Children and Youth Services Review*, *120*, 105711. https://doi.org/10.1016/j.childyouth.2020.105711

Montserrat, C., & Casas, F. (2018). What role do children play in social services? *Psicoperspectivas*, *17*(2), 1–13. https://doi.org/10.5027/psicoperspectivas-Vol17-Issue2-fulltext-1152

More, R. (2023). Inclusive child welfare services, disabled children, and their families: Insights from a European comparison of social policy and social (work) practice in Austria, Iceland, and Ireland. *European Journal of Social Work*, *27*, 478–489. https://doi.org/10.1080/13691457.2023.2219033

Muench, K., Diaz, C., & Wright, R. (2017). Children and parent participation in child protection conferences: A study in one English local authority. *Child Care in Practice*, *23*(1), 49–63. https://doi.org/10.1080/13575279.2015.1126227

Pösö, T. (2022). Children's consent to child welfare services: Some explorative remarks. *Children & Society*, *36*(1), 52–65. https://doi.org/10.1111/chso.12483

Robinson, C. (2021). Lost in translation: The reality of implementing children's right to be heard. *Journal of the British Academy*, *8*(s4), 29–39. https://doi.org/10.5871/jba/008s4.029

Robinson, C., & Taylor, C. (2007). Theorising student voice: Values and perspectives. *Improving Schools*, *10*(1), 5–17. https://doi.org/10.1177/1365480207073702

Roche, S. (2019). Childhoods in policy: A critical analysis of national child protection policy in the Philippines. *Children & Society*, *33*(2), 95–110. https://doi.org/10.1111/chso.12295

Salkauskiene, I., Husby, I. S. D., & Juul, R. (2024). Building trust with children in collaborative processes within in-home child welfare services. *Journal of Public Child Welfare*. Advance online publication. https://doi.org/10.1080/15548732.2024.2411047

Skauge, B., Skårstad, A., & Marthinsen, E. (2021). The what, why and how of child participation—A review of the conceptualization of "child participation" in child welfare. *Social Sciences*, *10*(2), 54. https://doi.org/10.3390/socsci10020054

Strømland, M., Bahus, M. K., & Andersen, A. J. W. (2022). Too vulnerable to participate? A systematic literature review of the gap between a right to participate and participation in welfare services. *Journal of Human Rights Practice*, *14*(1), 331–351. https://doi.org/10.1093/jhuman/huab061

Taylor, J., Stalker, K., & Stewart, A. (2016). Disabled children and the child protection system: A cause for concern. *Child Abuse Review*, *25*(1), 60–73. https://doi.org/10.1002/car.2386

Toros, K. (2021). A systematic review of children's participation in child protection decision-making: Tokenistic presence or not? *Children & Society*, *35*(3), 395–411. https://doi.org/10.1111/chso.12418

Toros, K., DiNitto, D. M., & Tiko, A. (2018). Family engagement in the child welfare system: A scoping review. *Children and Youth Services Review*, *88*, 598–607. https://doi.org/10.1016/j.childyouth.2018.03.011
United Nations. (1989). *Convention on the rights of the child*. https://www.ohchr.org/en/instruments-mechanisms/instruments/convention-rights-child
United Nations Committee on the Rights of the Child. (2003, 27 November). *General comment no. 5 (2003): General measures of implementation of the Convention on the Rights of the Child (CRC/GC/2003/5)*. United Nations.
United Nations Committee on the Rights of the Child. (2009a). *General comment No. 12: The right of the child to be heard*. https://digitallibrary.un.org/record/671444
United Nations Committee on the Rights of the Child. (2009b). *General comment No. 11: Indigenous children and their rights under the convention*. https://digitallibrary.un.org/record/648790
van Bijleveld, G. G., Dedding, C. W. M., & Bunders-Aelen, J. F. G. (2015). Children's and young people's participation within child welfare and child protection services: A state-of-the-art review. *Child & Family Social Work*, *20*(2), 129–138. https://doi.org/10.1111/cfs.12082
Vis, S. A., Holtan, A., & Thomas, N. (2012). Obstacles for child participation in care and protection cases—Why Norwegian social workers find it difficult. *Child Abuse Review*, *21*(1), 7–23. https://doi.org/10.1002/car.1155
Winter, K. (2010). *Building relationships and communicating with young children: A practical guide for social workers*. Routledge. https://doi.org/10.4324/9780203836729
Winter, K. (2011). The UNCRC and social workers' relationships with young children. *Child Abuse Review*, *20*(6), 395–406. https://doi.org/10.1002/car.1203.

# 8 Facilitating and Responding to Children's Participation in Social Work Decision-Making Processes

*Kristina Edman and Paul McCafferty*

## Introduction: Reframing Children's Participation in Social Work

Participation is a cornerstone of children's rights, rooted in the recognition that children are not merely passive recipients of adult care but active agents with valuable insights into their lives and preferred futures. The United Nations Convention on the Rights of the Child (UNCRC; United Nations, 1989), particularly Article 12, enshrines the child's right to express their views freely in matters affecting them, with due weight given according to their age and maturity. This principle has inspired significant shifts in how social workers engage children because it emphasises participatory practices that respect and amplify children's voices.

Participation is often conceptualised through established frameworks, such as Hart's (1992) ladder of participation, Shier's (2001) pathways to participation, and Lundy's (2007) model of participation. These models have made important contributions to the field by providing valuable tools for reflecting on participation and facilitating its implementation in various contexts. However, they are based on adult-authored documents (UNCRC) rather than practice-related data on how children exercise participation and how it is facilitated and responded to. Their foundation in adult-authored documents (e.g., UNCRC) and linear and hierarchical designs may limit their capacity to address the relational, dynamic, and nuanced aspects of participation in practice. This is particularly evident in the complex and emotionally sensitive domain of child protection, where the intricate nature of face-to-face social work dialogues demands more granular, dynamic and adaptable approaches (e.g., Bromark et al., 2023; Edman, 2025; Edman et al., 2024; Eriksson, 2024).

Building on this foundation, this chapter advances the field by presenting and exploring perspectives developed on practice-related data by Edman et al. (2022, 2024). It tailors their "participation compass" and its six distinct dimensions of participation—participatory, directive, positional, agentive, emotional, and narrative—for child protection decision-making processes. Additionally, the chapter discusses how this compass can be combined with practices that facilitate participation (e.g., Bromark et al., 2023; Edman et al., 2024).

DOI: 10.4324/9781003582410-12

Through an in-depth discussion of the participation compass and its six dimensions, supported by case studies, this chapter highlights its transformative potential in child protection decision-making processes.

## Evolution of Children's Participatory Rights: Historical Developments and Key Models

The evolution of children's participatory rights reflects a profound shift in societal attitudes towards children, recognising them as active agents with distinct voices (McCafferty, 2017). Historically, children have often been viewed as passive dependents (James & James, 2004; Qvortrup, 2009) with limited opportunities to influence decisions affecting their lives. This perspective was challenged in the early 20th century, notably with the adoption of the Declaration of the Rights of the Child by the League of Nations in 1924, which acknowledged the need for special safeguards for children. Significant advancements to children's rights were made in 1959, when the United Nations General Assembly adopted the Declaration of the Rights of the Child, then again in 1989 with the adoption of the UNCRC. This comprehensive treaty enshrined various rights for children, including the right to participate in decisions affecting them. Article 12 of the UNCRC explicitly states that children capable of forming views have the right to express those views freely in all matters affecting them, with due weight given according to their age and maturity. The UNCRC's emphasis on participation marked a paradigm shift in both social work research and practice, inspiring scholars and practitioners to develop and employ models for advancing children's participation in decision-making processes. Three prominent models emerged: Hart's ladder of participation, Shier's pathways to participation, and Lundy's model of participation. Each offers a unique framework for understanding and implementing children's participation rights.

Hart's ladder of participation, introduced by Roger Hart in 1992, presents eight levels of participation, ranging from non-participation (manipulation, decoration, tokenism) to genuine participation (assigned but informed, consulted and informed, adult-initiated shared decisions, child-initiated and directed, child-initiated shared decisions with adults). Although meant to stimulate reflection (Hart, 2007), this model has come to serve as a diagnostic tool, helping practitioners assess the degree of children's participation in various activities. In 2001, Harry Shier introduced pathways to participation, outlining five levels to advance children's participation: (1) children are listened to, (2) children are supported in expressing views, (3) their views are considered, (4) they are involved in decision-making processes, and (5) they share power and responsibility for decision-making. Each level is associated with three stages of commitment: openings (which occur when social workers are ready to operate at the level they are at or are approaching), opportunities (which occur when the social workers' needs to operate at this level are met), and obligations (which occur when there is an agreed-upon policy that social workers should operate at this level). Building on the foundations laid by the UNCRC, Lundy's model of participation, proposed by Laura Lundy in 2007, offers a rights-based framework centred on four interrelated elements: space (providing a safe environment to express views), voice (facilitating expression), audience (ensuring views are listened to), and influence (ensuring views are acted upon). This model emphasises that genuine participation requires more than listening to children; it necessitates creating environments where their voices can influence decisions.

These models offer distinct yet complementary perspectives on enhancing children's participation. In social work, particularly child protection, they collectively inform practices that respect and amplify children's participation, contributing to the upholding of children's rights in complex decision-making processes. Further advances in the field, however, are needed to capture more granular, nuanced, and relational aspects of participation processes, particularly in the complex and emotionally-sensitive context of child protection.

## The Participation Compass: A Complementary Framework

The participation compass introduces six distinct yet interconnected dimensions of participation—participatory, directive, positional, emotional, agentive, and narrative—each contributing uniquely to child protection decision-making processes (see Edman et al., 2022, p. 3494, for a pictorial representation of the compass). These dimensions are non-hierarchical and non-linear, acknowledging that participation is not about striving for a "higher" or "better" level but responding to and facilitating different ways that children express themselves. Participation itself is neither inherently positive nor negative; its quality is more important than quantity.

By reframing participation as a dynamic and context-sensitive process with no set or predetermined pathway, the compass serves as a versatile tool for navigating child protection complexities and fostering meaningful participation. The compass enriches theoretical understandings of participation while providing practical guidance to social workers. Building on Edman et al.'s (2022) earlier studies, each dimension of participation is outlined here to reflect its relevance to child protection decision-making processes.

### *Participatory Participation*

When children actively contribute to and sustain a dialogue, they are exercising participatory participation. This type of participation is characterised by collaborative and interactive elements that help sustain and drive dialogues forward. Examples include generic listening responses and responding to questions, signalling that the child is present, attentive, and engaged. Without participatory participation, decision-making processes would be severely impaired, if not entirely unworkable. In child protection, recognising these subtler forms of participation ensures that children's voices remain integral to the process. Importantly, non-compliance or resistance does not necessarily indicate an absence of participation. As illustrated in subsequent sections, non-compliance and resistance can also be valid forms of participation, such as directive or positional participation.

#### *Directive Participation*

This dimension is expressed when children influence the direction and flow of discussions, asserting control over how the decision-making process unfolds. In this form of participation, the child plays a guiding role—comparable to how a film director or music conductor orchestrates conversations to align with their preferences, needs, and perspectives. Without this type of active participation, a decision-making process might veer off in directions not in line with a child's intentions.

#### *Positional Participation*

Children exercise positional participation when they express their stance or explain the reasoning behind their stance. This form of participation reflects the child's viewpoint or opinion, revealing their preferences, values, or choices regarding various aspects of life. Similarly to directive participation, positional participation plays a crucial role in decision-making processes; when a child's position is not voiced and acknowledged, the decision-making process may unintentionally lead to outcomes misaligned with their preferences, needs, and perspectives.

#### *Emotional Participation*

When children exercise emotional participation, they engage in the decision-making process at an emotional level. Emotional participation can manifest in various ways, including crying, laughing, or talking with a trembling voice. When a child is not participating on an emotional level, they may struggle to relate to the subject matter. Highlighting the nuanced nature of participation, emotional detachment may at times play a constructive role, allowing children to communicate their thoughts without becoming overwhelmed.

#### *Agentive Participation*

When children express their past, present, or potential actions, they exercise agentive participation. Through agentive participation, children embody a form of participation that highlights their agency, such as responding to and dealing with hardship. This form of participation emphasises the child's capacity to act and make choices rather than merely being a passive recipient of actions or decisions made by others. Without agentive participation, how children manage challenges and successes is less apparent. Again, participation itself is neither inherently positive nor negative. When children are dealing with situations for which adults are responsible, their agentive participation may require adjustment to ensure it aligns with the support they need and to which they are entitled.

#### *Narrative Participation*

When someone—be it the child, social worker, or another person—brings attention to a child's participation, they contribute to shaping a narrative of the child as an active subject rather than a passive object. Unlike agentive participation, which focuses on the child's actions and their visibility, narrative participation emphasises the broader account of the child's role in decision-making processes. Narrative participation can be visualised as a string of beads, with each bead symbolising a moment when the child's participation is acknowledged. The length of the string and variety of the beads—different shapes, sizes, and colours—reflect the participation that is being acknowledged. The narrative evolves through dialogue, documentation, and final decisions. Without this perspective, a child's participation risks being overlooked, which can leave them feeling excluded and reduce their willingness to participate in the future.

#### *The Participation Compass in Practice*

The participation compass highlights the coexistence and interplay of diverse participatory dimensions. It frames participation as a dynamic and context-sensitive process, moving beyond linear progression or an "ideal" form (Edman et al., 2022). The compass encourages social workers to recognise that children exercise participation in multiple ways, often simultaneously. A child may, for instance, respond to a question (participatory participation), assert their position on a topic (positional participation), and express their emotions (emotional participation) in a single utterance. These participatory actions are co-constructed through dialogues shaped by individual, interactional, relational, and contextual factors (e.g., Edman, 2025; Edman et al., 2024). The participation compass reimagines participation as a shared and jointly achieved process that honours both children's and social workers' contributions. It signals that children's capability to express themselves (per the UNCRC) is shaped less by their age and assessed maturity and more by how the dialogues and decision-making process evolve (e.g., Edman, 2025; Edman et al., 2024).

### Case Study: Stephen's Journey in Therapeutic Child Protection

Stephen, a 10-year-old boy, is referred to therapeutic child protection services following allegations of domestic abuse and neglect at home. He is placed in foster care and begins attending weekly therapy sessions with Maria, his assigned social worker. These sessions aim to provide Stephen with a safe space to process his experiences and contribute to decisions about his care. Initially,

Stephen engages through participatory participation, using nonverbal gestures like nodding to indicate his attentiveness. As trust develops, he begins expressing his preferences verbally, such as his desire to remain with his foster family rather than return home. This shift demonstrates positional participation because Stephen articulated his reasoning and values, thus emphasising his sense of safety and stability in his current placement.

During a conversation addressing visitation with his mother, Stephen exhibits emotional participation by crying and expressing anxiety. His fear of being left alone with his mother prompts Maria to explore his feelings further. This emotional input becomes a pivotal factor in shaping decisions, leading to supervised visitations in a neutral location to ensure Stephen's comfort and safety. Stephen's directive participation emerges as he steers conversations towards topics he feels confident discussing, such as his friendships and achievements at school. These discussions reveal his agentive and directive participation, with Stephen proposing drawing activities to communicate his emotions and ideas visually. His contributions inform Maria's therapeutic strategies and foster a collaborative environment. Maria also emphasises narrative participation by reflecting on Stephen's contributions, reinforcing the importance of his role in shaping his care plan. For example, Maria acknowledges how Stephen's input about visitation directly influenced the final decision. This recognition illuminates and validates Stephen's participation, which encourages him to continue participating.

Stephen's case illustrates the multifaceted nature of participation, highlighting how children exercise various dimensions simultaneously. Recognising and responding to these dimensions allows social workers to tailor both the ongoing dialogue and interventions to align with each child's unique needs and circumstances. The participation compass offers a flexible and responsive framework to navigate these complexities.

**Box 8.1 Reflective Questions for Social Workers: Encouraging Participation**

How can I help regulate children's emotional participation when they express strong feelings about sensitive topics?

In what ways can I utilise narrative participation to reinforce a child's sense of agency and ensure their contributions are acknowledged and integrated into care plans?

How can I recognise and balance the interplay of positional, emotional, directive, and narrative participation in shaping decisions that reflect a child's needs and preferences, as seen in Stephen's case?

How can I foster and respect directive participation, as seen in Stephen's ability to steer conversations towards topics he feels confident discussing, such as friendships or school?

In what ways might I further develop my capacity to recognise, facilitate, and respond to the diverse dimensions of participation?

**Case Study: Leah's Voice in Decision-Making**

Leah, a 9-year-old girl, enters the child protection system following reports of neglect and exposure to domestic violence. Assigned to her case, social worker Anna adopts the participation compass framework to guide her interactions with Leah. During early sessions, Leah appears withdrawn, offering minimal verbal responses but nodding occasionally when asked about her preferences. By nodding when asked about her preferences, Leah exercised both participatory and positional participation, providing Anna with initial insights into Leah's experiences and perspectives.

Over time, as Leah and the social worker's dialogue evolves, Leah becomes more comfortable, and she begins expressing her preferences more explicitly. During a discussion about potential school placements, she states her desire to stay in her current school to maintain friendships. This is an example of more explicit positional participation, whereby Leah articulated her priorities and values. Anna uses this information to advocate Leah's educational stability in the care planning process.

During a family group conference, Leah displays emotional participation when her mother suggests increasing visitation. Leah begins crying and expresses fears about unsupervised visits, which she associates with past traumatic experiences. Anna explores Leah's concerns in a private session, leading to a decision to arrange supervised contact in a neutral location. This emotional participation provided critical insights into Leah's needs and directly shaped the decision-making process (arranging a private session) and the visitation plan.

**Box 8.2 Reflective Questions for Social Workers: Forms of Child Participation**

What specific cues or behaviours, such as Leah's nodding or emotional responses, can help me identify different dimensions of a child's participation?

How can I adapt my work to both facilitate and respond effectively to these dimensions?

What can I do to ensure that emotional participation is recognised and valued as a critical dimension of participation?

When a child, like Leah, articulates clear preferences (positional participation), how can I balance respecting the preferences with safeguarding their well-being? What challenges might arise, and how can I address them?

What role does the child's unique context and history, such as Leah's experiences of trauma, play in shaping their participation? How can I remain sensitive to these factors while fostering meaningful participation?

Leah also exhibits directive and agentive participation by initiating ways to make her foster placement feel more secure. She suggests creating a "safe space" in her foster home where she can keep personal items and artwork. This demonstrates her capacity to act and influence her immediate environment. Throughout these interactions, Anna emphasises narrative participation by voicing her reflections on Leah's contributions and acknowledging her impact on care decisions. For example, Anna highlights how Leah's input about school and visitation directly influenced the final care plan. By reinforcing the significance of Leah's participation, Anna helps Leah feel more empowered and valued in the decision-making process.

Leah's case illustrates the interplay of multiple participation dimensions and their collective impact on the decision-making process. By using the participation compass, Anna navigated these dimensions effectively, ensuring Leah's voice remained central to her care.

## Discussion: Expanding and Facilitating Participation in Child Protection

Children's participation in social work decision-making is far from being a singular or uniform concept. Instead, it unfolds as dynamic and multifaceted processes shaped by continuous dialogues among children, their family members, extended network, social workers, and other professionals (Henze-Pedersen & Bengtsson, 2024). Understanding this complexity requires moving beyond simplistic notions of children providing input for adults to consider (Kennan et al., 2017). Instead, participation should be recognised as a nuanced, constantly evolving and jointly achieved process that encompasses a range of dimensions that reflect the diverse ways children interact with and influence decision-making (Jørgensen et al., 2023). By recognising the dynamic and multifaceted nature of participation, this chapter invites social workers to foster inclusive, responsive, and rights-respecting environments for children in social work contexts. Participation, based on this view, is not a static action but an active and iterative process. The participation compass framework encapsulates this multidimensionality, offering a conceptual tool to understand and navigate the varied ways children may participate in decision-making in child protection. This perspective challenges the notion of participation as a linear or hierarchical pathway and instead emphasises its fluidity and responsiveness.

Participatory participation reflects moments when children actively sustain dialogue through verbal or nonverbal contributions, such as nodding and responding to questions. These actions, although seemingly subtle, are vital for creating collaborative spaces where decisions are shaped through mutual engagement. Without such foundational participation, the decision-making process risks becoming a one-sided endeavour. In contrast, directive participation shifts the focus to the child's ability to guide the conversation, steering it towards issues they deem important (Edman et al., 2022). For example, a child in foster care may redirect a discussion to emphasise the importance of staying with a particular foster family to which they feel connected, rather than discussing school placement options. This dimension to participation highlights the importance of ensuring the child feels empowered and encouraged to lead certain aspects of the conversation while also making room for them to express their priorities without feeling constrained. Balancing this directive input with safety and well-being considerations remains a critical responsibility for practitioners.

Positional participation, meanwhile, enables children to assert their preferences or viewpoints on specific matters, offering insights that are often critical to decision-making. A child might express, for instance, that they do not feel safe during unsupervised visits with a parent. Such statements, grounded in the child's experiences, provide valuable guidance for professionals. Positional participation helps keep the focus on the child's immediate priorities, ensuring their expressed preferences directly inform the decision-making process. Emotional participation represents another vital yet complex dimension, wherein children convey their feelings and emotional states during the decision-making process. For example, a child who appears distressed when discussing reunification with their biological family may reveal underlying fears or anxieties that warrant careful consideration. Emotional expressions offer a depth of understanding that might otherwise be overlooked, but they also require sensitivity and skill from practitioners to navigate effectively. Adjusting the intensity of dialogue becomes especially crucial here because practitioners must carefully regulate the emotional tone of the conversation to ensure children feel safe expressing their feelings (Edman et al., 2024). This can involve using techniques like pausing to provide reassurance or shifting focus to lighter topics momentarily before returning to sensitive matters.

Agentive participation underscores the child's role as an active agent in their life. By articulating their actions, choices, and aspirations, children demonstrate their capacity to influence outcomes. Supporting this form of participation not only illuminates the child's agency but also encourages them to engage constructively with the decision-making process. Finally, narrative participation focuses on the broader story of the child's participation. This dimension involves acknowledging and validating the child's contributions, helping them see how their input has shaped decisions. Social workers play a pivotal role in this process by reflecting on and highlighting the significance of the child's participation. For example, practitioners might revisit key moments in the dialogue to emphasise how a child's preferences influenced a particular outcome. This practice not only strengthens the child's engagement but also fosters a sustained sense of agency, empowering them for future interactions.

By facilitating and embracing these dimensions of participation, social work practice can move towards a more inclusive and context-sensitive approach. The dynamic and multidimensional nature of the compass reflects the reality that children's participation is not a singular act but a layered and evolving process. The participation compass offers a valuable framework to navigate this complexity, allowing practitioners to adapt their methods to the child's needs and the specific circumstances of each case. In doing so, it ensures that children's voices are heard, validated, and acted on in ways that genuinely reflect their experiences and aspirations.

Participation itself is not inherently positive or negative; its value depends entirely on the context, how it is exercised, and the response it generates. In specific situations, limiting one aspect of participation might be more conducive than seeking to expand it (Edman et al., 2022). This highlights the importance of continuously tailoring decision-making processes to the individual needs of the child and the uniqueness of each dialogue. By emphasising the quality of participation over its quantity, the compass emerges as a versatile and insightful framework for child protection. It challenges the assumption that increased participation always leads to better outcomes, advocating instead a nuanced approach that prioritises relevance and contextual fit.

This adaptability allows practitioners to tailor their work according to each child and their unique circumstances, fostering a more inclusive and relational model of participation. Because participation does not necessarily equate to improved decision-making processes or outcomes for a child—though it can undoubtedly do so (e.g., Heimer et al., 2017, 2018; Wågby & Englander, 2019)—the compass preserves an important complexity.

### *Implications for Practice*

The participation compass offers important insights for child protection decision-making processes. First, it calls for a paradigm shift in how participation is understood and operationalised. Rather than communicating participation in a linear and hierarchical structure, the compass encourages practitioners to view participation as a multifaceted, dynamic, and context-sensitive process (Skauge et al., 2021). In other words, social workers need to be mindful of the quality and direction of participation rather than its frequency or extent. For example, continuous participatory participation might indicate that a child is maintaining social norms by being polite and attentive on a procedural level rather than being engaged. These implications demand attunement and adaptability because children's ways of exercising participation and the usefulness of each dimension vary, not only between individual children but also during dialogues with children. By integrating these dimensions into practice, professionals can move beyond the tokenistic approaches recognised by Toros (2020) and foster meaningful and context-sensitive participation.

Second, training is essential to equip social workers with skills to recognise, facilitate, and respond to the six dimensions of participation. For example, addressing emotional participation—whether by enhancing, sustaining, or alleviating—requires a combination of theoretical understanding and hands-on expertise. Recent advancements, such as King et al.'s (2022) triangular model, Bromark et al.'s (2023) dialogical cards, and Edman et al.'s (2024) dynamic framework for facilitating children's in-session participation, offer practical tools and guidance in this area. Additionally, as McCafferty (2024) suggested, organisations must address systemic barriers, such as time constraints and high caseloads, which can hinder meaningful participation. Allocating adequate resources to support social workers is critical for ensuring that children's voices are truly integrated in decision-making processes.

Finally, the participation compass highlights the value of relational practice. Social workers must, therefore, prioritise building trust and rapport with children because these are prerequisites for meaningful participation (van Bijleveld et al., 2019). By fostering safe and supportive relationships, social workers can enable children to exercise different dimensions of participation, enhancing the quality and impact of children's voices in decision-making processes.

### *Future Developments*

Rather than discarding traditional frameworks, a hybrid or revised model could emerge as a practical solution. This model would need to be adaptable to varying circumstances, recognising that different levels and forms of participation are appropriate depending on the specific context (Bromark et al., 2023; Edman et al., 2024). Safeguards would be essential to prevent tokenistic applications and establish clear accountability mechanisms. Additionally, the model should directly address asymmetries inherent in child protection by proposing strategies to balance the responsibilities of professionals with the agency of children. Finally, it must be designed to work effectively in both resource-rich and resource-limited environments, ensuring scalability and practicality across diverse settings while remaining responsive to unforeseen challenges.

Future developments in child protection practice should focus on integrating the participation compass into training programmes and decision-making frameworks. Research should explore the compass's practical application in diverse contexts, to develop its usefulness in improving dialogical processes and outcomes for children. Longitudinal studies could provide valuable insights into how children's participation evolves over time and how different dimensions interact to shape decision-making processes.

The use of digital tools offers another avenue for innovation. For example, digital platforms could facilitate narrative participation by providing a space for children to create and share multimedia stories about their experiences. Similarly, virtual reality tools could be used to simulate decision-making scenarios, helping social workers practice recognising and responding to different dimensions to participation. Finally, policy development must align with the principles of the participation compass to ensure that participatory practices are embedded in organisational structures and culture (McCafferty & Mercado García, 2024). By prioritising participation as a dynamic and relational process, future advancements can create more inclusive and responsive systems that honour children's rights and voices in child protection.

## Conclusion: Advancing Multidimensional Participation in Child Protection

This exploration of the six dimensions of children's participation—participatory, directive, positional, agentive, emotional, and narrative—reveals the inherent complexity and richness of children's participation in decision-making processes. Participation, as shown throughout this chapter, is not a one-size-fits-all concept that can be reduced to a single formula or approach. Instead, it is a fluid, dynamic, and iterative process, deeply influenced by a child's unique needs, experiences, and the relational, cultural, and systemic contexts in which decisions are made (Keddell, 2023).

The participation compass emerges as a transformative framework for understanding and responding to this complexity. It moves beyond the UNCRC and traditional models, which although foundational often imply hierarchical and linear progressions of participation. These models tend to overlook the non-linear, multifaceted nature of participation, whereby children may simultaneously engage across multiple dimensions or shift between them depending on the situation.

The compass equips social workers with the tools to recognise and nurture diverse dimensions of participation, ensuring that children's voices are not only heard but are meaningfully integrated into decision-making processes. For example, emotional participation—often overlooked or undervalued—can provide critical insights into a child's fears, joys, hopes, or concerns, which might otherwise remain hidden. Similarly, positional and directive participation empower children to assert their preferences and influence the trajectory of discussions, ensuring their perspectives are central to outcomes that directly influence their lives. In practice, the participation compass encourages social workers to adopt flexible and responsive approaches. This involves viewing participation as an ongoing process. By recognising that a child's participation may vary, not only between contexts but also in a single interaction, practitioners are better equipped to adapt their strategies to align with the child's preferences, needs, and circumstances. For instance, a child expressing emotional distress during discussions about reunification might also demonstrate agentive participation by proposing alternative arrangements for contact with a parent. These overlapping dimensions challenge practitioners to remain attuned to the complexities of participation and respond with sensitivity and care.

The implications of this approach extend beyond individual practice to organisational and systemic levels. The participation compass provides a framework for fostering a culture of inclusivity and responsiveness in child protection systems, where children's voices are consistently prioritised and valued. By integrating this framework into training, supervision, and policy development, social work practitioners and organisations can move towards a more participatory ethos that honours children's rights and amplifies their agency. Moreover, the participation compass highlights the relational nature of participation. It positions social workers not as gatekeepers of participation but as facilitators of a co-constructed process in which children and adults work collaboratively to shape outcomes. Practice-focused research on the collaborative, relational dimensions of facilitating children's participation (Edman et al., 2024) has highlighted the importance of timing conversational elements and pacing dialogue to fit children's everyday lives and immediate needs. It also requires continuously fine-tuning the emotional intensity of interactions—for example, by initiating a break or contextualising topics so they resonate with the child. In addition, it involves ensuring the child can participate on their own terms, using language or props they prefer and rearranging who is present or absent in the dialogue. By facilitating children's participation, practitioners can support children in navigating the complexities of decision-making, ensuring their voices are not only included but also instrumental in shaping decisions.

Ultimately, the participation compass invites us to rethink participation as a multidimensional, dynamic process that reflects the diversity of children's experiences and actions. It provides a robust and adaptable tool for social workers to recognise and navigate the intricacies of children's participation, particularly in the high-stakes and emotionally- charged context of child protection. By embracing this framework, the field can advance towards a more inclusive, equitable, child-centred approach, ensuring that every child's voice is recognized, respected, and integrated into the decisions that shape their lives. This shift not only fulfils the promise of children's rights but also enhances the quality and effectiveness of child protection systems, paving the way for more informed, compassionate, and impactful practice. This approach not only enhances children's diverse voices in child protection but also ensures that their way of participating is being acknowledged and valued. Importantly, children have the right to participate but are not obliged to participate.

## References

Bromark, K., Knutsson, O., & Spånberger Weitz, Y. (2023). Co-designing a dynamic tool to enhance participation for young people: A participatory design project with young service users and social workers. *Children and Youth Services Review*, *147*, 106856. https://doi.org/10.1016/j.childyouth.2023.106856

Edman, K. (2025). Conversational democracy: Facilitating children's "unprompted talk" in social work dialogues. *Child & Family Social Work*. Advance online publication. https://doi.org/10.1111/cfs.13318

Edman, K., Gustafsson, A. W., & Cuadra, C. B. (2022). Recognising children's involvement in child and family therapy sessions: A microanalysis of audiovisual recordings of actual practice. *The British Journal of Social Work*, *52*(6), 3480–3500. https://doi.org/10.1093/bjsw/bcab248

Edman, K., Gustafsson, A. W., & Cuadra, C. B. (2024). Facilitating children's in-session involvement in child and family therapies: A dynamic framework of clinical practices. *Psychotherapy*, *61*(4), 55–67. https://doi.org/10.1037/pst0000511

Eriksson, M. (2024). Enabling children's participation: Putting the "good dialogues" model into practice. *Children & Society*, *38*(2), 334–348. https://doi.org/10.1111/chso.12702

Hart, R. A. (1992). *Children's participation: From tokenism to citizenship*. UNICEF International Child Development Centre.

Hart, R. A. (2007). Stepping back from "the ladder": Reflections on a model of participatory work with children. In A. Reid, B. B. Jensen, J. Nikel, & V. Simovska (Eds.), *Participation and learning: Perspectives on education and the environment, health and sustainability* (pp. 19–31). Springer.

Heimer, M., Näsman, E., & Palme, J. (2017). *Rättighetsbärare eller problembärare? Barns rätt att komma till tals och socialtjänstens insatser*. Stiftelsen Allmänna Barnhuset.

Heimer, M., Näsman, E., & Palme, J. (2018). Vulnerable children's rights to participation, protection, and provision: The process of defining the problem in Swedish child and family welfare. *Child & Family Social Work*, *23*(2), 316–323. https://doi.org/10.1111/cfs.12424

Henze-Pedersen, S., & Bengtsson, T. T. (2024). Developing a model for child participation in child welfare services. *Child & Family Social Work*, *29*(4), 1086–1095. https://doi.org/10.1111/cfs.13150

James, A., & James, A. L. (2004). *Constructing childhood: Theory, policy and social practice*. Palgrave Macmillan.

Jørgensen, T., Seim, S., & Njøs, B. M. (2023). How children and young people understand and experience individual participation in social services for children and young people: A synthesis of qualitative studies. *European Journal of Social Work*, *27*(3), 546–559. https://doi.org/10.1080/13691457.2023.2256490

Keddell, E. (2023). Recognising the embedded child in child protection: Children's participation, inequalities and cultural capital. *Children and Youth Services Review*, *147*, 106815. https://doi.org/10.1016/j.childyouth.2023.106815

Kennan, D., Brady, B., & Forkan, C. (2017). Supporting children's participation in decision making: A systematic literature review exploring the effectiveness of participatory processes. *The British Journal of Social Work*, *48*(7), 1985–2002. https://doi.org/10.1093/bjsw/bcx142

King, G., Chiarello, L. A., Phoenix, M., D'Arrigo, R., & Pinto, M. (2022). Co-constructing engagement in pediatric rehabilitation: A multiple case study approach. *Disability and Rehabilitation*, *44*(16), 4429–4440. https://doi.org/10.1080/09638288.2021.1910353

Lundy, L. (2007). "Voice" is not enough: Conceptualising Article 12 of the United Nations Convention on the Rights of the Child. *British Educational Research Journal*, *33*(6), 927–942. https://doi.org/10.1080/01411920701657033

McCafferty, P. (2017). Implementing Article 12 of the United Nations Convention on the Rights of the Child in child protection decision-making: A critical analysis of the challenges and opportunities for social work. *Child Care in Practice*, *23*(4), 327–341. https://doi.org/10.1080/13575279.2016.1264368

McCafferty, P. (2024). Children's participation in child welfare decision making: Recognising dichotomies, conceptualising critically informed solutions. *Child Care in Practice*, *30*(2), 112–129. https://doi.org/10.1080/13575279.2021.1896990

McCafferty, P., & Mercado García, E. (2024). Children's participation in child welfare: A systematic review of systematic reviews. *The British Journal of Social Work*, *54*(3), 1092–1108. https://doi.org/10.1093/bjsw/bcad167

Qvortrup, J. (2009). Childhood as a structural form. In J. Qvortrup, W. A. Corsaro, & M. S. Honig (Eds.), *The Palgrave handbook of childhood studies* (pp. 21–33). Palgrave Macmillan.

Shier, H. (2001). Pathways to participation: Openings, opportunities and obligations. *Children & Society*, *15*(2), 107–117. https://doi.org/10.1002/chi.617

Skauge, B., Storhaug, A. S., & Marthinsen, E. (2021). The what, why and how of child participation: A review of the conceptualization of "child participation" in child welfare. *Social Sciences*, *10*(2), 54. https://doi.org/10.3390/socsci10020054

Toros, K. (2020). A systematic review of children's participation in child protection decision-making: Tokenistic presence or not? *Children & Society*, *35*(3), 395–411. https://doi.org/10.1111/chso.12418

United Nations. (1989). *Convention on the rights of the child*. https://www.ohchr.org/en/instruments-mechanisms/instruments/convention-rights-child

van Bijleveld, G. G., Bunders-Aelen, J. F. G., & Dedding, C. W. M. (2019). Exploring the essence of enabling child participation within child protection services. *Child & Family Social Work*, *25*(2), 286–293. https://doi.org/10.1111/cfs.12684

Wågby, A., & Englander, M. (2019). Barns delaktighet i vårdnads-, boende- och umgängesutredningar. *Socialvetenskaplig Tidskrift*, *26*(2), 173–194.

# 9 In Their Own Words

## Adolescent Participation in Group Social Intervention Programs in Madrid

*Linda Ducca Cisneros and Andrés Arias Astray*

### Introduction: The Right of Participation and Social Interventions

In Spain, most social intervention programmes designed to address or prevent teenagers' social exclusion are aimed at promoting participation. However, there is no consensus on the definition, meaning, and scope of participation.

Prevailing perceptions of youth and varying interpretations of participation shape the nature of social interventions. These perspectives manifest in diverse practices, ranging from a risk-focused, control-oriented approach to one centred on empowerment, critical awareness, and social transformation.

Participation is one of the most contested and criticised rights of children. Thus, it is crucial to define the concept through adolescents' experiences and points of view, mainly because they are the so-called subjects or objects of intervention yet have a scant presence in research on social work.

The right to participation of children is found in Article 12 of the United Nations Convention on the Rights of the Child (UNCRC; United Nations, 1989), although the word is not mentioned directly. Commentary No. 20 (United Nations, 2016) on the implementation of these rights in adolescence adds that member states should:

> introduce measures to guarantee adolescents the right to express their views in all matters concerning them, in accordance with their age and maturity, and ensure that they have a say, for example, in decisions relating to their education, health, sexuality, family life, and judicial and administrative proceedings.
>
> (p. 7)

In addition, it emphasises the political dimension, urging states to increase opportunities for civic and political participation to enhance the personal agency of adolescents so that they can make informed decisions and fight for their rights.

It should be noted that the right to be heard has been one of the UNCRC's most revised and debated points (Lansdown, 2009). It is still considered "radical and difficult to achieve" and the most neglected and transgressed in its

DOI: 10.4324/9781003582410-13

developments (Shier, 2001, p. 110). Criticisms persist about the limitation of rights implied by the article. For example, phrases such as "who is in a position to form his or her judgement" or "matters affecting the child" may lead to different interpretations by adults, which may limit these rights (Gaitán, 2015).

Providing a vision of adolescence aligned with a comprehensive view of individuals and the particular and collective circumstances that should be incorporated into social work seems too ambitious for this space. The definition of adolescence incorporates the different complexity of human development and social relationships, together with the social representations of adolescence and youth and their impact on the opportunities provided for participation (Ducca Cisneros et al., 2024).

The concept of adolescence has changed over time and differs depending on the place, but most scholars agree that this period is marked by significant changes and developments (Bendit & Miranda, 2017; Feixa, 2006; Gómez del Toro, 2015; Schlegel & Hewlett, 2011).

Something similar happens when we attempt to frame and explain the concepts of empowerment and participation and the consequences of social intervention. When a professional intervenes to facilitate a group, their perceptions of the intervention and the social and institutional representations that justify the action come into play. At the same time, social work with adolescents constitutes a sociopedagogical practice that mediates between individual aspirations and social expectations in a structural context (Ávila Cantos et al., 2019).

Due to this complexity and the characteristics of the evaluation of participation in the Spanish context, it is very hard to identify the degree and manner of participation in intervention programmes. However, participation in research in Spanish social work journals could offer insight. Adolescents' and young people's points of view are scant in research dealing with issues related to these age groups. During the 10 years before the fieldwork that informs this chapter took place (2010–2019), only 11% of published articles involving adolescents or youth had some kind of involvement of the participants, and that percentage is much lower (2%) if we consider the previous decade (2000–2009; Ducca Cisneros, 2021).

Participation is continuously associated in the literature with the concept of citizenship and its various meanings, contributing to overlapping approaches (Barber, 2007). Public policies have focused on challenging the image of youth as alienated by involving young people at different levels and bringing institutions closer to citizens to improve democracy (Ganuza Fernández, 2006). Similarly, numerous efforts have been made at European and local levels to engage adolescents in civic participation (Gaitán & Liebel, 2011; Santana Clavijo et al., 2016).

Marshal's (1950) classification is the most common, distinguishing civil, social, and political citizenship when discussing youth citizenship and participation. Willow's (1997) adaptation emphasises youth participation. Politically, the literature frequently references the "democratic deficit" among youth—low civic involvement attributed to perceptions of passivity or alienation. However, recent years have seen polarised views on youth interest in politics, highlighted by recent social movements that exemplify active citizenship (Figueras et al., 2011). Nevertheless, many age groups feel excluded, leading to apathy (Francés García, 2008).

This creates a paradox: Youth movements face societal criticism despite initiatives promoting citizenship. Such initiatives often follow adult-centric logic, aiming to consult or train youth in citizenship rather than fostering emancipation.

Legally, youth citizenship rights are supported by international frameworks like the UNCRC (United Nations, 1989) and regional laws. These laws emphasise participation, though interpretations by adults can limit this right. European and national laws in Spain similarly promote youth civic rights but highlight gaps between legal frameworks and practical implementation.

Socially, adolescent participation challenges assumptions of their indifference, reflecting their concerns and rights (Lansdown, 2009). Participation empowers individuals beyond political influence, fostering connections, responsibility, and conflict resolution (Zimmerman & Rappaport, 1988). Nevertheless, public policies often treat youth as passive "clients" rather than active participants, exacerbating the gap between policy intentions and actual practices (Ganuza Fernández, 2006; Graham et al., 2010).

This chapter relies on evidence from PhD research (Ducca Cisneros, 2021) that included older young people. It focuses on defining the term participation by emphasising the perspectives and experiences of participation among adolescents (ages 13–18 years) throughout their lives. More than 90 participants who were part of two social intervention programmes in the academic year 2018–2019 took part in this research, giving their opinions and points of view on the meaning of participation, how participation can be encouraged or hindered, and opportunities available for participating in society. This qualitative study of children's perceptions of participation used grounded theory for general guidance on obtaining data and completing analysis from discourses and experiences, stressing situated and critical perspectives. The research techniques—participant observation and focus groups—were adapted to each case study.

Though the study initially had other objectives—to systematise group intervention programmes and promote participation through social work with groups—in this chapter, we focus on the identification of circumstances and practices that favour or hinder participation by listening to and considering the young people and adolescents who participated; identifying areas of participation; and analysing adult roles, types of activities proposed, and circumstances pointed out by participants.

This chapter is divided into four sections, incorporating research case studies to illustrate the discourses among children and adolescents. The first part brings us closer to the challenges of participation and implementation of the guidelines set out in the UNCRC. In the second part, the objectives that guided the research are presented, along with the methodology implemented in the study. The third part presents the findings, giving prominence to the voices of children and adolescents, and discusses the roles played by adults and institutions in fostering spaces that support youth decision-making. The chapter concludes with recommendations and reflections on implications for practice.

## Methodology

This study employed a qualitative, non-experimental, cross-sectional, and exploratory approach based on a constructivist paradigm. It adopted grounded theory (Strauss & Corbin, 2015) as the overarching framework, focusing on a contextual and critical view of the research process. The interpretative framework, shaped by the chosen paradigms, theories, and methodologies, served as both a guide and a limitation, offering structure and organisation. Additionally, the data collection methods were selected to align with both the epistemological stance and the study's theoretical framework.

In this study, the researcher also served as the facilitator of the groups, whether ad hoc or long-term. This dual role as a professional and researcher necessitated exploring how these roles intersect. The researcher was positioned as a component of the complex relationships being studied, participating alongside the adolescents in a process of translating and interpreting reality, moving away from the role of the "all-knowing" professional (Doel & Orchard, 2006).

More than 90 individuals aged 13 to 17 voluntarily participated during the 2018–2019 academic year. The sampling criteria was designed to ensure diversity, capturing a range of social intervention contexts while allowing for group-based activities. Given the focus on experience-based participation, it was essential to include participants' stories and experiences, highlighting specific participatory processes. Thus, a group was formed to meet the study's requirements.

This research involved two distinct case studies. Six focus groups based on an art activity took place at Enredadero, a space for adolescents to spend their free time provided by the city government after a petition made by the Commission for the Participation of Children and Adolescents, an organisation focused on child participation.

Four other focus groups were held at La Caixa Pro Infancia, a programme of La Rueca, a non-governmental organisation. This programme is designed to support children considered at risk of social exclusion and consists of financial help with education expenses, after-school lessons, and a space for leisure and free time to promote participation. At the same time, a participatory groupwork process was conducted and analysed in this institution.

The study employed theoretical sampling (Gaete Quezada, 2014) to select participants based on their potential to inform the research. This structural approach highlights diversity in perspectives and relationships (Hernández Pedreño, 2016) by ensuring representation of different forms of group intervention and social sectors. Sampling (see Table 9.1) was guided by theoretical criteria, emphasising heterogeneity to enrich the discourse on participation in social interventions rather than aiming for stratification (Padgett, 2017).

*Table 9.1* Sampling Criteria

| | *La Rueca Asociación Proyecto La Caixa Pro-Infancia* | *INJUCAM Proyecto Enredadero* |
|---|---|---|
| *Structural Criteria* | | |
| Level of education | Public education (secondary education or vocational training) | Public or semi-private education (mostly secondary education, high school, or vocational training) |
| Social exclusion | At risk of social exclusion (prerequisite for programme involvement) | General public |
| Ethnic or cultural origin | Almost all but two were immigrants or second-generation immigrants; their origins varied: Dominican Republic, Morocco, Romania, Peru, and Ecuador | Varied origins; four groups were mainly made up of immigrants, one involved Roma people, and another with mostly Spaniards |
| Gender | Mixed (70% boys) | Mixed (60% boys) |
| *Special Criteria* | | |
| Type of association | Non-profit non-governmental organisation | Non-profit non-governmental organisation: Federation of Neighbourhood Associations |
| Project funding | Bank foundation | Local government |
| Purpose of social intervention | Promoting and supporting integral development | Promoting participation and healthy leisure |
| Methodology of social intervention | Groupwork; integral education and school support | Support to promote participation; rights-based approach; group work is not conducted a priori, although groups are eventually established |
| Promotion of participation | Main objective | Promotion of self-management and children's participation |

### ***Data Collection***

Each group engaged in diverse participatory activities (Table 9.2), with methodologies designed to connect with participants, facilitate discussions, and promote engagement. Various data collection methods and techniques were employed, including participant observation; recorded group processes, with subsequent analysis of generated materials; and focus groups. The latter used two modalities: conversations based on specific themes and artistic experiences, whereby participants collaboratively created a drawing to simulate participatory processes, then they reflected on what participation means to them, incorporating expressive languages beyond verbal communication.

*Table 9.2* Data Collection Methods and Techniques

| *Organisation and Project* | *Ages* | *Participants* | *Sessions*[a] | *Data collected*[b] |
|---|---|---|---|---|
| La Rueca: La Caixa Pro Infancia | 13–15 | 15 | 1 FGA, 6 GP | FGA and FG: recording and literal transcription GP: audio recording and selective transcription |
| | 15–17 | 12 | 1 FGA, 1 FG | |
| | 13–15 | 13 | 1 FGA | |
| | 15–17 | 9 | 1 FGA | |
| INJUCAM: Enredadero | 14–17 | 7 | 1 FGA | Recording and verbatim transcription |
| | 15–17 | 7 | 1 FGA | |
| | 12–16 | 8 | 1 FGA | |
| | 12–15 | 9 | 1 FGA | |
| | 13–16 | 8 | 1 FGA | |
| | 15–17 | 6 | 1 FGA | |

*Note:* FG = focus group; FGA = art-based focus group; GP = group process.
[a] Participant observation was carried out in both entities.
[b] A fieldwork journal was kept during participant observation, group process, and focus groups.

### *Data Analysis*

Qualitative research is characterised by a comprehensive, analytic, and interpretative orientation during analysis, making it a flexible and open-ended process that requires continuous decision-making, creativity, and methodological rigour (Coffey & Atkinson, 2005).

Grounded theory guided the analysis, aiming to generate substantive ideas later abstracted into more general theoretical insights. The process included: (a) open coding, involving conceptual categorisation and selection of labels for events, actions, interactions, and verbal expressions, which were then grouped into categories; (b) axial coding, or connecting groups to subcategories to form abstract categories considering theoretical aspects and macro-contexts; and (c) triangulation (Carter et al., 2014), using various methods and techniques to cross-verify findings, including participant validation.

Two criteria guided data selection: relevance, or whether the information was pertinent to the theme of participation; and significance, or whether the contributors made frequent or insightful contributions to the topic. Saturation (Callejo Gallego, 1998) was used as a validation criterion, ensuring no new significant insights emerged from additional data.

The analysis was conducted using ATLAS.ti 9.0 qualitative research software that although not replacing the interpretative work of the researcher enhances coherence and rigour in analytic processes (San Martín, 2014).

## Results and Discussion

This section examines the findings from the 10 focus groups and the process group, aiming to integrate participants' perspectives on youth participation with the theoretical framework. The dialogue highlights the dynamic interplay among three key elements: The role of adolescents, with emphasis on their level and quality of involvement in participation; the role of adults and institutions, especially how they either enable or hinder participatory processes; and how decision-making processes materialised.

These elements are interconnected and shaped by contextual factors. They determine the degree and nature of adolescent participation and citizenship. Youth empowerment emerges as a product of their interactions with adults and institutions. The insights can be used to bridge theoretical concepts with practical applications, supporting the development of policies and practices that reflect the realities of social intervention.

#### *Role of Adolescents*

This section highlights the influence of individual qualities and social perceptions on youth participation. Age was seen both as a barrier and an asset, whereas maturity was often used to justify inclusion or exclusion. Participants challenged adult perceptions of youth as immature, arguing that they demonstrate responsibility when the situation demands it. All names are pseudonyms

*Jaime:* We want to be heard so that people realise that everyone can participate, and age doesn't matter when it comes to sharing our opinion.
*Gaia:* We want to feel the same way when, for example, we want to give our opinion. Even though we are minors, we still want to be able to say it.
(Enredadero Villaverde)

*Karen:* Whether you are a child or an adult, the opinion is the same. You can express your opinion just the same. Just because you're a child doesn't mean your opinion doesn't matter.
(La Rueca)

Key factors like vitality, curiosity, and leadership skills were deemed crucial for participation, though they often need to be proven to adults. Depending on the context, these characteristics are perceived variably, sometimes admired and sometimes dismissed.

Participants emphasised the importance of enjoyable, engaging, and fun activities. Their interest in an activity often dictated their level of participation, with disengagement occurring when activities failed to resonate with them individually or as a group. Educators have noted fluctuating participation levels, often attributed to youth stereotypes of being "uncommitted" (González Salcedo, 2011). However, participants said such variability is common, even in adult participation.

*Cuchi:* Do you know who has the initiative? The one who likes the project.
*Researcher:* And what do the rest do?

*Several:* They follow it.
*Cuchi:* They follow the leader.
*Khalid:* They follow the crowd.
*Cuchi:* [Sings] Follow the leader, leader.

(Enredadero Fuencarral)

Participants critiqued activities that disregarded their perspectives, stressing the need for initiatives that align with their interests, enable skill development, and prioritise quality over quantity in participation. This preference creates a positive feedback loop: Enjoyment fosters motivation and increases involvement. Nevertheless, participants acknowledged the role of responsibility-driven participation in activities like voting or completing domestic tasks. They critiqued institutional reliance on attendance as a measure of participation, noting that active engagement was more meaningful.

Although not initially a focus, diversity emerged as a significant theme. Participants framed diversity as a positive and natural aspect of group identity, emphasising respect for values and challenging stereotypes aligned with social work principles (Malekoff, 2016). Participants raised questions about ethnic representation, highlighting the underrepresentation of native Spaniards in specific groups and systemic neglect of immigrant experiences.

*José:* Well, if we're always considered worthless—
*Omar:* Of course, because your word doesn't matter, just because you're Black.
*Elías:* Even if we have citizenship.

(La Rueca)

The phenomenon of "colour blindness," whereby institutions promote equality without addressing lived discrimination, perpetuates social inequalities (Eliassi, 2017). Young (2014) argued that social justice requires acknowledging conditions of oppression to enable equitable participation, a principle often overlooked by institutions. Racism surfaced during activities when participants shared personal experiences of discrimination, illustrating its profound impact.

Gender discrimination emerged as a structural issue linked to patriarchy, though participants did not explicitly name it as such. Female participants, mainly from Roma communities, reported more restrictions on leisure activities and greater household responsibilities, limiting their participation in society generally. Additionally, educators observed lower participation rates among girls aged 15–17, often due to caregiving duties. Both male and female participants associated caregiving with traditional gender roles.

*Carmen:* Yes. Maybe I will ask these guys for the bike, and they will not let me have it.
*Lucas:* Why not?
*Antonio:* Because girls should not ride bikes.

*Carmen:* Why?

*Lucas:* It is bad for your genitals. [They continue joking and talking about pain related to riding bikes: "Can Carmen take it? For her ovaries?"]

*Researcher:* Are there other things that happen to you just because you're girls?

*Carmen:* Things happen to us because we're girls; they won't let us do a ton of stuff.

*Jenni:* They don't let us participate in many things just because we're girls.

*Carmen:* Just because we're girls.

*Jenni:* Yeah, because they're assholes.

*Antonio:* It's just that they don't know how to drive.

*Lucas:* They don't know how to play, they don't know how to ride—

*Carmen:* They won't let me play cards.

(Enredadero Moratalaz)

***Role of Adults and Institutions: Spaces of Participation and Decision-Making***

Adolescents defined participation based on its relevance to their lives, the levels of involvement allowed, and the degree of independence from adult supervision. Adolescents often questioned how their participation affects social change and decision-making, in both institutions and their personal lives.

The concept of political efficacy, defined as the belief that social and political change is possible and individuals can contribute (Campbell et al., 1954; González Salcedo, 2011), framed much of the discussion. Participants expressed disillusionment with politicians and institutions, viewing political participation as distant and ineffective. Some attributed this ineffectiveness to systemic issues in political parties rather than democracy (Canal, 2017).

*Mía:* For example, voting does not really matter to me. I do not believe in any political party. I do not think anyone who gets elected is going to change the world, not even the country, or something smaller.

*Héctor:* Then, I think you must start with small sectors. The idea that you cannot change the world or the country by voting for a political party is because either that party has not tried hard enough or they have goals that are very different from what the people want.

(Enredadero Centro)

Some participants viewed opportunities for formal participation, such as Madrid's Commission for Participation of Childhood and Adolescence, as performative rather than impactful. For instance, participants from La Rueca and Enredadero often regarded such initiatives as token gestures, emphasising the importance of fundamental change to sustain motivation. Experiences like contributing to the beginning of the Enredadero project demonstrated the potential for meaningful engagement but were the exception (some participants had been part of the petition to create the project). Other avenues for participation included volunteering and providing mutual aid. Adolescents emphasised helping others or the environment as a key contribution.

Although family participation is rarely prioritised in social programmes, adolescents viewed it as crucial. They associated it with decision-making, household responsibilities, and caregiving, aligning with Bertrán et al.'s (2009) definition of family participation. However, gendered expectations persisted, with caregiving and domestic work viewed as primarily falling on young women.

*Jaime:* It is easier, like when the adults are talking, and they tell you—

*Luna:* Adults' stuff.

*Victoria:* Yes! They do not let you give your opinion because you are younger. Yeah, it does not work.

*Celia:* I have a 12-year-old sister, and one day we were talking about things we did not even know she knew, and in the end, she was interrupting, and we were like, "Shut up," and she said something that made both of us shut up. She knew more about the topic than we did. That is what they say—that sometimes they exclude us because we are told we are too young, that it is an adult conversation, but in the end, we know more than they do.

*Luna:* Because, in the end, us young people go out more, we see more of the world, so to speak. The adults are at work, at home, busy, whatever. We are out all day; we are on the streets all day.

(Enredadero Villaverde)

Participants noted educational spaces as significant because they have spent several years in these settings. Active participation, not just consultative but involvement in decision-making processes, has been highlighted in the academic literature and good practice guides (O'Kane et al., 2020). UNICEF's guidelines on adolescent and youth participation underscore that in education participation should be a goal in itself, a means to improve teaching processes, and the core principle guiding educational planning (O'Kane et al., 2020). However, participants in this study viewed school participation as passive, associating it with traditional education requiring only their attendance or responses to adults' directives.

*Cristina:* The lessons, teaching—

*Rober:* It is boring [laughter]. You get bored in class, I do not know—

*Natalia:* The teacher talks too much. … [cross-talk] We get bored and do not participate.

*Educator:* Mía [who uses sign language] wanted to say that class is boring and that she does not feel like you can participate in class. To participate, it must be fun [participants start talking about their row in class].

(La Rueca)

Participants emphasised that schools must foster participation in both the institution and the broader community, suggesting that education should go beyond academic success (Gastañaga Moreno, 2004). They identified motivating activities as those that allow them to apply practical and theoretical knowledge, particularly those that involve self-management and decision-making. Adolescents highlighted the need for fun, motivating activities aligned with their interests, suggesting that a tedious activity could not be considered participatory.

A few participants mentioned participation at the representative level, particularly class representatives, but they said these roles are rarely transformative. The institutional rules governing participation were noted to be strict and unagreed upon, with participation often framed around rewards and punishments rather than as a social right. For example, some schools appointed class representatives without democratic selection processes.

Activities play a key role in defining participation in social intervention and daily life. In this research, activities were central to how participants understood and practised participation because they were seen as essential for achieving goals and fostering group cohesion. The focus group participants identified activities like sports, play, and engagement in different settings (school, free time, and social organisations) as key ways to participate.

*Francisco:* Participate, play in a group. That is, it.
*Cristina:* Sports—
*Several:* Football.
*Rober:* Basketball.

(La Rueca)

The research distinguished between self-organised leisure activities (sports, play, and being "out on the street") and activities related to social intervention (which are guided by public policies). Sports and play were directly linked to participation in all groups, often symbolised by sports-related images such as balls or fields in participants' drawings. The participants recognised that for games to happen, active involvement was necessary, emphasising that teamwork and cooperation were integral to participation.

Virtual social media has also emerged as an important tool for participation, particularly in leisure. The adolescents' use of social media focused more on personal relationships, self-expression, and creating content rather than political or social activism, which aligns with García-Galera et al. (2014). Although some adolescents engaged in passive forms of participation (such as liking posts), others were active participants, creating content or organising offline meetups.

The analysis also revealed a reluctance among youth workers to use social media to promote participation. This aligns with findings by de Lucas y Murillo de la Cueva and D'Antonio Maceiras (2020), who argued that a lack of training and limited access to technology reduce opportunities for utilising digital tools to foster active participation in modern society.

Public spaces were important for these youths regarding free time. They viewed the street as a place where they could engage in activities independently. However, adults often viewed it negatively, mainly when youth engaged in behaviours considered illegal (e.g., drinking or smoking). This perception of being judged and monitored by the police limited their sense of participation in these spaces.

The study also highlighted how participants perceived different public spaces: Universities and wealthier neighbourhoods were seen as "free" spaces, whereas other areas were seen as "targeted" by authorities. The participants often perceived this disparity as an injustice, contributing to their reluctance to participate in leisure activities.

Racial discrimination emerged as another barrier to participation, as seen in the experiences of participants in Fuencarral. These youths, often subjected to stereotyping and marginalisation, demonstrated attitudes and behaviours that align with Webster's (2009) migration marginalisation thesis, which suggests that youths from immigrant families face more significant challenges integrating into society despite being born in the country.

Finally, the study found that the lack of public spaces was not limited to ethnic minority youth but also affected Spanish youth regarding social exclusion. One suggested solution to improve participation was the creation of more public spaces where youth could spend time, reflecting the goals of spaces like Enredadero. However, the tension between autonomy and control in organising free time in social organisations was evident, with these entities often trying to manage leisure activities, which contrasted with the youths' desire for independent engagement.

Participants spent a significant amount of time in social entities, making them essential because they offer various forms of participation. In general, they viewed the possibility of a positive experience in a social entity as surprising, exceptional, and unfamiliar. Many participants described institutions that promote participation (such as Enredadero and La Rueca) as "different" places. For example, they described how institutions treat them better than schools and offer them more freedom.

*Flor:* It is a self-managed space for teenagers [talking about Enredadero].
*David:* And we all participate—
*Flor:* From 12 to 17 years old.
*Vani:* And what does "self-managed" mean?
*David:* It is managed by us.
*Flor:* And for leisure! I remember putting leisure, but I don't know where.
*Vani:* Does "self-managed" mean it's managed by you all?
*David:* Yes. By teenagers.
*Jaime:* By those who make it up.
*Flor:* It is a space free from consumption. Well, there can be juices (soft drinks).
*David:* Consumption, but not weed. That is it.

(Enredadero Villaverde)

Arias and Di Leo (2020) found in their study on youth relations with social entities that participants identified these institutions as different. Much like in the stories shared by participants in this research, the difference lies in the experience itself, to which they attributed positive value to factors such as the expression of opinions and "good treatment."

The spaces where they experienced positive interactions were not compulsory. Participants even viewed La Rueca's programme, which requires continuous attendance—to avoid leaving their families without the support of the La Caixa Foundation—as a place they choose to attend. In the same manner as the participants, Albertos et al. (2020) highlighted voluntariness as a key criterion for leisure activities because they require intrinsic motivation, leading individuals to feel "awake, alive, and open to developmental experiences" (p. 209).

However, contradictions emerged in the organisations. For example, La Rueca often expressed the need to promote participation in institutional decision-making in their policy and practice. However, when attempts were made to organise activities fostering such participation, the organisation's custom and practice reduced its likelihood—a point recognised by the participants. In these cases, even formal attempts at participation were often repurposed to align with adult-driven agendas, which led to frustration and reduced motivation among the youth.

The influence of economic and social transformations on the concept of citizenship was evident, particularly with policies emphasising youth education, while limiting participation to adult-defined experiences. France (1998) discussed how these policies focus on individual responsibility while ignoring the need to recognise youth rights. Larson and Angus (2011) argued that professionals face paradoxes when implementing empowerment and participation objectives in highly controlled institutions, where authority and responsibility are hierarchical. They emphasised that such environments often undermine the initial goals of empowerment because adult authority often takes precedence when problems arise.

A paradox occurred between institutional guidelines and adolescents' willingness to engage in issues that affect them. Efforts to involve youth in processes initiated by adults often led to frustration, resignation, and a loss of motivation. However, there were examples of promoting participation adapted to the participants' characteristics. For instance, in Enredadero, assemblies were generally seen as tedious, but in Vallecas, a fun "gymkhana" or "escape room" approach was used to make assemblies engaging. Participants enjoyed this method.

### *Socio-structural Context: Social Exclusion as an Obstacle and Imperative for Participation*

A literature review revealed connections between the concept of participation and the socio-structural context in which the lives of youth and adolescents unfold. Several difficulties identified by the adolescents as barriers to participation were linked to aspects of social exclusion. Zambrano Constanzo (2005) noted that citizenship is only exercised through participation and the ability to build a life project with real execution possibilities, with social movements playing a key role in advocating rights.

The participants' accounts highlighted two key issues related to the concept of participation tied to citizenship and social inclusion, shaped by the tension between individual agency and the constraints imposed by social structures. The first refers to a conception of participation based on following normative or linear life trajectories. The second focuses on how these youth experienced social exclusion and reflected on segmented efforts to promote participation and prevent risk.

In several groups, especially those aged 16 or 17, participants associated social inclusion and everyday participation with following normative and linear life trajectories (Du Bois-Reymond & López-Blasco, 2004). This included studying, working, becoming independent from their family, and forming a family. Although similarities existed among the groups, everyone defined a linear trajectory differently regarding timing, rhythm, and order of life events.

| | |
|---|---|
| *Researcher:* | We're getting super pessimistic about all this. ... [they laugh] But do you think there's a positive future for you all? |
| *Arnold:* | Maybe. |
| *Omar:* | I don't think so, to be honest. |
| *Researcher:* | You don't think? |
| *Omar:* | What for? |
| *Elías:* | I just want to work. |
| *Francisco:* | Without studying, you don't have anything. |
| *José:* | If you don't study, well, you figure it out, get a normal job. |
| *Francisco:* | What job? |
| *José:* | Any job. One in construction, one in offices, or whatever. |
| *Researcher:* | What you are saying is that it is more complicated if you do not study. |

(La Rueca)

At times, youth expressed a sense of apathy due to the lack of future opportunities, as seen in discussions with participants who had disengaged from participatory processes. Adolescents in poverty have been shown to experience higher levels of learned helplessness, which contributes to motivational deficits (Leung & Shek, 2011).

Despite being the focus of public policies, they did not consider social interventions adequate. Linear policies addressing life trajectories fail because they neglect individuals' subjective perspectives, focus on containing risks, overlook structural mismatches, and address social inequality in educational and labour trajectories with bureaucratic, one-size-fits-all criteria (Julkunen, 2009).

Vincenzino (2017) highlighted the paradox of defining adolescents as subjects of rights while inequality and poverty continue to increase in this demographic. He questioned whether youth rights can genuinely exist when the neoliberal system fails to guarantee basic needs, creating a barrier to citizenship. Participants emphasised two key topics related to social exclusion and difficulties in participating in society, which they described as enabled by institutions: the role of social entities and citizen security devices. Ávila Cantos (2012) defined the governance of difference as power practices based on differentiating population sectors, whereby access to certain rights depends on one's social sector. This is reflected in interventions that prevent many people from perceiving themselves as citizens, a shared experience among the youth in this study. For instance, segmented public policies, differences in legal and police treatment, and programmes limited to low-income areas all contribute to this issue.

*Researcher:* So, even if you do not like it, sometimes you participate.
*Rober:* Yes.
*Dina:* Sometimes they force you, which is different.
*Darío:* Just like now.
*Dina:* There are cases where they force you.
*Rober:* They do not force me. I just go because I have nothing to do at home.
*Dina:* Just to try it.
*Rober:* Not to try it. I just have nothing to do.

(La Rueca)

Thus, the contradiction between rights and citizenship intensified: Adolescents in social exclusion faced more difficulties being considered citizens, yet they were pressured to participate more.

Social entities act exclusively with populations considered excluded or at risk of exclusion, creating a paradox about the institution's ability to foster social change in segregated areas. Several authors have criticised citizenship participation efforts that are often aimed only at those at risk of exclusion, as if citizenship were achieved by reaching a certain socioeconomic status or social inclusion (France, 1998; Marchioni, 1999; Martí, 2005; Price & Mencke, 2013). Choudhury and White (2010) argued that the pressure for participation at all costs often ignores the structures that facilitate social action, overestimating individual autonomy and underestimating people's real difficulties.

Most projects identified during the exploratory phase, fieldwork, and document review in this study were aimed at adolescents and young people in situations of social exclusion in low-income neighbourhoods. Consequently, people who would like to engage in these exchanges cannot do so because their daily lives are confined to specific, segregated spaces (Ballester Brage & Vecina Merchante, 2011).

During the research, it became clear that many participants engaged in leisure activities not because they were interested but because they had no other options. Hopper and Iwasaki (2017) reviewed the literature on leisure and free time for youth at risk of exclusion, concluding that programmes often aim to fix perceived deficits to integrate them into society and avoid risks.

Examples from the La Caixa Pro Infancia programme at La Rueca highlighted the typical social action directed at youth at risk of social exclusion, often referred by schools or social services. La Rueca exclusively serves adolescents identified as being at risk, whereas Enredadero has no explicit target. However, regardless of neighbourhood, most participants belong to families facing economic and social difficulties. Furthermore, the new government has shifted the target population of these kinds of programmes from the general public to those at risk of exclusion.

**Box 9.1 Reflective Questions for Social Workers: Considerations for Facilitating Participation**

How do you ensure that the power dynamics between professionals and children are balanced, especially when facilitating participatory processes in diverse social contexts?

Given the diversity of participants in the case studies (ethnically, socially, and culturally), how can social workers adapt their approaches to facilitate meaningful participation that is culturally sensitive and contextually relevant?

What are the challenges of promoting participation in social interventions when participants have different lived experiences?

How might group-based activities (such as art sessions or focus groups) affect opportunities for participation?

What can be learned from the differing methods employed across the two case study settings in terms of fostering group cohesion and participation?

How can the social worker's role be adjusted to best support adolescents at risk of social exclusion, as seen in the study with La Caixa Pro Infancia?

How might the lessons from these case studies inform your practice regarding self-management and advocacy in social work with young people?

***Implications for Practice***

The findings of this study underscore the vital importance of integrating theory and practice in social work, particularly when working with adolescents. Active and consistent engagement with young participants offers a richer understanding of their experiences and needs. Practitioners should be mindful of the inconsistency in how participation is framed by various social entities, which ranges from tokenistic involvement to opportunities for genuine decision-making. Adolescents often face barriers to meaningful participation due to rigid institutional structures and social inequalities that hinder their access to fundamental rights and opportunities.

Effective social work with adolescents, therefore, should aim to dismantle these systemic barriers and create environments that encourage both inclusive decision-making and equitable access to resources. Practitioners must consider adolescents' unique needs, preferences, and the social contexts that shape their ability to participate. This requires creating opportunities for engagement that extend beyond formal settings and into everyday spaces like schools, families, and leisure activities, where adolescents naturally interact and feel comfortable.

### *Recommendations for Practice*

Institutions should move beyond formalised, one-time events and integrate participation into regular activities and everyday settings. Social work practitioners should work towards embedding participatory practices in schools, community centres, and even family environments, ensuring that participation is not an exceptional or externally imposed activity but a continuous and valued part of adolescents' lives.

To promote authentic participation, social work interventions must challenge systemic inequalities. This includes advocating policies and practices that prioritise inclusivity and equitable access to resources for all adolescents. Practitioners should aim to create platforms where young people from diverse backgrounds can express their opinions without fear of being disregarded.

Adolescents highly value being listened to in an authentic and respectful manner. Social work practices should be grounded in building genuine relationships based on trust, in which young people feel heard and understood, rather than merely being asked for their input as part of a formal process. Recognising and valuing their voice fosters a deeper sense of agency and empowerment that promotes participation.

Public policies and institutional practices should move away from administrative timelines and focus more on aligning with the actual needs and desires of young people. This means not only creating policies that facilitate participation but also ensuring they are flexible and responsive to the dynamic and diverse realities of adolescents.

## Conclusion

This study highlights the critical need for a paradigm shift in how adolescent participation is conceptualised and implemented in social work practice. The research findings emphasise that participation cannot be reduced to a mere procedural act but must be embedded in the daily lives and lived experiences of young people. By prioritising inclusion, respect, and addressing the systemic challenges adolescents face, social work can support meaningful engagement that fosters true agency and empowerment.

On a broader scale, the study's conclusions offer valuable insights for global practices. Whether in local community settings or international social work contexts, the need to address structural inequalities and create spaces for adolescents to participate meaningfully is universal. Social work practice should be grounded in solidarity and an understanding of the complex interplay among individual agency, social structures, and institutional practices. By promoting inclusive, creative, and respectful environments for adolescent participation, practitioners worldwide can help ensure that young people are not only heard but also empowered to shape the decisions that affect their lives.

## References

Albertos, A., Osorio, A., & Beltramo, C. (2020). Adolescentes y ocio: Desarrollo positivo y transición hacia la vida adulta. *Educación y Educadores*, *23*(2), 201–220. https://doi.org/10.5294/edu.2020.23.2.3

Arias, A. J., & Di Leo, P. F. (2020). Complejidades, responsabilidades e invenciones: Construcciones de subjetividades y de derechos en el encuentro entre instituciones y jóvenes de sectores populares. *Cuadernos de Trabajo Social*, *33*(1), 53–75. https://doi.org/10.5209/cuts.61551

Ávila Cantos, D. (2012). El gobierno de la diferencia: De las lógicas de gestión de lo social [Doctoral thesis, Universidad Complutense de Madrid]. https://docta.ucm.es/rest/api/core/bitstreams/62bea8c3-49ce-49b6-a748-706b9e083d11/content

Ávila Cantos, D., Cassián Yde, N., García García, S., & Pérez Pérez, M. (2019). *Por una acción social crítica: Tensiones en la intervención social*. Editorial UOC.

Ballester Brage, L., & Vecina Merchante, C. (2011). Intervención comunitaria, diversidad y complejidad social: El problema de la segregación social en la escuela. *Prisma Social 6*, 1–29. http://dialnet.unirioja.es/servlet/oaiart?codigo=3686008

Barber, T. (2007). Young people and civic participation: A conceptual review. *Youth & Policy*, *96*, 19–39.

Bendit, R., & Miranda, A. (2017). La gramática de la juventud: Un nuevo concepto en construcción. *Última Década*, *25*(46), 4–43. https://doi.org/10.4067/S0718-22362017000100004

Bertrán, I., Casas, F., Figuer, C., González, M., Malo, S., & Navarro, D. (2009). *Informe técnico sobre experiencias de participación social efectiva de niños, niñas y adolescentes*. Institu de Recerca sobre Qualitat de Vida. https://grupodeinfancia.org/wp-content/uploads/2021/06/3.Participacioninfantijulio2008.pdf

Callejo Gallego, J. (1998). Los límites de la formalización de las prácticas cualitativas de investigación social: La situación. *Sociológica: Revista de Pensamiento Social*, *3*, 93–120. http://hdl.handle.net/2183/2707

Campbell, A., Gurin, G., & Miller, W. E. (1954). *The voter decides*. Row, Peterson, and Co.

Canal, R. (2017). ¿Queremos decir lo mismo cuando hablamos de participación? Perspectivas de activistas, técnicos y políticos locales reveladas con metodología Q. *Reis: Revista Española de Investigaciones Sociológicas*, *158*, 23–40.

Carter, N., Bryant-Lukosius, R., DiCenso, A., Blythe, J., & Neville, A. (2014). The use of triangulation in qualitative research. *Oncology Nursing Forum*, *41*(5), 545–547. https://doi.org/10.1188/14.ONF.545-547

Choudhury, S., & White, S. (2010). Children's participation in Bangladesh: Issues of agency and structures of violence. In B. Percy-Smith & N. Thomas (Eds.), *A handbook of children and young people's participation* (pp. 39–50). Routledge.

Coffey, A., & Atkinson, P. (2005). *Encontrar el sentido a los datos cualitativos: Estrategias complementarias de investigación* (2nd edn.). Publicaciones de la Universidad de Alicante.

de Lucas y Murillo de la Cueva, F., & D'Antonio Maceiras, S. (2020). ICT, young people and social work: Distances and opportunities. *Social Work Education*, *39*(6), 813–824. https://doi.org/10.1080/02615479.2019.1691163
Doel, M., & Orchard, K. (2006). Groupwork researchers as "temporary insiders". *Groupwork*, *16*(3), 4670. https://doi.org/10.1921/gpwk.v16i3.603
Du Bois-Reymond, M., & López-Blasco, A. (2004). Transiciones tipo yo-yo y trayectorias fallidas: Hacia las políticas integradas de transición para los jóvenes europeos. *Revista de Estudios de Juventud*, *65*(4), 11–29.
Ducca Cisneros, L. (2021). La participación en la intervención grupal con jóvenes y adolescentes en la ciudad de Madrid: Entre el control y el empoderamiento [Doctoral thesis, Universidad Complutense de Madrid]. https://produccioncientifica.ucm.es/documentos/624bbdd5e9790a3dbd042f61
Ducca Cisneros, L., Cañas Lerma, A. J., & González Casas, D. (2024). ¿Dónde está la juventud en el trabajo social? Hormonas, exclusión e intervención social. In J. Garcés Ferrer (Ed.), *Tratado general de trabajo social, servicios sociales y política social* (pp. 753–782). Tirant Humanidades.
Eliassi, B. (2017). Conceptions of immigrant integration and racism among social workers in Sweden. *Journal of Progressive Human Services*, *28*(1), 6–35. https://doi.org/10.1080/10428232.2017.1249242
Feixa, C. (2006). Generación XX: Teorías sobre la juventud en la era contemporánea. *Revista Latinoamericana de Ciencias Sociales, Niñez y Juventud*, *4*(2), 21–45. https://dialnet.unirioja.es/servlet/oaiart?codigo=4657548
Figueras, M., Soler Masó, P., Casal, J., Saura, J., Romaní, J., Trilla Bernet, J., & Feixa, C. (2011). La ciudad indignada. In J. C. Trilla Bernet, J. Casal, C. Feixa, M. Figueras, A. Planas, J. Romaní, J. Saura, & P. E. Soler Masó (Eds.), *Jóvenes y espacio público: Del estigma a la indignación* (pp. 193–244). Edicions Bellaterra.
France, A. (1998). 'Why should we care?': Young people, citizenship and questions of social responsibility. *Journal of Youth Studies*, *1*(1), 97–111. https://doi.org/10.1080/13676261.1998.10592997
Francés García, F. J. (2008). El laberinto de la participación juvenil: Estrategias de implicación ciudadana en la juventud. *OBETS: Revista de Ciencias Sociales*, *2*, 35–51.
Gaete Quezada, R. (2014). Reflexiones sobre las bases y procedimientos de la teoría fundamentada. *Ciencia, Docencia y Tecnología*, *25*(48), 149–172. http://dialnet.unirioja.es/servlet/oaiart?codigo=4751827
Gaitán, L. (2015). Protagonismo en la infancia, o la participación de los niños en los procesos de intervención social. *Servicios Sociales y Política Social*, *32*(107), 25–39.
Gaitán, L., & Liebel, M. (2011). *Ciudadanía y derechos de participación de los niños*. Universidad Pontificia de Comillas: Síntesis.
Ganuza Fernández, E. (2006). *Tendencias de la participación ciudadana en Europa y España*. CSIC. https://digital.csic.es/handle/10261/14388
García-Galera, M., Del-Hoyo-Hurtado, M., & Fernández-Muñoz, C. (2014). Jóvenes comprometidos en la red: El papel de las redes sociales en la participación social activa. *Comunicar: Revista Científica de Comunicación y Educación*, *22*(43), 35–43.
Gastañaga Moreno, J. L. (2004). Trabajo social, familia y escuela. *Cuadernos de Trabajo Social*, *17*, 255–271.
Gómez del Toro, R. (2015). Adolescencia y violencia desde el Trabajo Social: Un estudio etnográfico [Doctoral thesis, Universidad Pablo de Olavide]. https://rio.upo.es/xmlui/handle/10433/2142
González Salcedo, A. (2011). Cultura política y participación en España. *Studia Politicae*, *24*, 5–24.
Graham, A., Fitzgerald, R., Smith, A., & Taylor, N. (2010). Children's participation as a struggle over recognition: Exploring the promise of dialogue. In B. Percy-Smith & N. Thomas (Eds.), *A handbook of children and young people's participation: Perspectives from theory and practice* (pp. 293–305). Routledge.

Hernández Pedreño, M. (2016). La muestra en la investigación cualitativa. In N. Caparros Civera & E. Raya Díez (Eds.), *Métodos y técnicas de investigación en trabajo social* (pp. 77–94). Grupo 5.
Hopper, T., & Iwasaki, Y. (2017). Engagement of "at-risk" youth through meaningful leisure. *Journal of Park and Recreation Administration*, *35*(1), 20–33. https://doi.org/10.18666/JPRA-2017-V35-I1-7289
Julkunen, I. (2009). Youth unemployment and marginalization. In A. Furlong (Ed.), *Handbook of youth and young adulthood: New perspectives and agendas* (pp. 157–166). Routledge.
Lansdown, G. (2009). The realisation of children's participation rights: Critical reflections. In B. Percy-Smith & N. Thomas (Eds.), *A handbook of children and young people's participation* (pp. 11–23). Routledge.
Larson, R., & Angus, R. (2011). Pursuing paradox: The role of adults in creating empowering settings for youth. In M. S. Aber, K. I. Maton, & E. Seidman (Eds.), *Empowering settings and voices for social change* (pp. 65–93). Oxford University Press.
Leung, J., & Shek, D. (2011). Poverty and adolescent developmental outcomes: A critical review. *International Journal of Adolescent Medicine and Health*, *23*(2), 109–114. https://doi.org/10.1515/ijamh.2011.019
Malekoff, A. (2016). *Group work with adolescents: Principles and practices* (3rd edn.). Guildford Press.
Marchioni, M. (1999). *Comunidad, participación y desarrollo*. Editorial Popular.
Marshall, T. (1950). *Citizenship and social class*. Cambridge University Press.
Martí, J. (2005). Diagnósticos comunitarios y participación local: El diagnóstico comunitario de la Zona Ponent de Tarragona. In J. Martí (Ed.), *Participación y desarrollo comunitario en medio urbano: Experiencias y reflexiones* (pp. 181–198). IEPALA Editorial.
O'Kane, C., Haj-Ahmad, J., & Friscia, F. (2020). *Engaged and heard! Guidelines on adolescent participation and civic engagement*. UNICEF. https://www.unicef.org/documents/engaged-and-heard-guidelines-adolescent-participation-and-civic-engagement
Padgett, D. (2017). *Qualitative methods in social work research* (3rd edn.). Sage.
Price, P., & Mencke, P. (2013). Critical pedagogy and praxis with Native American youth: Cultivating change through participatory action research. *The Journal of Educational Foundations*, *27*(3–4), 85–102.
San Martín, D. (2014). Teoría fundamentada y Atlas.ti: Recursos metodológicos para la investigación educativa. *Revista Electrónica de Investigación Educativa*, *16*(1), 104–122. https://dialnet.unirioja.es/servlet/oaiart?codigo=4679899
Santana Clavijo, S., Gasca Collazos, P., & Fernández Cediel, M. (2016). La participación de los niños y las niñas: Un aporte al estado del arte. *Revista de Psicología GEPU*, *7*(1), 244–267.
Schlegel, A., & Hewlett, B. (2011). Contributions of anthropology to the study of adolescence. *Journal of Research on Adolescence*, *21*(1), 281–289. https://doi.org/10.1111/j.1532-7795.2010.00729.x
Shier, H. (2001). Pathways to participation: Openings, opportunities and obligations. *Children & Society*, *15*(2), 107–117. https://doi.org/10.1002/chi.617
Strauss, A., & Corbin, J. (2015). *Basics of qualitative research: Techniques and procedures for developing grounded theory* (4th edn.). Sage.
United Nations. (1989). *Convention on the rights of the child*. https://www.ohchr.org/en/instruments-mechanisms/instruments/convention-rights-child
United Nations. (2016). *General comment No. 20 on the implementation of the rights of the child during adolescence*. https://www.ohchr.org/en/documents/general-comments-and-recommendations/general-comment-no-20-2016-implementation-rights
Vincenzino, M. (2017). Sobre el derecho de niños y adolescents: Subjetividad reguladora versus ciudadanía emancipadora. *Margen: Revista de Trabajo Social y Ciencias Sociales*, *87*, 1–7.

Webster, C. (2009). Young people, "race" and ethnicity. In A. Furlong (Ed.), *Handbook of youth and young adulthood: New perspectives and agencies* (pp. 66–73). Routledge.
Willow, C. (1997). *Hear! Hear! Promoting children and young people's democratic participation in local government*. Local Government Information Unit.
Young, I. M. (2014). Five faces of oppression. In S. Asumah & M. Nagel (Eds.), *Diversity, social justice, and inclusive excellence: Transdisciplinary and global perspectives* (pp. 3–32). State University of New York Press.
Zambrano Constanzo, A. (2005). *Participación y empoderamiento comunitario: Rol de las metodologías implicativas [Paper]*. X Congreso Internacional del CLAD sobre la Reforma del Estado y de la Administración Pública, Santiago, Chile. https://repositoriocdim.esap.edu.co/bitstream/handle/20.500.14471/8996/6739-1.pdf
Zimmerman, M., & Rappaport, J. (1988). Citizen participation, perceived control, and psychological empowerment. *American Journal of Community Psychology*, *16*(5), 725–750.

## Section IV

# Children's Rights to the Provision of Services in Social Work

# 10 Rights, Recognition, and Residential Childcare

## An Exploration of Identity Formation Using Honneth's Recognition Theory

*Gerry Marshall and Paul McCafferty*

### Introduction

Article 8 of the United Nations Convention on the Rights of the Child (UNCRC; United Nations, 1989) places obligations on states for the preservation of a child's identity. It reads as follows:

> States Parties undertake to respect the right of the child to preserve his or her identity, including nationality, name and family relations as recognized by law without unlawful interference.
>
> Where a child is illegally deprived of some or all of the elements of his or her identity, States Parties shall provide appropriate assistance and protection, with a view to re-establishing speedily his or her identity.

Some commentators have characterised Article 8 as outlining "a foundational but underdeveloped right" (Tobin, 2019, p. 281). They suggested this underdevelopment is because the term "identity" is somewhat fluid and ambiguous (Scolnicov, 2017). Nonetheless, some elements of identity seem to be more readily identifiable—for example, genetic origin, ethnicity, physical appearance, and family history. In contrast, other aspects are shaped in an ongoing way through parental, community, and wider sociocultural influences intertwined with the child's personal experiences. These factors integrate into their emerging sense of self during their childhood. So, in some respects, identity is an evolving process that contains a combination of static and dynamic elements.

Article 8 is considered a natural progression from Article 7, in which a child is understood as having the rights to be registered at birth, receive a name and nationality, and be cared for by parents. Additionally, Article 8 makes a demand on the state to take actions that will preserve the child's identity. Reference is made to family relations, which are understood as having a broader meaning than only the child's parents. In this instance, preservation can be interpreted as the child:

- being enabled to understand their unique life history.
- being allowed to explore, define, and express the elements of their identity without unlawful interference.

DOI: 10.4324/9781003582410-15

So, the state has been issued with clear obligations in respect of the child. As one commentator noted, "States must assist children to preserve not only their right to know their identity but also their right to express, protect, discover and live it" (Tobin, 2019, p. 296). Here, obligations are established to have measures in place that preserve and protect the child's identity. So, what could Article 8 mean for children looked after in a residential childcare setting? How can we interpret these obligations from a social work practice and research perspective for this group?

Moskal and Sime (2022) noted "a scarcity of literature that explores young people's response to unsettling events such as Brexit or the COVID-19 pandemic and the impact on their identity formation" (p. 190). The main focus of their study was the impact of disruption and change on the identity process of young people. As a result of these seismic events in their lives, the young people defined their identity as "fragmented, dynamic, and changeable" (Moskal & Sime, 2022, p. 195). Many children and young people in care experience movements from family life to group care, then further moves within the residential care system. There is no doubt that such movements qualify as "unsettling events," deeply affecting their personal development and life course trajectory.

So, Article 8 of the UNCRC places twin responsibilities on states with respect to children and young people: first, to preserve the child's identity, and second, to assist and protect a child with a view to speedy re-establishment of their identity if elements are illegally deprived. We can conclude that inherent in the UNCRC is a clear relationship between the emerging individual and the state that requires some form of regulation if the individual is to actualise who they are and who they will become fully:

> While the article is a consequence of a specific historical period, it has many applications—from helping children who have been displaced to re-establish contact with their family to assisting children in State care to trace aspects of their identity they are too young to remember. In essence, it protects the personal characteristics, relationships and histories that make children who they are.
>
> (Child's Rights International Network, n.d., para. 4)

## Residential Childcare and Identity

In this context and set of obligations, we situate this discussion on identity and residential childcare. Although in recent years there has been some broad discussion about identity formation and children and young people in care (J. Thomas & Holland, 2010; Thrana, 2016), some authors have argued that identity remains theoretically underdeveloped and has yet to reach its apotheosis either in social work practice or research (Ferguson, 2018). Positive interrelational experiences in childhood and adolescence support the development of positive identity formation and contribute to long-term positive outcomes and well-being into adulthood (Honneth, 1995; Houston, 2015). A combined view of both psychological and sociological research concludes that identity is constructed through interactions with people, culture, and environment (Crocetti et al., 2017; Morsünbül et al., 2014; Oyserman & Destin, 2010; J. Thomas & Holland, 2010). These external and internal influences provide key messages to young people about where they belong, expectations about their role in society, and an evolving sense of their individuality and identity (Burke & Stets, 2009; Juhila & Abrams, 2011; Tikkanen, 2016).

Our sense of self being influenced by internal and external psychosocial experiences is of direct significance to young people in care, many of whom have first-hand experience of disenfranchisement from their family circle, local community, and wider society (Bellonci et al., 2018). Marginalised young people seek positive identity formation, but due to discrimination, intolerance, and invisibility, they can be coerced into socially negative roles (Way & Rogers, 2015). This can lead to the acquisition of a negative identity role, confirming further disenfranchisement and societal stigma (Way et al., 2013). In this context, we need to reflect more profoundly on the residential childcare milieu. Not only is it the environment in which many vulnerable children grow up, it is also the place in which their evolving sense of self is shaped and formed by the culture of care that surrounds them. Anglin (2002) reflected that a living environment in a children's home is crafted in the interrelationship between young people and staff members and is "more akin to making pottery than to building a house" (p. 79). This task of co-constructing the living environment is a symbiosis between the staff and young people, a fact that has deep implications for how we support positive identity formation in this setting.

Additionally, this chapter reflects on national and international research that has highlighted that young people in residential child care facilities have often been exposed to traumatic incidents and personal adversity, are often exceptionally vulnerable, and require professional specialist care and support (Bellonci et al., 2018; Moore et al., 2017, 2018). A body of research has indicated that trauma affects a young person's emerging sense of identity (Côté, 2018). Furthermore, organisational and structural issues in the sector present a further challenge to the development of positive identity. For example, frequent staff changes and multiple placements have been found to have a negative impact on the self-esteem of children and young people (Holmes et al., 2018). Memories of traumatic events can represent turning points in life and become component parts of a person's identity and autobiography (Delker & Freyd, 2017). Yet lack of time and space, and access to accurate information, official records, letters, and photographs, can mean that children and young people have diminished opportunities to knit together their personal life story in a dynamic and living way that helps them form a clear life narrative and sense of self.

For children and young people in residential childcare, opportunities for positive identity formation form an essential part of their well-being (Sindi & Strompl, 2019). The process of identity formation is understood as an intersubjective process and rooted in the context of each young person's life experience (McMurray et al., 2011; Winter & Cohen, 2005). Such findings reinforce the need to focus more intently on the psychosocial dynamics that provide the conditions for the flourishing of the human identity in a residential setting. This chapter argues in favour of connecting identity formation, adolescence, and trauma in such a way that it can contribute to national and international debates relating to what works for young people and how we understand and subsequently facilitate positive identity formation. Approaching identity formation from these sociological, psychological, and practice-based perspectives provides a wider theoretical context through which to situate the approach from Axel Honneth, whose model emerged from a distinctly philosophical tradition. Although acknowledging that the work of Honneth is not directly focused on the care system, it does offer a new way of understanding the psychosocial dynamics and processes that exist in residential childcare.

## Residential Care: Recognition Theory and the Honneth Model

The potential contribution of recognition theory in social care has been foregrounded by other authors (Husby et al., 2018; Marthinsen & Skjefstad, 2011; N. Thomas, 2012; Turney, 2012). These studies all concluded that the quality of the interpersonal engagement has the potential for transforming the working relationship between the professional and service user. Importantly, this relationship emerges in a specifically crafted environment in which the key empowering dynamic is interrelational. The service user experiences being respected and valued as a unique individual with skills and talents, alongside their hopes and aspirations for the future—findings that are directly transferable to the residential childcare context for deeper consideration.

Much of what has been written to date about recognition theory discusses the concept from a largely theoretical perspective, using the theory as a lens for deeper reflection on the experiences of a service user, and there is considerable merit to this approach. In this chapter, we move the discussion more directly into the arena of children's homes, highlighting the work of Smith et al. (2017), who argued that the theory has potential application in residential care. Smith et al. (2017) noted recognition theory as an "attractive" concept because it not only emphasises the importance of emotional connection but also "sets this alongside legal protection and civil engagement. It thus gives legitimacy and force to societal responsibility and the inter-connections of individual to other" (p. 1619). These authors drew attention to the wider dimensions of life for a young person in care and the potential for recognition theory to provide a more holistic perspective on this service.

One strength of recognition theory acknowledged in their paper is that Honneth foregrounds the intersubjective aspect alongside the moral and legal responsibilities that society has towards the individual (Smith et al., 2017). Recognition theory, therefore, potentially offers an innovative approach by which it is possible to critique the interrelational, legal, ethical, and practice framework that surrounds and supports young people in care. Moreover, as already evidenced in the prior studies, recognition theory contains not only breadth of scope but also a versatility that makes its application as an analytic lens valuable across the breadth of social care provision—thereby increasing its usefulness to academics, policy makers, and practitioners alike.

This chapter reflects on this body of work as the basis to explore further how recognition theory might have practical application in a residential care setting in such a way that it takes account of processes, mechanisms, and relationships in the sector and contributes to the discussion about the necessary conditions for human flourishing in a group care setting.

Honneth's (1995) seminal work *The Struggle for Recognition* provides a bespoke framework with respect to the formation of human identity. Honneth's theory is constructed around the writings of Hegel but also incorporates the social psychology of Mead (1967) and psychoanalytic theory (Turney, 2012, p. 153). One author wrote that recognition theory "offers a moral philosophically and social psychologically grounded normative foundation of recognition as a moral requirement for social work practice" (Warming, 2015, p. 250). Recognition theory is centred on the importance of social recognition as a requirement for the development of psychoemotional autonomy and self-realisation. It is constructed around three forms of recognition that are facilitated through the relationships in our lives: our interrelational experience of love, rights, and solidarity. From the point of our birth onwards, we internalise our sense of personal value based on the quality of the relationships with those around us on whom we are interdependent. In their empirical analysis of a Danish survey of 1,400 young people in care, Lausten and Frederiksen (2016) used the theory as their analytic tool and commented that "the well-being and social integration of a human being is determined by the level of recognition that he or she receives from his or her surroundings" (p. 94). This is diagrammatically represented in Honneth's (1995, p. 129) book (see Table 10.1 for an adapted version). These forms of recognition and their application to residential childcare are explored next.

As shown in the table, Honneth outlined the forms and modes that recognition takes, the dimensions of personality to which they relate, the forms of disrespect, and the threatened component of the personality. Importantly for this chapter, Honneth outlined the practical relation to self—namely, self-confidence, self-respect, and self-esteem—which are consistently reported as issues of concern for young people growing up in residential care (Berridge et al., 2012).

The Canadian philosopher Charles Taylor (1994) described recognition as a "vital human need" (p. 26). Sennett (2003) defined recognition as a synonym for respect. Webb (2010) referred to it as a paradox of the human condition that the journey to fully becoming oneself can only be achieved through relationships with others in the inter-subjective turn known as recognition. As previously discussed, young people in care often have adverse experiences that are stigmatising and can lead to reduced self-esteem and, for some, disenfranchisement from family, local community, and wider society (Bellonci et al., 2018;

*Table 10.1* Adaptation of Honneth's (1995) Conceptual Framework regarding Recognition

| *Forms of Recognition* | *Primary Relationships (Love, Friendship)* | *Legal Relations (Rights)* | *Community of Value and Solidarity (Esteem)* |
|---|---|---|---|
| Mode of recognition | Emotional support | Cognitive respect | Social esteem |
| Dimension of personality | Needs and emotions | Moral responsibility | Traits and abilities |
| Practical relation to self | Basic self-confidence | Self-respect | Self-esteem |
| Forms of disrespect | Abuse and rape | Denial of rights and exclusion | Denigration and insult |
| Threatened component of personality | Physical integrity | Social integrity | Honour and dignity |

Daly et al., 2018). These experiences find resonance in the framework of recognition theory: "Members of marginalized and subaltern groups have been systematically denied recognition for the worth of their culture, or way of life, the dignity of their status as persons and the inviolability of their physical integrity" (Honneth, 1995, p. x).

Recognition theory potentially offers a lens through which to understand the interconnection between this experience of trauma and human identity formation in the context of residential childcare, which ironically has itself been denied recognition for many years by being viewed as inherently flawed and the option of last resort (Berridge et al., 2012; Holmes et al., 2018).

## Legal Relations Involving Rights

Honneth's conceptualisation of recognition through legal rights emerged from a wider discussion of the historic connection between social hierarchies and legal entitlements. As with relations of love, Honneth continued with the theme of interdependence in the context of rights, although this form of recognition does not emerge through psychosocial interiority (Houston, 2015). Honneth (1995) wrote: "With the uncoupling of traditional rights claims from the ascription of social status, a general principle of equality emerges for the first time, which henceforth requires of every legal order that it allow no exceptions and privileges" (p. 115).

In this form of recognition, an emphasis is placed on the central theme of equality—the worth of each person is recognised through their participation in universal freedoms to which all are automatically entitled. The critical turn is the shift from exclusion to inclusion; those in society who were formerly marginalised are now returned to equitable legal and moral status. This turn is made possible by the inclusion of concepts of equality in modern legal thinking, which Honneth argued had a two-fold effect. First, it engendered an increased consciousness around legally mandated social freedoms, and second, it led to an emerging set of "previously excluded or disadvantaged groups ... [being] granted the same rights as all other members of society" (Honneth, 1995, p. 118). As discussed at the start of this chapter, young people in a residential care setting often experience disenfranchisement and social exclusion; therefore, this shift towards inclusivity has direct relevance and application. Honneth (1995) marked the transformation through which one becomes a bearer of rights through social recognition inherent in equality and belonging. This transformation also develops a positive relation-to-self—namely, that of self-respect. This occurs through the symbolic act of recognition inherent in a legal structure affirming an individual's innate worth, concluding that "one is able to respect oneself because one deserves the respect of everyone else" (Honneth, 1995, p. 119).

Significant issues about inherent power imbalances between staff members and young people are, in part, addressed in this form of recognition (Marthinsen & Skjefstad, 2011). One key issue in residential childcare is how and in what way staff members deal with issues of adult power in their practice, especially given the historic abuse of power in this sector (Smith, 2009). Anglin (2002) denoted the sharing of power and decision-making as a key element of good quality care. Honneth situated the issue of rights in the context of respect. Reflecting this, Zurn (2015) wrote:

> Honneth's central claim here is that a person can fully develop healthy self-respect only when he or she is granted the appropriate social recognition expressed through the full legal rights granted to other members of his or her community. I can only realize my dignity as an irreplaceable, unique source of moral worth when I can understand myself as a morally autonomous agent.
>
> (p. 36)

Honneth's framework arguably has the potential to contribute to the discussion on children's rights and power-sharing because it connects the development of self-respect with human dignity in the specific context of rights. Rights and their consequent entitlements become the mechanism for social recognition in which young people have their status and moral worth affirmed. Nonetheless, it is necessary to bear in mind that a rights-based discussion cannot sit in isolation from the wider context of residential care. Rights are contingent, contextual, and conditional. Therefore, the theoretical application of rights becomes more complex when considered alongside the interface with the practical realities of the decision-making by adults that occurs daily; for example, about risk management, care planning, or restrictive practices. These decisions involving adult power and the child's best interests, in the final analysis, may disregard a rights-based approach in preference to protection concerns and risk reduction strategies. This inherent tension in residential practice arguably has yet to be fully explored.

**Legal Relations, Rights, and Residential Care**

Essential to recognition theory is the lived experience of having one's rights upheld. In her article on chilqqa21`1

dren attending welfare services in Norway, Thrana (2016) discussed young people gaining recognition from children's services as a "citizen by right" (p. 75) and located it in the context of equality. Smith et al. (2017) argued that legal recognition for young people in care is conceptualised in a type of citizenship. According to Smith et al. (2017), this takes the form of "an imperative to consult, pay attention and enable participation through structures of care about issues that are important to young people" (p. 1617). Both these articles advanced the original Honneth conceptualisation by expanding it into a defined social work structure under the concept of citizenship and exploring its application in practice. Although they interpret the concept of a citizen differently, the key focus is the concept of equity and participation in the context of recognition through legal relations.

Central to Honneth's thought is Kant's (1964) dictum that each of us is an end in ourselves and not a means to an end:

> Of particular importance, the respect involved here is not differential or graduated: it is not based upon a comparative evaluation of a person's traits, capabilities, or achievements. Respect, rather, is for a person as an end-in-herself, as an irreplaceable source of intrinsic worth.
>
> (Zurn, 2015, p. 35)

Because people are fundamentally dependent on recognition for the construction of their identity and personal self-worth, there is moral responsibility to recognise the worth of others. As such, each individual person is of intrinsic value, a participating member of the humanity, and ipso facto of moral worth. This moral worth is enshrined in legal protections to which we are all entitled, including young people in care. These legal entitlements mean that each is as worthy as the other with respect to the law. It is one of the few areas of life that children in care have the same status and privileges as everyone else because these rights accord everyone in society the same level of self-respect regardless of their social status (Zurn, 2015).

In that sense, rights represent the self-worth of the child enshrined in codified form and constitute "depersonalised symbols of social respect" (Honneth, 1995, p. 118). Children's rights and the broader legal framework for children and young people, therefore, can be thought of as equalizers, given previously they might have felt excluded from power structures and decision-making forums (Wijemanne, 2017). From the platform of shared rights, a young person living in residential care can theoretically look someone else in the eye from a position of equality, something they often are unable to do because of stigma, limited education, poorly developed social skills, and diminished sense of self-value (Barnes, 2012). Because of this recognition of worth through upholding of legal rights, the young person's personal self-respect is permitted to flourish (Honneth, 1995). However, it is important to acknowledge that the relationship between children's rights and residential childcare has been characterised as uneasy, with some practitioners remaining unconvinced of their intrinsic merit in this professional setting: "This is not necessarily because they have anything to hide or because they want to maintain adult power over children. It is because the whole concept of rights is, in conceptual and practical terms, neither neutral nor unproblematic" (Smith, 2009, p. 10).

To apply this better to residential childcare, through recognising the rights of others, we can understand ourselves to be "legal persons" (Honneth, 1995, p. 108). In this way, a rights-based consciousness emerges through reciprocal recognition of everyone else's legal entitlements and our own. A rights-based culture in residential childcare could elevate the status of everyone in the home, adults and children, as rights-bearers. Therefore, in the Honneth model, by recognising the rights of children, adult caregivers also have their entitlements acknowledged and upheld—a recognition double-turn. Developing a rights-based consensus between those who live or work in a children's home, therefore, becomes an act of mutual building-up and collective self-interest because everyone benefits from this reciprocity. However, this double-turn is not a simple task and requires a culture of care that is imbued with a rights consciousness in a way that has yet to be attained. Based on the reflection by Anglin (2002) that the caring environment is crafted by young people and staff members, the development of a rights culture must be a co-production, a programme designed collaboratively by the young people and professionals, for the young people and professionals.

### Case Study I: Co-Production of Children's Rights in a Children's Home

Sunny Hills Children's Home has three young people newly admitted to the house this month. The change in the group of young people leads to disruptive and challenging behaviours for several weeks. Underlying this tension is a desire for young people to access the kitchen after bedtime or when they come in late after being out in the community. The kitchen is automatically closed and locked by the staff at 10 p.m. each night. The young people are prohibited from entering and making snacks or food. They complain that they are very hungry and need something more substantial than the snacks that the staff offers them. Some staff members are assaulted, and two young people are cautioned by the police in this regard. The local authority has the option to press criminal charges against the young people. However, a senior manager suggests that the home manager, staff, and young people engage in an exercise where they jointly explore the rules in the home. To do this, they use the UNCRC to inform the discussion.

**Box 10.1 Reflective Questions for Social Workers: Discussing Children's Rights**

What articles in the UNCRC might be relevant to this discussion?
Whose rights do you need to consider here—young people's, adults, or both?
How might the staff develop comprehension of children's rights and their application in a real-life setting?
How might the day-to-day running of the home be changed positively because of this exercise?
What objections might there be to completing this exercise with young people?

## Misrecognition and Relations Involving Rights

Honneth (1995) wrote that forms of misrecognition occur through a denial of rights or being wilfully excluded from legal entitlements:

> For the individual, having socially valid rights claims denied signifies a violation of the intersubjective expectation to be recognized as a subject capable of forming moral judgements. ... The experience of this type of disrespect typically brings with it a loss of self-respect, of the ability to relate to oneself as a legally equal interaction partner with all fellow humans. (p. 134)

Honneth (1995) foregrounded that the upholding of rights is inextricably interlinked with the concept of respect. Misrecognition is any form of a downgrading that diminishes the individual's capacity to value their abilities (p. 134). In other words, a denial or disenfranchisement from participation in a rights-based community not only leads to a form of legal ostracism but also reduces a person's capability for self-validation. In residential care, rights-based misrecognition occurs when a young person does not have their legal rights upheld in their living environment. This can either be due to staff members in the home not being sufficiently conversant with the legal entitlements of young people in care or viewing such rights as an impediment to their work (Barnes, 2012). In that sense, misrecognition is a product of either the actions or inaction of staff members. Recognition theory can provide the lens to develop a much deeper understanding of the implications for young people that emerge from this reality. What staff members choose to do or not do towards young people in terms of relationship building and how they use their power and authority have consequences for the young people with respect to building a positive identity.

Honneth (1995) made a direct link between rights and ability of the young person regarding personal validation. This progressed the discussion from considering rights as an additional element of the statutory framework already in place to rights being a fundamental requirement for the psychoemotional development of the young person. This approach could and should underpin the effective provision of care. The young person's capacity to develop a sense of self-respect is contingent on their lived experience of being a rights-holder. Yet the literature has identified examples where this is not the case. Some commentators have noted concerns about the criminalisation of young people who enter residential care without a criminal record but leave care with a record due to staff members who call police to the home to address challenging but non-criminal behaviour (Shaw, 2016; Smith et al., 2017).

> When staff members did not have time for individual adolescents or when they did not listen to or understand what they had to say, adolescents were prone to experiencing more oppression … It was only when a sincere understanding of the adolescent's need was combined with staff behaviour that confirmed this understanding that empathy had the power to counter repression.
>
> (De Valk et al., 2019, p. 762)

The concept of misrecognition provides a lens through which to examine if a home is providing adult-centred rather than child-centred care. Examples include the punitive use of restrictive practices to impose the will of the staff on young people or maximise an unnecessary degree of control over the environment. Actions such as locking doors to restrict the movement of young people, sending young people to bed early without cause, or routinely preventing access to the kitchen at night are not indicative of a rights-based approach to the well-being of children in a residential setting (De Valk et al., 2019). Importantly, recognition theory suggests that the imposition of such a care environment by staff members impedes the natural development of the young person's self-respect, which is detrimental to their holistic well-being and an emerging sense of their entitlements as legal citizens and rights-holders in society.

So, what impact does this have on their developing sense of self and personal identity formation? The primary psychological task of adolescence is to develop a strong sense of identity (Erikson, 1968). Yet young people in care face a double challenge to achieving this task. Not only do they have to negotiate the stigma associated with being placed in care, but some also find it necessary to go to great lengths to conceal their identity in care from their peer group for fear of rejection and ridicule. So, how and in what ways can staff help young people to address this? Are there mechanisms in a residential setting that will support young people in developing a more positive identity despite these challenges?

## Case Study II: Analysis of an Incident Using Honneth's Recognition Theory and Children's Rights

You are an inspector carrying out an unannounced visit to Sunny Hills Children's Home. You are reviewing a case file and read the following report on John, a 15-year-old young person in the home:

> Psychiatric Assessment Report: October 2022
>
> John can display a lack of empathy around other people. We observed that his interpersonal communication can be poor, and he has limited development of emotional language to help him express his feelings and emotions. John has evident social and emotional difficulties, and he shows traits that indicate he may be on the autistic spectrum disorder.

A little later, you read through the daily event record for the home:

> There was an incident yesterday where John had kicked and punched a staff member. This started out as a bit of banter between John and the staff member. Unfortunately, John's ability to read cues and interpersonal expressions may be limited. John then lost his cool and assaulted the staff member.

The following day, the daily log includes the following entry:

> John has been well behaved today. The staff described him as sheepish and ashamed due to his behaviour last night.

In Honneth's framework, the first form of recognition, relations of love, emphasises how the quality of the relationship we experience shapes our evolving sense of identity. In other words, the human environment surrounding a

**Box 10.2 Reflective Questions for Social Workers: Analysing the Incident**

Were the staff members on duty aware of the psychiatric report and operating from a planned basis with John in line with his assessed needs? (Consider Article 39 of the UNCRC regarding rehabilitation)

What is the meaning and purpose of "banter" in this transaction for the staff member and for John? Did the staff member display empathy and emotional intelligence? Or was this interaction mishandled, leading to the possibility of an incident occurring? (Consider Article 19 regarding maltreatment)

The written records clearly indicate that the "problem" in this episode lay with John, who had a defined psychiatric diagnosis. Why is there a lack of empathy for John reflected in the written account of the incident? (Consider Article 19 regarding maltreatment)

John experienced shame as a result of this interaction (per Article 27 on standards of living and Article 8 regarding identity). How might any sense of unfairness and internalised shame affect John? (Consider Article 12 regarding voice of the child and Article 19 on maltreatment)

child directly affects the child psychologically and emotionally. As we see in the case study involving John, the actions and words that young people experience in residential childcare are deeply connected to their psychoemotional well-being. When living in residential childcare, young people can experience mis-recognition through the actions and attitudes of staff members that can undermine their confidence and esteem. Recognition theory suggests that engaging young people with good intentions but without a clear plan is not sufficient. Rather, staff members must calibrate their words and actions in accordance with the needs of the child and more fully consider the impact that their day-to day interactions have on them.

## Conclusion

This chapter suggests that there has been some but as yet limited discussion of the importance of identity formation for young people in residential care. This has occurred despite research that combined psychological and sociological approaches to understand that our identity is an intersubjective process constructed through interactions with people, culture, environment, and experiences (Crocetti et al., 2017; Honneth, 1995; Morsünbül et al., 2014; Winter & Cohen, 2005). It is important to re-evaluate residential care in the light of this interpretation because it gives deeper insight into why relationships are important. Additionally, we can reconfigure our understanding of residential care as the environment in which the dynamics, processes, and practices that enable and facilitate positive identity formation actually take place (Ferguson, 2018; McMurray et al., 2011; J. Thomas & Holland, 2010; Thrana, 2016). In this chapter, we argued that the absence of a focus on identity represents a significant gap in research and practice. It also begs a question about the state's obligation to preserve and restore the identity of the child. In his model of recognition, Honneth offered an approach that enables practitioners to develop and sustain a supportive environment in which young people can nurture and maintain positive identity formation. Finally, more fully understanding how the fundamental "data of self" emerges in group care arguably becomes one of the key measures by which we, the adults responsible for designing and delivering the care system, can judge the merits or quality of the care service being provided.

## References

Anglin, J. P. (2002). *Pain, normality and the struggle for congruence: Reinterpreting residential care for children and youth*. Routledge.

Barnes, V. (2012). Social work and advocacy with young people: Rights and care in practice. *The British Journal of Social Work*, *42*(7), 1275–1292. https://doi.org/10.1093/bjsw/bcr142

Bellonci, C., Holmes, L., & Whittaker, J. (2018). Re-thinking therapeutic residential care (TRC) as a preventative service: Examining developments in the US and England. *Residential Treatment for Children and Youth*, *36*(1), 35–53. https://doi.org/10.1080/0886571X.2018.1536495

Berridge, D., Biehal, N., & Henry, L. (2012). *Living in children's residential homes*. Department for Education.

Burke, P., & Stets, J. (2009). *Identity theory*. Oxford University Press.

Child's Rights International Network. (n.d.). *Article 8: Preservation of identity*. https://archive.crin.org/en/home/rights/convention/articles/article-8-preservation-identity.html

Côté, J. E. (2018). The enduring usefulness of Erikson's concept of the identity crisis in the 21st century: An analysis of student mental health concerns. *Identity*, *18*(4), 251–263. https://doi.org/10.1080/15283488.2018.1524328

Crocetti, E., Branje, S., Rubini, M., Koot, H., & Meeus, W. (2017). Identity processes and parent-child and sibling relationships in adolescence: A five-wave multi-informant longitudinal study. *Child Development*, *88*(1), 210–228. https://doi.org/10.1111/cdev.12547

Daly, D. L., Huefner, J. C., Bender, K. R., Davis, J. L., Whittaker, J. K., & Thompson, R. W. (2018). Quality care in therapeutic residential programs: Definition, evidence for effectiveness and quality standards. *Residential Treatment for Children and Youth*, *35*(3), 242–262. https://doi.org/10.1080/0886571X.2018.1478240

Delker, B. C., & Freyd, J. J. (2017). Betrayed? That's me: Implicit and explicit betrayed self-concept in young adults abused as children. *Journal of Aggression, Maltreatment & Trauma*, *26*(7), 701–716. https://doi.org/10.1080/10926771.2017.1308982

De Valk, S., Kuiper, C., Van der Helm, G. H. P., Maas, A. J. J. A., & Stams, G. J. J. M. (2019). Repression in residential youth care: A qualitative study examining the experiences of adolescents in open, secure and forensic institutions. *Journal of Adolescent Research*, *34*(6), 757–782. https://doi.org/10.1177/0743558417719188

Erikson, E. (1968). *Identity, youth and crisis*. Norton and Company.

Ferguson, L. (2018). "Could an increased focus on identity development in the provision of children's services help shape positive outcomes for care leavers?" A literature review. *Child Care in Practice*, *24*(4), 76–91. https://doi.org/10.1080/13575279.2016.1199536

Holmes, L., Connolly, C., Mortimer, E., & Hevesi, R. (2018). Residential group care as a last resort: Challenging the rhetoric. *Residential Treatment for Children and Youth*, *35*(3), 209–224. https://doi.org/10.1080/0886571X.2018.1455562

Honneth, A. (1995). *The struggle for recognition: The moral grammar of social conflicts*. Polity Press.

Houston, S. (2015). "When I look, I am seen, so I exist to change": Supplementing Honneth's recognition model for social work. *Social Work and Society*, *13*(2), 1–34.

Husby, I. S. D., Kiik, R., & Juul, R. (2018). Children's encounters with professionals—Recognition and respect during collaboration. *European Journal of Social Work*, *22*(6), 987–998. https://doi.org/10.1080/13691457.2018.1473841

Juhila, K., & Abrams, L. S. (2011). Special issue editorial: Constructing identities in social work settings. *Qualitative Social Work*, *10*(3), 277–292.

Kant, I. (1964). *Groundwork of the metaphysics of morals*. Harper Row.

Lausten, M., & Frederiksen, S. (2016). Do you love me? An empirical analysis of the feeling of love amongst children in out-of-home care. *Scottish Journal of Residential Child Care*, *15*(3), 90–103. https://doi.org/10.14324/111.444.ijsp.2017.07

Marthinsen, E., & Skjefstad, N. (2011). Recognition as a virtue in social work practice. *European Journal of Social Work*, *14*(2), 195–212. https://doi.org/10.1080/13691451003744317

McMurray, I., Connolly, H., Preston-Shoot, M., & Wigley, V. (2011). Shards of the old looking glass: Restoring the significance of identity in promoting positive outcomes for looked-after children. *Child and Family Social Work*, *16*(2), 210–218. https://doi.org/10.1111/j.1365-2206.2010.00733.x

Mead, G. H. (1967). *Mind, self and society*. University of Chicago Press.

Moore, T., McArthur, M., Roche, S., Death, J., & Tilbury, C. (2017). Young people's views on safety and preventing abuse and harm in residential care: "It's got to be better than home." *Children and Youth Services Review*, *81*, 212–219. https://doi.org/10.1016/j.childyouth.2017.08.010

Moore, T., McArthur, M., Roche, S., Death, J., & Tilbury, C. (2018). Sticking with us through it all: The importance of trustworthy relationships for children and young people in residential care. *Children and Youth Services Review*, *84*, 68–75. https://doi.org/10.1016/j.childyouth.2017.10.043

Morsünbül, Ü., Crocetti, E., Çok, F., & Meeus, W. (2014). The Utrecht-Management of Identity Commitments Scale (U-MICS): Gender and age measurement invariance and convergent validity of the Turkish version. *Journal of Adolescence*, *37*, 799–805. https://doi.org/10.1016/j.adolescence.2014.05.008

Moskal, M., & Sime, D. (2022). Young Europeans in Brexit Britain: Unsettling identities. *Global Networks*, *22*(2), 183–196. https://doi.org/10.1111/glob.12338

Oyserman, D., & Destin, M. (2010). Identity-based motivations: Implications for intervention. *The Counselling Psychologist*, *38*(7), 1001–1043. https://doi.org/10.1177/0011000010374775

Scolnicov, A. (2017). *The child's right to religious freedom and formation of identity*. Routledge.

Sennett, R. (2003). *Respect*. Penguin.

Shaw, J. (2016). Policy, practice and perceptions: Exploring the criminalisation of children's home residents in England. *Youth Justice*, *16*(2), 147–161. https://doi.org/10.1177/1473225415617858

Sindi, I., & Strompl, J. (2019). Who am I and where am I from? Substitute residential home children's insights into their lives and individual identities. *Child and Youth Services*, *40*(2), 120–139. https://doi.org/10.1080/0145935X.2019.1591272

Smith, M. (2009). *Rethinking residential child care: Positive perspectives*. Policy Press.

Smith, M., Cameron, C., & Reimer, D. (2017). From attachment to recognition for children in care. *The British Journal of Social Work*, *47*(6), 1606–1623. https://doi.org/10.1093/bjsw/bcx096

Taylor, C. (1994). The politics of recognition. In A. Gutmann (Ed.), *Multiculturalism: Examining the Politics of Recognition* (pp. 25–73). Princeton University Press.

Thomas, J., & Holland, S. (2010). Representing children's identities in core assessments. *The British Journal of Social Work*, *40*(8), 2617–2633. https://doi.org/10.1093/bjsw/bcp154

Thomas, N. (2012). Love, rights and solidarity: Studying children's participation using Honneth's theory of recognition. *Childhood*, *19*(4), 453–466. https://doi.org/10.1177/0907568211434604

Thrana, H. M. (2016). Love: Recognising relationships in work with vulnerable youth. *Scottish Journal of Residential Care*, *15*(3), 72–89. https://doi.org/10.14324/111.444.ijsp.2017.06

Tikkanen, J. (2016). Concern or confidence? Adolescents' identity capital and future worry in different school contexts. *Journal of Adolescence*, *46*, 14–24. https://doi.org/10.1016/j.adolescence.2015.10.011

Tobin, J. (2019). *The UN Convention on the Rights of the Child: A commentary*. Oxford University Press.

Turney, D. (2012). A relationship-based approach to engaging involuntary clients: The contribution of recognition theory. *Child and Family Social Work*, *17*(2), 149–159. https://doi.org/10.1111/j.1365-2206.2012.00830.x

United Nations. (1989). *Convention on the rights of the child*. https://www.ohchr.org/en/instruments-mechanisms/instruments/convention-rights-child

Warming, H. (2015). The life of children in care in Denmark: A struggle over recognition. *Childhood*, *22*(2), 248–262. https://doi.org/10.1177/0907568214522838

Way, N., Hernández, M. G., Rogers, L. O., & Hughes, D. L. (2013). "I'm not going to become no rapper": Stereotypes as a context of ethnic and racial identity development. *Journal of Adolescent Research*, *28*(4), 407–430. https://doi.org/10.1177/0743558413480836

Way, N., & Rogers, O. (2015). "[T]hey say Black men won't make it, but I know I'm gonna make it": Ethnic and racial identity development in the context of cultural stereotypes. In K. C. McLean & M. Syed (Eds.), *The Oxford handbook of identity development* (pp. 269–285). Oxford University Press.

Webb, S. A. (2010). (Re)Assembling the left: The politics of redistribution and recognition in social work. *British Journal of Social Work*, *40*(8), 2364–2379. https://doi.org/10.1093/bjsw/bcq070
Wijemanne, H. (2017). Child's rights imperatives for children in alternative care. *Scottish Journal of Residential Child Care*, *16*(2).
Winter, K., & Cohen, O. (2005). Identity issues for looked after children with no knowledge of their origins: Implications for research and practice. *Adoption & Fostering*, *29*(2), 44–52. https://doi.org/10.1177/030857590502900206
Zurn, C. F. (2015). *Axel Honneth: A critical theory of the social*. Polity Press.

# 11 Upholding Children's Rights to Services in the Face of Structural Inequality

## Social Work, Poverty, and Global Declarations

*Mary McColgan and Paul McCafferty*

### Introduction

The global picture about the extent to which services for children promote and protect their well-being and security does not offer much assurance that their rights are centre stage (Joseph Rowntree Foundation, 2024), nor that their voices are being valued in contributing to and developing policies that affect their lives (Bessell, 2022). This chapter explores themes related to this topic and examines two case studies with global influence, addressing poverty as a child's rights issue that affects social work services and the Kigali Declaration (Commonwealth Heads of Government, 2022).

The two case studies consider how core rights are marginalised, contested, and ameliorated, and they analyse the implications for social work, drawing out lessons for practice and examining how the underpinning conceptual frameworks pose challenges for social workers. The chapter adopts a critical stance to examine key reports regionally, nationally, and internationally that focus on key aspects of well-being—e.g., health, mental health, and education—that are impacted by structural inequalities such as poverty, social consequences of violence and abuse, and discrimination.

### Case Study: Why is Poverty a Children's Rights Matter?

Poverty is not merely a question of material deprivation; it is also a profound and enduring children's rights issue. When children live in poverty, their access to essential rights enshrined in international law is systematically undermined. Increasingly, our understanding of this relationship is framed against the wider backdrop of global economic inequality, deepening austerity policies, and the long-term social and economic fallout from the COVID-19 pandemic. These conditions have disproportionately affected children and families already experiencing disadvantage, amplifying structural inequalities and severely curtailing children's life chances.

DOI: 10.4324/9781003582410-16

For children, poverty is experienced as a daily erosion of dignity, opportunity, and security. It affects every aspect of their lives—health, education, relationships, identity, and well-being. Social work professionals, therefore, must understand poverty not only as a social policy concern but also as a direct breach of children's rights, demanding both preventive and rights-based responses at all levels of intervention.

Although the United Nations Convention on the Rights of the Child (UNCRC; United Nations, 1989) does not explicitly use the term "poverty" (Bessell, 2022), the concept is deeply embedded in its framework. Articles have directly addressed the material and socioeconomic conditions essential to the full realisation of children's rights. The convention recognises that children cannot realise their rights in isolation from their social and economic contexts. The following articles are particularly relevant.

#### *Article 6: Right to Life, Survival, and Development*

"State Parties recognize that every child has the inherent right to life."

This article establishes the foundation for all other rights. The child's right to survival and development is indivisible from the socioeconomic conditions that enable them to thrive. Poverty jeopardises this right at its core.

#### *Article 26: Right to Social Security*

"State Parties shall recognize for every child the right to benefit from social security, including social insurance."

This article places a clear obligation on states to establish and maintain systems of social protection that proactively address poverty. If social security is inadequate or inaccessible, states risk violating their obligations under the convention.

#### *Article 27(1): Right to an Adequate Standard of Living*

"State Parties recognize the right of every child to a standard of living adequate for the child's physical, mental, spiritual, moral and social development."

This is a central article for understanding poverty as a rights issue. It reinforces the notion that material deprivation directly impairs a child's development across multiple dimensions—educationally, emotionally, and physically.

#### *Article 27(2): Parental Responsibility and Economic Capacity*

"The parents or others responsible for the child have the primary responsibility … within their abilities and financial capacities."

Here, the convention acknowledges the realities of parental economic constraints. It recognises that the responsibility to secure adequate living conditions cannot rest solely on individuals, especially in conditions of structural poverty.

***Article 27(3): State Responsibility for Material Assistance***

"States ... shall take appropriate measures to assist parents and others ... and shall in case of need provide material assistance and support programmes."

This clause places direct responsibility on the state to provide material support when families are unable to meet their children's needs. It shifts the focus from personal failure to structural injustice and mandates state intervention to mitigate poverty's effects on children.

***Article 23: Rights of Children with Disabilities***

"Recognizing the special needs of a disabled child ... the right to enjoy a full and decent life ... and to achieve the fullest possible social integration and individual development."

Article 23 reinforces the importance of intersectionality in rights-based work. Children with disabilities are often at heightened risk of poverty and exclusion. The convention demands a tailored, equitable response that accounts for both disability and deprivation.

Understanding poverty through a children's rights lens compels us to move beyond surface-level indicators and consider the structural injustices that underpin inequality. Social workers, policymakers, and practitioners have a professional and moral responsibility to challenge poverty not only as a barrier to well-being but also as a systemic rights violation.

This framing aligns with international obligations and ethical practice, demanding that we advocate structural change, resource redistribution, and social justice. In doing so, we reaffirm the indivisibility of social and economic rights and the central role of the state in realising the promise of the UNCRC for all children, especially those most marginalised by poverty.

This is important because poverty continues to be one of the most significant determinants of inequality in children's lives, shaping not only their immediate experiences but also their access to fundamental rights, services, and future opportunities. It is both a cause and a consequence of social exclusion, and its effects are magnified by policy inaction, fragmented welfare systems, and the erosion of state obligations to children as rights-holders.

In both the Global North and Global South, poverty is a defining structural condition that shapes childhoods, limiting access to education, housing, healthcare, nutrition, and participation in community life. Recent data from the Northern Ireland Assembly's (2024) Public Accounts Committee provide a stark example: In a population of 1.9 million, 1 in 4 children lives in relative poverty and 9% of children grow up in households without access to basic goods or essential social activities. These figures speak to not only deprivation but also an erosion of dignity and rights, signalling a failure of governance to uphold the rights enshrined in the UNCRC.

Although the Northern Ireland Executive introduced a 4-year child poverty strategy in 2016, the Public Accounts Committee's assessment revealed a deeply concerning pattern of failure. The lack of prioritisation of early intervention, combined with a persistent silo mentality across government departments, has led to policy incoherence and poor outcomes for children. From a rights-based perspective, such fragmentation of service delivery is not merely inefficient—it undermines the core principles of the UNCRC, particularly the obligation to act in the best interests of the child (Article 3) and ensure rights are implemented in a coherent, systemic manner (Article 4).

This concern is echoed in Professor Philip Alston's 2018 report as United Nations Special Rapporteur on Extreme Poverty and Human Rights. He noted the United Kingdom's regression in terms of poverty-related policy, warning that up to 50% of children could be living in poverty by 2022. Although this projection was seen as stark at the time, it has proven prescient: By 2024, 4 million children in the United Kingdom lived in poverty and 800,000 were reliant on food banks to meet basic nutritional needs (Cabinet Office, 2024). These figures are not only statistics; they represent lived realities of exclusion, hunger, cold, and humiliation for millions of children. As the Joseph Rowntree Foundation (2024) described, poverty has become increasingly visceral, with the associated stigma and human cost increasingly visible and politically unacceptable.

Despite the near-universal ratification of the UNCRC, the degree to which it is integrated into domestic legislation varies considerably. As Kilkelly et al. (2021) argued, progress in embedding the UNCRC into national policy is uneven, and children's socioeconomic rights often remain aspirational rather than enforceable. Todres (2021) highlighted the specific case of the United States, where early momentum to adopt the UNCRC was ultimately replaced by resistance, leaving 13.4 million children in poverty without access to the full protections of the convention. His analysis underscored how racial and economic injustice intersect, creating entrenched disadvantage among children from minoritised communities.

Even in countries that have ratified the UNCRC, implementation gaps persist. In Ireland, for example, Forde and Kilkelly (2021) identified ongoing poverty challenges—7.7% of children living in poverty and a further 15.9% at risk of poverty—despite formal commitments to children's rights. In Sweden, Thorburn Stern (2021) raised similar concerns, noting the absence of targeted legislation addressing child poverty despite the country's strong welfare reputation.

These issues are not simply about resource distribution; they are about the failure to treat children as full rights-bearers whose well-being should be central to all aspects of policy and practice. As UNICEF's (2023b) *Innocenti Report Card 18* noted, national wealth alone does not determine progress in reducing child poverty. Political will, rights-based governance, and participatory policymaking are essential. UNICEF strongly advocated the inclusion of children's views (Article 12 in the UNCRC) in shaping poverty policy, emphasising that only by listening to children can we truly understand how poverty affects their lives—and how we might design systems that respond with dignity, empathy, and justice.

**Upholding Children's Rights Through Service Provision: Social Work Responses to Poverty**

Poverty fundamentally compromises children's ability to realise their rights. It is not simply a context in which rights are more difficult to access; it is a structural condition that actively obstructs children's entitlements to health, education, safety, play, and participation. For social workers, whose professional mandate is grounded in social justice and human rights, responding to poverty is not a peripheral concern—it is central to ensuring that services meet children's needs and protect their rights.

McCartan et al. (2018) argued convincingly that poverty must be understood as a social justice issue, not only an economic one. They challenged the notion that poverty is the "wallpaper" of social work practice—always visible yet too familiar to challenge effectively. Drawing on Morris et al. (2018, p. 370), they described poverty as "too big to tackle and too familiar to notice." This framing urges practitioners to see poverty not as the background noise of practice but as a defining force in the lives of the children and families they serve.

In Northern Ireland, efforts have been made to move poverty closer to the centre of professional concern. The Office of Social Services' anti-poverty practice framework for social work seeks to make the link between poverty and rising child protection referrals explicit. It recognises that children in the most deprived communities were overrepresented on child protection registers and calls for social work responses that go beyond risk management. The framework promotes a more holistic and preventive model of service delivery, including:

- Income maximisation and welfare advice
- Advocacy of adequate living standards
- Access to affordable childcare
- Parenting support
- Enhanced professional understanding of the causes and consequences of poverty

Yet this initiative has suffered from implementation fatigue. According to the Public Accounts Committee (Northern Ireland Assembly, 2024), key mechanisms intended to deliver the framework—such as cross-departmental collaboration and stakeholder engagement—have failed to materialise. The lack of political urgency and interagency coordination has rendered such frameworks largely symbolic, reinforcing the disconnection between policy commitments and frontline realities.

The Northern Ireland Commissioner for Children and Young People (2024) echoed these concerns in a health and social care briefing, highlighting the absence of a rights-based approach to planning and budgeting. The commissioner called for:

- Greater visibility of children in public spending decisions
- Systematic inclusion of children's voices in decision-making processes (UNCRC Article 12)
- Mandatory children's rights impact assessments across all legislation, policy, and service developments

These critiques underscore a recurring pattern: Rights-based intentions are undermined by operational inertia. Without robust implementation, meaningful participation, and integrated service delivery, children's rights risk being relegated to aspirational rhetoric rather than enforceable standards.

Central to a rights-based approach is a critical understanding of how poverty functions—not as an individual or parental failing but as a structural injustice. As Bessell (2022) and others have argued, dominant discourses often frame poverty as the result of poor choices or inadequate parenting. These narratives deflect attention from the real sources of harm: inadequate welfare systems, austerity measures, and economic models that prioritise efficiency over equity.

Treanor and Troncoso (2024) emphasise the need for social workers to reject these deficit-based assumptions and instead address poverty as a violation of rights and a risk to child development. Their research illustrates how poverty affects not only material well-being but also emotional security, mental health, and family relationships. The cumulative stress of financial precarity can erode children's sense of stability and dignity, with long-term implications for their capacity to thrive.

Social work responses, therefore, must be both structural and relational. As Hingley-Jones and Kirwan (2023, p. 135) argued, effective practice requires attention to both the macro-level causes of poverty and the micro-level experiences of children and families. This dual lens enables practitioners to provide meaningful support while also advocating systemic change. Service provision becomes not only a vehicle for meeting immediate needs but also a site of resistance—challenging the normalisation of poverty and asserting children's rights to live with security, dignity, and opportunity.

Realising a poverty-aware, rights-based approach to social work practice and service provision, therefore, is essential—but it is not without profound challenges. The post-COVID-19 context has exposed the fragility of welfare systems and intensified the pressures experienced by frontline practitioners. As McFadden et al. (2024) observed, the profession is increasingly stretched by unsafe staffing levels, rising caseloads, and the long-term effects of austerity. Funding cuts and the erosion of public sector infrastructure have compromised not only the availability of services but also the ability of practitioners to deliver sustained, relational support to children and families. Compounding this challenge, many social workers are affected by the economic pressures they are tasked with mitigating: rising living costs, stagnating wages, and personal experiences of financial strain.

In such conditions, the capacity to engage in justice-oriented, poverty-aware practice can feel diminished. Yet paradoxically, this is precisely the moment when such approaches are most needed. Social workers are on the frontline of inequality—and with that position comes a powerful opportunity and responsibility to challenge the systems that perpetuate inequality.

The *Anti-Poverty Practice Guide* (British Association of Social Workers & Child Welfare Inequities Project, 2023) offers a practical and principled roadmap for navigating these tensions. It encourages a shift in mindset and method, calling on practitioners to:

- Develop a deep understanding of the local community profile, grounding intervention in lived realities
- Build meaningful alliances with the voluntary and community sector, recognising the value of non-statutory partnerships
- Work collaboratively across disciplines and agencies to promote integrated, holistic responses
- Engage in direct advocacy, particularly regarding income maximisation and access to entitlements, viewing these not as add-ons but as core social work functions

Crucially, the guide also tackles one of the profession's enduring discomforts: the reluctance to speak openly with families about poverty and financial insecurity. Many social workers express concern that such conversations may seem intrusive or inappropriate, potentially harming the relationship. However, the guide (British Association of Social Workers & Child Welfare Inequities Project, 2023) is unequivocal that avoiding these conversations not only obscures the reality of families' lives but also risks reinforcing stigma and silencing their experiences. When approached with empathy, transparency, and respect, these discussions become a powerful act of solidarity—an expression of core social work values in action.

Social work's response to poverty, then, cannot be seen as optional or peripheral. It is central to the profession's ethical identity and international obligations. In a context of rising child poverty and heightened public awareness, social workers must position themselves as both critical allies and systems-level advocates, supporting families in immediate need while also challenging the structures that produce inequality. Doing so requires more than individual skill; it demands organisational cultures and policy frameworks that value rights-based, anti-poverty practice and equip practitioners with the resources to act.

## Reframing Poverty Through a Children's Rights and Service Provision Lens

Understanding poverty through a children's rights lens shifts the focus from abstract measurement to the real-world implications of deprivation for children's everyday lives and their access to services. It challenges professionals and policymakers to go beyond narrow income-based indicators and consider how poverty obstructs children's rights to health, education, protection, participation, and an adequate standard of living, as articulated in the UNCRC.

Traditionally, poverty has been defined using income-based measures, such as those advanced by Lister (2004), or by efforts to develop universal benchmarks, such as the international poverty threshold proposed by Townsend et al. (1979). Although these models have contributed significantly to comparative poverty research, they often fail to capture the day-to-day realities that children face. As Bessell (2022, p. 541) observed, there is still no globally accepted definition of child poverty. Sustainable Development Goal 1, which aims to "end poverty in all its forms everywhere," remains tied to subsistence-level definitions of poverty, offering limited scope for a holistic, rights-based approach that centres on dignity, well-being, and inclusion.

Emerging frameworks seek to move beyond this limitation by conceptualising poverty as multidimensional—a lived experience that intersects with children's access to services, relationships, and participation in society. These models integrate not only income but also factors such as education, housing, health, and social connectedness, creating a more meaningful basis for assessing how poverty affects the realisation of children's rights.

One of the most influential contributions to this approach is Bessell's (2022) rights-based model of poverty, developed through extensive research with children in the Global South. Her framework redefines poverty through the lens of children's lived experience, offering a powerful foundation for the design and delivery of child-focused services. It identifies three interrelated dimensions:

- Material poverty: the absence of adequate income and physical resources to meet basic needs such as food, clothing, and housing
- Opportunity poverty: barriers to accessing education, health care, recreational activities, and other services essential for development
- Relational poverty: structural inequalities and stigma that limit children's social inclusion, their voice in decision-making, and support available from trusted adults and institutions

This model carries significant implications for social work practice and service provision. It recognises that poverty is not only an economic problem but also a relational and rights-based issue that cuts across all domains of a child's life. For social workers, this means that effective intervention cannot rely solely on crisis response or material aid. It must also engage with the systems and structures that shape children's opportunities—and critically, amplify their voices in service planning and policy design (UNCRC Article 12).

Applying this framework in practice requires services to move from reactive models to preventive, participatory, and relational approaches. This includes:

- Designing services that reflect children's perspectives on what poverty means in their lives
- Building relational trust with families experiencing financial hardship
- Ensuring service delivery is culturally responsive and inclusive of diverse experiences (e.g., children with disabilities, ethnic minorities, children with experiences in care)
- Advocating structural change when systems reproduce or exacerbate disadvantage

Framing poverty as a violation of rights, rather than a failure of individual or parental responsibility, fundamentally shifts how social workers engage with children and families. It demands that practitioners become not only providers of support but also advocates of justice, navigators of systems, and collaborators in co-producing solutions that are grounded in dignity, equity, and respect.

### Practice Illustration: Living on the Breadline

Cherie Lewis is a single parent with three children aged 10 years, 8 years, and 3 years; she is expecting another child in 4 months. She had been in a long-term relationship that involved intimate partner violence, coercion, and financial control, but 3 years ago, with the help of family and friends and support from Women's Aid, she moved into privately-rented accommodation. She receives Universal Credit (social security support), and until recently she worked as a home caregiver for an older couple with complex health problems.

**Box 11.1 Reflective Questions for Social Workers: Poverty and Children's Rights**

How does poverty affect the realisation of the children's rights to health, education, and an adequate standard of living (Articles 24, 28, and 27 of the UNCRC) in Cherie's family situation? Consider how socioeconomic conditions are limiting the children's development and well-being and what this means for your professional responsibilities.

In what ways might the intersection of poverty, domestic abuse history, and mental health shape Cherie's ability to parent, and how can your practice avoid reinforcing stigma or blame? Reflect on how structural inequalities contribute to parenting challenges and whether support plans are responsive to these realities.

How can you advocate for Cherie and her children's rights in the broader system—such as housing, education, and welfare—while maintaining your statutory responsibilities? Think about your role as both a protector and an advocate and where systemic responses are needed beyond individual casework.

What are the ethical considerations in balancing legal access arrangements with the expressed wishes and emotional safety of the children? Reflect on how you centre children's voices (UNCRC Article 12) and assess risk, particularly when children reject contact with a parent who has a history of violence.

How can your practice challenge the hidden harms of poverty-related shame and stigma experienced by children, especially in school and peer environments? Consider how schools, social services, and community partners can work together to promote inclusion, dignity, and protection from social exclusion.

Her children attend school on a regular basis; they receive free school meals and sometimes attend an afterschool group. Cherie experiences bouts of depression and low mood and feels unable to cope financially. Her rent has increased, and her landlord has indicated the rent is likely to increase again next year. Her gas heating costs mean that she only uses heating when the children are at home and only for a few hours each day. The children complain of feeling cold, and they are all prone to respiratory infections; the youngest child has asthma. Feeding her family nutritious food is a concern for Cherie. She regularly has to borrow money from family, and although she had only occasionally used a food bank before, she now goes there on a weekly basis. She often skips meals for herself to make sure there is enough food for the children.

Social services has been involved with the family because of ongoing issues related to access by their father, and this has caused anxiety and distress. Despite an access order in place, none of the children wants to have supervised access because they have ongoing concerns about their father's unpredictable behaviour. Cherie has concerns about the children's anxiety, especially her middle child, who is struggling academically and is prone to bouts of aggression.

At school, the children have been bullied and called names, and other children reference to the fact that the family uses the local food bank and gets free meals at school.

**Case Study: The Kigali Declaration: Global Declarations and the Provision of Services amid a Polycrisis**

The landscape for professional social work practice in the context of a polycrisis is undoubtedly challenging. Social workers are increasingly caught in a vortex where global challenges—economic uncertainty, climate breakdown, forced migration—collide with national dilemmas, including poverty, inequality, and escalating demands in child protection systems. These intersecting crises constrain the profession's ability to secure adequate resources, influence policy direction, and provide timely, empathetic, and rights-focused support to children and families.

In such contexts, the stakes are high. Children living in poverty, experiencing displacement, or affected by fragile social infrastructures are particularly vulnerable to having their rights denied or delayed. Social workers are on the frontline of these challenges and are often asked to operate in underfunded systems while maintaining their ethical and professional commitments. Reconstructing professional practice under these conditions does not mean reinventing social work. Rather, it involves reaffirming its core values—human dignity, social justice, and relational ethics—and equipping practitioners to understand and challenge the structural forces shaping the lives of children.

This also requires recognising that international declarations and global frameworks, such as the UNCRC, must be translated into local service delivery. They are not simply aspirational tools but also provide guiding principles that should underpin professional practice. For social workers, this includes translating global commitments into meaningful service responses, advocating reforms that promote equity and justice, and working collaboratively across systems to co-produce integrated responses to children's needs. In this way, a rights-based approach is not simply theoretical; it becomes a practical and necessary framework for decision-making, service planning, and ensuring that children's dignity, voice, and agency are prioritised.

An important example of this effort is the Kigali Declaration on Child Care and Protection Reform, adopted by the Commonwealth Heads of Government in June 2022. Signed by 56 member countries representing 39% of the world's child population, the declaration acknowledges the collective responsibility of states to address global failures in upholding children's rights—particularly in relation to violence, poverty, and access to services. Its development was shaped by UNICEF data that exposed widespread global concerns: child marriage, female genital mutilation, the impact of poverty and disability, educational disruption, and deteriorating mental health following COVID-19.

Although initially framed more as a development agenda than a rights-based instrument, the declaration's reference to key frameworks such as the UNCRC (United Nations, 1989), United Nations Convention on the Rights of Persons with Disabilities (United Nations, 2006), and United Nations Declaration on the Rights of Indigenous Peoples (United Nations, 2007) anchored its goals in broader human rights commitments. More recently, the declaration has taken a stronger position, calling for an "accelerated shift in legislation, policy solutions and financial decisions" to place children at the centre of societal priorities (UNICEF, 2023a). Among its seven goals, one stands out as central to realising a rights-based approach: "Consult children and young people in the process of legal and policy reform and other matters that concern them." This alignment with Article 12 of the UNCRC reinforces the value of child participation in designing the very services that aim to protect and support them.

For social workers, the Kigali Declaration underscores a growing recognition of their role in advancing children's rights. As Schier (2019) argued, states are the primary duty bearers under international human rights law, but the responsibility for realising these rights is shared by professionals tasked with delivering services on behalf of the state. Realising children's rights depends not only on legal frameworks but also on enabling environments, practitioner capability, and a belief in the agency of children. The Kigali Declaration, in its evolving form, provides a valuable opportunity to embed this thinking into national policies, professional training, and everyday practice.

However, significant barriers to realising children's rights in service provision remain. As Byrne (2024) illustrated, systemic discrimination continues to prevent marginalised groups—such as Roma children—from accessing education, healthcare, and protection. Despite international obligations, state responses have been slow, framed more by legal deflection than by a commitment to children's rights. Byrne identified the need for an integrated model that brings together statutory child protection and social welfare approaches, grounded in family support and anti-discrimination principles. This, he argued, is fundamental to moving from rights in theory to rights in practice.

UNICEF (2023a) highlighted similar challenges in a recent analysis of global youth perspectives that revealed a landscape shaped by intersecting geopolitical instability, economic downturn, and environmental breakdown. These global forces have direct consequences for children's lives, often manifesting as service gaps, funding cuts, and deteriorating access to rights. UNICEF outlined trends such as food insecurity, inflation, civic space erosion, and educational instability—each directly affecting how services are resourced and delivered.

In this context, professional social workers must act as translators between policy declarations and frontline realities. Global statements like the Kigali Declaration provide direction, but it is through relational practice, advocacy, and collaborative service provision that these commitments are realised. This means embedding participation frameworks, ensuring children's voices are heard in service design, and advocating systems that uphold—not undermine—children's dignity and rights.

Ultimately, a rights-based approach to service provision is most powerful when it is lived through practice. It requires not only structural reform but also a commitment to relational care, professional integrity, and the co-production of solutions with children and their families. In a time of polycrisis, this is both the greatest challenge and the most vital task for the profession.

The implications of global crises for children's rights are not abstract; they directly shape how services must respond. Table 11.1, adapted from UNICEF's (2023a) analysis, offers a succinct illustration of how current global trends affect children's lives and well-being and how these in turn map onto specific UNCRC obligations. It underscores the critical importance of ensuring that service responses are rooted in a children's rights framework.

## National Reflections on Global Commitments

At a national level, the challenges outlined here are reflected in local contexts. In the United Kingdom, the Children's Society (2021) documented a troubling decline in young people's subjective well-being, linked to post-COVID-19 anxiety, educational disruption, and limited access to mental health services. Waiting lists are long, and service provision is often fragmented or underresourced. The report also highlights the absence of systematic monitoring of children's well-being, noting a lack of data on children's perspectives. A recent study by the Food Foundation (2024) suggested that poverty continues to affect children's physical health, contributing to reduced growth and increased illness. These findings illustrate the direct relationship among poverty, service provision, and children's rights.

In global contexts, participatory research in the Pacific region by Gilbert et al. (2023) reinforced the importance of embedding rights-based practice at

*Table 11.1* Global Crises and Children's Rights

| *Trend* | *Action* | *Link to UNCRC* |
|---|---|---|
| Curbing inflation will have unintended consequences on poverty and well-being of children and families | Implement policy measures to protect and prioritise investment in vulnerable children and families, including mitigating rising poverty, low income, and increased costs of food and heating | Article 6 on the right to life, survival and development: "State Parties recognize that every child has the inherent right to life" |
| Food and nutrition insecurity | Climate and food system adaptation to avoid food poverty; nutrition of women and children | Article 27(1) recognises child's right to a range of standards of living affecting their development: "State Parties recognise the right of every child to a standard of living adequate for the child's physical, mental, spiritual, moral and social development" |
| Threats to freedom of expression | Social movements by women and children; potential benefits to civic engagement and activism | Article 15(1): "State Parties recognise the rights of the child to freedom of association and to freedom of peaceful assembly"<br>Article 15(2): "No restrictions may be placed on the exercise of these rights other than those imposed in conformity with the law and which are necessary in a democratic society in the interests of national security or public safety, public order, the protection of public health or morals or the protection of the rights and freedoms of others" |
| Risk to global human rights amid geopolitical tensions; impact on women and children | Potential for common ground from a global perspective | Article 27(3): "State Parties, in accordance with national conditions and within their means, shall take appropriate measures to assist parents and others responsible for the child to implement this right and shall in case of need provide material assistance and support programmes, particularly with regard to nutrition, clothing and housing" |

*Note:* Compiled by the authors from Section 9 of the UNICEF (2023a) report.

**Box 11.2 Reflective Questions for Social Workers: Provision of Services**

How effectively do you translate global commitments—such as the UNCRC and Kigali Declaration—into local service planning and delivery for children and families? Consider how these declarations shape your day-to-day decisions, priorities, and advocacy efforts.

In what ways does your current service provision support or hinder children's access to their rights, particularly in contexts of poverty, displacement, or systemic discrimination? Reflect on who may be excluded or underserved by current systems.

How do you ensure children's voices are meaningfully included in shaping services, in line with Article 12 of the UNCRC and the Kigali Declaration's emphasis on participation? Think about formal mechanisms, informal practices, and cultural responsiveness.

What structural barriers (e.g., funding, policy, interagency collaboration) limit your ability to deliver timely, rights-based services in times of crisis—and how can these be addressed? Focus on how resource constraints, policy silos, or workforce pressures affect practice.

How do you stay grounded in the core values of social work—human dignity, social justice, and relational care—when delivering services under pressure from intersecting global and national crises? Reflect on how these values guide your work during times of uncertainty or instability.

community level. Their work, informed by children with lived experience of violence, calls for culturally relevant, participatory decision-making structures that integrate formal and informal systems of protection. Their study echoed findings by Doel-Mackaway (2022), who advocated child-led models of participation that reflect local cultural knowledge and priorities.

## Conclusion: Reclaiming Rights, Reframing Services

This chapter has explored how both poverty, both as a structural injustice and lived experience, and national declarations and obligations intersect with children's rights, along with how social work services are both challenged and called to respond in a time of global instability. Drawing on two case studies—poverty as a child rights issue and the Kigali Declaration—this analysis has highlighted that upholding children's core rights is not simply about protecting individuals but also about transforming the systems and narratives that shape their lives.

From the Global North to the Global South, the evidence points to a shared crisis: Children are being failed not because of an absence of knowledge or commitment but due to systemic inertia, fractured services, and the marginalisation of their voices in policy and practice. The effects of poverty on children's well-being—on their education, mental health, family life, safety, and participation—are profound and often invisible. When services treat poverty as background noise rather than as a direct assault on children's rights, they risk colluding in its perpetuation.

The case for a rights-based approach has never been stronger. Such a model offers a powerful corrective to deficit-based understandings of families and narrow service responses. It reframes poverty as a violation of dignity and justice, placing the onus not on individual resilience but on state accountability and collective responsibility. As demonstrated, articles of the UNCRC offer a legally and ethically robust foundation for policy and service reform, from ensuring adequate standards of living and access to social protection to embedding child participation and ensuring freedom from discrimination.

Importantly, the chapter has illustrated that global declarations, such as the Kigali Declaration, have the potential to catalyse change—if they are matched by professional leadership and grounded in everyday practice. For social workers, this means reclaiming their role not only as practitioners and protectors but also as advocates, system challengers, and relational allies.

In a context marked by polycrisis, rights violations, and public fatigue, the task of social work may appear overwhelming. But it is also profoundly hopeful. It is in the smallest acts of recognition—hearing a child's fear, validating a parent's struggle, advocating a basic right—that the ideals of the UNCRC are made real. In transforming services, social workers can help reclaim a future where every child's rights are more than aspirational—they are lived, upheld, and honoured.

## References


Alston, P. (2018). *Visit to the United Kingdom of Great Britain and Northern Ireland: Report of the Special Rapporteur on Extreme Poverty and Human Rights (A/HRC/41/39/Add.1)*. United Nations Human Rights Council.

Bessell, S. (2022). Rethinking child poverty. *Journal of Human Development and Capabilities*, *23*(4), 539–561. https://doi.org/10.1080/19452829.2021.1911969

British Association of Social Workers & Child Welfare Inequities Project. (2023). *Anti-poverty practice guide for social work* (2nd edn.). https://basw.co.uk/policy-and-practice/resources/anti-poverty-practice-guide-social-work

Byrne, K. (2024). *Europe's forgotten children: Roma children and their families in Europe 2000–2020: A child rights perspective*. UNICEF. https://www.unicef.org/innocenti/reports/europes-forgotten-children

Cabinet Office. (2024). *Tackling child poverty: Developing our strategy*. https://assets.publishing.service.gov.uk/media/685d11823e6b7941f4e00a74/Child_Poverty_Strategy_Launch_Publication.pdf

Children's Society. (2021). *The good childhood report 2021*. https://www.childrenssociety.org.uk/sites/default/files/2021-08/GCR_2021_Full_Report.pdf

Commonwealth Heads of Government. (2022). *Kigali declaration on child care and protection reform*.

Doel-Mackaway, H. (2022). *Indigenous children's rights to participate in law and policy development*. Routledge.

Food Foundation. (2024). *A neglected generation: Reversing the decline in children's health in England*. https://foodfoundation.org.uk/sites/default/files/2024-06/TFF_Children%27s%20Health%20Report.pdf

Forde, L., & Kilkelly, U. (2021). Incorporating the CRC in Ireland. In U. Kilkelly, L. Lundy, & B. Byrne (Eds.), *Incorporating the UN convention on the rights of the child into national law* (pp. 177–201). Intersentia.

Gilbert, K., Doel Mackaway, H., Law, M., Mercer, C., Low, I., Ma'u Fatiaki, K., Yamba, A., Maetala, R., & Pakoa, A. (2023). *Regional child protection situation analysis*. Save the Children.

Hingley-Jones, H., & Kirwan, G. (2023). Poverty: Social work perspectives. *Journal of Social Work Practice*, *37*(2), 131–135. https://doi.org/10.1080/02650533.2023.2233845

Joseph Rowntree Foundation. (2024). *UK poverty 2024: The essential guide to understanding poverty in the UK*. https://www.jrf.org.uk/uk-poverty-2024-the-essential-guide-to-understanding-poverty-in-the-uk

Kilkelly, U., Lundy, L., & Byrne, B. (Eds.). (2021). *Incorporating the UN convention on the rights of the child into national law*. Intersentia.

Lister, R. (2004). *Poverty*. Polity Press.

McCartan, C., Morrison, A., Bunting, L., Davidson, G., & McIlroy, J. (2018). Stripping the wallpaper of practice: Empowering social workers to tackle poverty. *Social Sciences*, *7*, 193. https://doi.org/10.3390/socsci7100193

McFadden, P., Davies, H., Manthorpe, J., MacLochlainn, J., McGrory, S., Naylor, R., Mallett, J., Kirby, K., Currie, D., Schroder, H., Nicholl, P., Mullineux, J., & McColgan, M. (2024). Safe staffing and workload management in social work: A scoping review of legislation, policy and practice. *British Journal of Social Work*, *54*(5), 2006–2026. https://doi.org/10.1093/bjsw/bcae017

Morris, K., Mason, W., Bywaters, P., Featherstone, B., Daniel, B., Brady, B., Hooper, J., Bunting, L., Nughmana, M., Scourfield, J., & Webb, C. (2018). Social work, poverty, and child welfare interventions. *Child and Family Social Work*, *23*(3), 364–372. https://doi.org/10.1111/cfs.12423

Northern Ireland Assembly. (2024). *Report on child poverty in Northern Ireland* (Report NIA 54/22-27). Public Accounts Committee.

Northern Ireland Commissioner for Children and Young People. (2024). *Health and social care briefing*. https://www.niccy.org/publications/health-and-social-care-briefing-july-2024/

Schier, H. (2019). Student voice and children's rights: Power, empowerment, and "protagonismo." In M. Peters (Ed.), *Encyclopedia of teacher education*. Springer. https://doi.org/10.1007/978-981-13-1179-6_27-1

Thorburn Stern, R. (2021). Incorporating CRC in Sweden. In U. Kilkelly, L. Lundy, & B. Byrne (Eds.), *Incorporating the UN convention on the rights of the child into national law* (pp. 205–227). Intersentia.

Todres, J. (2021). Incorporating the CRC and its optional protocols in the United States. In U. Kilkelly, L. Lundy, & B. Byrne (Eds.), *Incorporating the UN convention on the rights of the child into national law* (pp. 123–143). Intersentia.

Townsend, P. (1979). *Poverty in the United Kingdom: A survey of household resources and standards of living*. Penguin Books.

Treanor, M., & Troncoso, P. (2024). *The impacts of poverty on children's social, emotional and behavioural outcomes*. University of Glasgow and University of Edinburgh, Scottish Centre for Administrative Data Research.

UNICEF. (2023a). *Prospects for children in the polycrisis: A 2023 global outlook*. Global Office of Research and Insight.

UNICEF. (2023b). *Child poverty in the midst of wealth: Executive summary (Innocenti Report Card 18)*. Global Office of Research and Foresight.

United Nations. (1989). *Convention on the rights of the child*. https://www.ohchr.org/en/instruments-mechanisms/instruments/convention-rights-child

United Nations. (2006). *Convention on the rights of persons with disabilities*. United Nations. https://www.un.org/disabilities/documents/convention/convention_accessible_pdf.pdf

United Nations. (2007). *United Nations declaration on the rights of indigenous peoples (A/RES/61/295)*. United Nations General Assembly. https://digitallibrary.un.org/record/607406

# 12 Keeping the Promise

## Workforce Retention as a Children's Rights Obligation

*Liz Tanner, Paul McCafferty, and Davy Hayes*

### Introduction: Keeping the Promise

This chapter extends our earlier work, which synthesised organisational, personal, and structural influences on social work retention. Here, we shift the focus from why workers stay to why it matters for children. Our central claim is that workforce retention is a precondition for the realisation of children's rights in child protection.

We adopt the United Nations Convention on the Rights of the Child (UNCRC; United Nations, 1989) as the organising frame and specify the mechanisms through which staff stability translates into rights outcomes: (a) relationship continuity, enabling authentic participation (Article 12) and coherent planning for family life and permanence (Article 20); (b) protected time for professional judgement, enabling proportionate protection (Article 19) and best interests decision-making (Article 3); and (c) reflective supervision and learning cultures that sustain access to health, education, and development (Articles 6, 24, 28, and 29). Rather than treating retention as a workforce problem alone, we frame it as an accountability obligation for governments, regulators, educators, and employers.

Our contribution is threefold. First, we offer a practice-proximate, rights-based explanatory model linking concrete conditions (caseloads, continuity, supervision) to the effects of specific rights. Second, we propose a small set of practical indicators (e.g., worker change rate, percentage of protected direct-work time, supervision quality) to evidence when rights are being realised or hollowed out. Third, we ground the analysis in two fictionalised case studies constructed from recurring practice patterns and use brief international contrasts to show that rights-enabling conditions are policy-contingent, not inevitable. Our aim is to refine concepts and provide an actionable bridge between retention reforms and children's rights obligations.

We structure the chapter to move from frontline mechanisms and rights effects (including two case vignettes), through structural and political drivers, to a practical matrix of indicators and a set of actionable recommendations for policy, education, and organisations.

DOI: 10.4324/9781003582410-17

**Understanding the Retention Problem**

Across the globe, social workers engage with millions of children, making some of the most complex and consequential decisions in society (McCafferty et al., 2021). In the United States, for instance, child protection workers may be called on to decide whether a child can safely remain at home when allegations of neglect are raised, often under intense media and political scrutiny. In Norway, practitioners balance strong commitments to family preservation with the state's duty to intervene when children's rights to protection and stability are at risk. In South Africa, social workers contend with the additional challenge of extreme poverty and HIV-related orphanhood, where decisions about kinship care or residential placement carry profound implications for children's right to survival and development. In England, social workers conducting Section 47 enquiries under the Children Act 1989 must weigh competing accounts from parents, schools, and children, determining whether statutory thresholds for intervention are met. In New Zealand, the Oranga Tamariki system requires practitioners to integrate child protection assessments with Māori cultural frameworks, recognising the rights of Indigenous children to identity and participation.

Although contexts differ, the stakes are consistently high and rights are engaged. A decision to remove a child may protect against immediate harm yet disrupt family life (Article 20); a decision to leave a child at home may respect parental autonomy yet risk undermining protection (Article 19). The universality of such dilemmas underlines the global significance of social work in realising children's rights through everyday practice.

Social workers require strong skills, sound judgement, and resilience to safeguard children and promote well-being (Koprowska, 2024). The role spans advocacy, social justice, and human rights while working in policy, law, and welfare frameworks. As Peart (2024) observed, practitioners are asked to work both with and against the state—enforcing its decisions while speaking out when systems fail children and families. This dual position creates intense moral and emotional pressures (McCafferty & Taylor, 2020), especially in child protection and family support, where workers weigh risks and balance competing rights: Should a child return home following neglect? How should contact be supervised between siblings separated by care placements? How can a young person be supported best through court?

The foundation of this work is children's rights, particularly those set out in the UNCRC. These rights include the right to be safe from harm (Article 19), to be heard in decisions that affect them (Article 12), to family life and stability (Article 20), and to develop and thrive through access to health, education, and support (Articles 6, 24, 28). In practice, this means social workers act as key guardians of rights for children who are most vulnerable—whether due to abuse, poverty, or experience of care—by ensuring that everyday decisions uphold their dignity and long-term well-being.

For these rights to be more than aspirations on paper, however, children need consistent, skilled practitioners who can build trusting relationships over time. This is where workforce stability becomes critical. Yet in many countries, social work services face a retention crisis (British Association of Social Workers, 2023). High turnover, workforce shortages, and instability not only undermine the profession but also the very rights of the children it seeks to uphold (Research in Practice, 2025). There is an urgent need to focus on retaining experienced social workers, whose expertise is vital for not only workforce sustainability but also safeguarding children's rights through consistent, informed, and ethical practice (Department of Health Northern Ireland, 2022). Stable teams with a healthy balance of experience uphold service continuity (McFadden, 2020). In contrast, high turnover results in the loss of skilled staff members and the valuable knowledge they bring to their role, disrupting the relationships that are central to rights-based practice with children and families (Cook et al., 2025).

Retention concerns are not new. The Children's Bureau in the United States identified staffing shortages and poor retention efforts as early as the 1960s (Rycraft, 1994). Research in subsequent decades has echoed these concerns, highlighting persistent systemic failures in addressing retention in child welfare (Ewalt, 1991; Mor Barak et al., 2001; Webb & Carpenter, 2012). Today, these challenges remain global in scope and unresolved in many countries (Astvik et al., 2020; Burns et al., 2020; McFadden et al., 2015; McLaughlin et al., 2023). Numerous studies have identified longstanding factors contributing to poor retention, including unsupportive working conditions and organisational culture, stress and burnout, limited training opportunities, poor leadership and management, and high workloads (Cook et al., 2025; McLaughlin et al., 2023). Stress in particular has been widely cited as a critical driver of attrition (Coffey et al., 2004). The British Association of Social Workers (2023) recently warned that the profession is at breaking point, and John McGowan (Social Workers Union, 2024), general secretary of the Social Workers Union, stated: "The social work workforce is on the brink of a collective breakdown" (p. 6). These stressors are not abstract: they translate directly into compromised service delivery, especially for vulnerable children, whose rights depend on reliable, engaged, and experienced practitioners.

## How Workforce Instability Erodes Rights

Although staff turnover may introduce new ideas and fresh perspectives (Healy & Oltedal, 2010; McFadden, 2020)—for example, international recruits sharing alternative models of family engagement or newly qualified staff members embracing participatory methods—the benefits are typically short-lived and uneven. Organisationally, turnover can catalyse reflection, prompting managers to question established systems. Yet these potential positives rarely outweigh the destabilising effects of continual attrition, which weakens teams, inflates workloads, and diminishes quality of care (Cook et al., 2025; McFadden, 2020). The impacts travel through three mechanisms introduced earlier: the erosion of relationship continuity, the squeeze on protected time for professional judgement and direct work, and the fraying of reflective supervision and learning cultures—each with direct implications for Articles 12, 19, and 20 of the UNCRC.

Research has shown that staff shortages lead to rising caseloads and reduced time for meaningful engagement (McFadden et al., 2024; McFadden et al., 2015; McLaughlin et al., 2023). This directly undermines children's rights to participation and protection (Articles 12 and 19). In child protection, consequences can be significant. High turnover has been linked to failures in safeguarding and case oversight (Gomez et al., 2010; Healy & Oltedal, 2010), with children's best interests often compromised due to workforce instability (McFadden, 2020). A frontline practitioner in McFadden et al.'s (2024) study illustrated the reality of this crisis: "Fewer staff due to vacancies but no reduction in caseloads and still expected to manage incoming work. No wonder more and more staff are leaving their post" (p. 1967). The departure of experienced workers also leads to gaps in mentorship and weakens team expertise (Healy & Oltedal, 2010; Mor Barak et al., 2001), affecting not only professional development (Cook et al., 2022) but also children's access to safe, informed interventions.

The consequences of poor retention ripple across multiple rights. Most immediately, it undermines the continuity of relationships that make participation under Article 12 meaningful. When children must repeatedly retell traumatic experiences to a succession of new workers, trust is eroded and their involvement risks becoming tokenistic rather than authentic. For example, a young person in care who has had three social workers in a single year may learn to withhold their views, feeling there is little point in opening up when the next worker will soon replace the last. This instability not only weakens participation (Article 12) but also compromises protection from harm (Article 19) and disrupts continuity of family life and care (Article 20). Without stability, innovative ideas are difficult to embed, and any benefits are quickly lost as workers move on. Instead, teams fall into a cycle of starting over, with new staff members redoing assessments, rebuilding relationships, and revisiting decisions—leaving little space for sustained progress. In practice, the disruption caused by turnover almost always outweighs the potential positives.

Studies have shown the scale of this disruption: In the United Kingdom, a quarter of children in care had three or more social workers in a single year (Samuel, 2025), and Carter (2019) reported that more than 45,000 children experienced a change of social worker in 2017 and 2018. Young people describe this instability as deeply traumatic, with one child in Strolin-Goltzman et al.'s (2010) study stating:

> I had a deep relationship with one worker and could talk with her about everything; she had answers about things that were important. When she left, I shut down, it wasn't the same, it didn't feel right. I didn't talk with her [the new caseworker], tried to stay away from her and deal with my problems by myself.
>
> (p. 51)

Such disruptions fracture therapeutic alliances, compromise the effectiveness of services, and may constitute breaches of Article 12.

The right to family life and stability (Article 20), health (Article 24), and education (Article 28) are also compromised when turnover disrupts case management and planning. Inconsistent worker involvement can lead to gaps in assessment, placement planning, and reunification efforts, sometimes resulting in unnecessary moves and instability. Redmond et al. (2010) found striking differences in outcomes: Children with a single consistent caseworker had a 74.5% chance of achieving permanency, compared to only 0.1% for those with six or seven caseworkers. Similarly, the disruption of social work input can delay access to mental health support, medical treatment, or educational resources, undermining children's development and well-being.

Finally, retention failures place children's right to protection from harm (Article 19) at direct risk. Serious case reviews in the United Kingdom have repeatedly linked high caseloads, staffing shortages, and turnover to safeguarding failures (Harlow et al., 2013). When overstretched workers cannot sustain regular visits, build trust, or detect early warning signs of abuse, risks go unnoticed and opportunities for early intervention are lost (Research in Practice, 2022).

Administrative and target pressures are also displacing direct work with children. The Independent Review of Children's Social Care (2021) found that practitioners in direct roles spend less than one third of their time with families; when contact is squeezed, early warning signs are more easily missed and opportunities for early intervention are lost. This undermines children's rights to protection from harm (Article 19), to be heard in decisions that affect them (Article 12), and to have their best interests treated as a primary consideration (Article 3). A subsequent review (Independent Review of Children's Social Care, 2022) reported that child protection practitioners are especially vulnerable to burnout, reflecting persistently high workloads, elevated stress, and role overload (Department for Education, 2020). These patterns are longstanding: Earlier research identified poor working conditions and cumbersome bureaucratic arrangements (Anderson, 2000). A central driver across all accounts is the volume of paperwork that diverts time from the relational practice needed with children and families (Department for Education, 2020), contributing to drift that jeopardises stability and family life (Article 20). Comparable evidence has appeared in the United States: deVaron Reynolds et al. (2008) linked understaffing, worker turnover, and fewer contacts with families to weaker performance in child and family services reviews regarding maltreatment recurrence, placement stability, and timeliness of permanency—outcomes closely tied to protection (Article 19), continuity of care (Article 20), and children's best interests (Article 3).

The problem was starkly illustrated in a United Kingdom High Court case (Stevenson, 2015), in which a child had eight social workers during care proceedings. The judge concluded that this revolving door of professionals led to "a lack of cohesive, comprehensive management and care," amounting to a breach of both the Human Rights Act 1998 and international conventions. Similar concerns have been echoed internationally. Elsewhere, research has found that frequent changes of caseworkers are strongly associated with higher rates of placement breakdowns, longer stays in foster care, and child deaths (Cook et al., 2022).

The risks are not only systemic but also profoundly personal for children. A child who has been exposed to repeated violence at home may go weeks without being seen because their allocated worker is covering double caseloads after colleagues resign. Another may disclose abuse to a trusted worker, only to find that the worker has left before protective action is taken, leaving them with a sense of betrayal and hopelessness. These situations are not isolated failings of individual practitioners but symptoms of structural weaknesses in workforce planning and retention.

Ultimately, the erosion of workforce stability undermines not only Article 19 but also a wider constellation of rights. Failure to detect harm compromises children's right to health (Article 24) and development (Article 6), whereas repeated changes of workers can disrupt placement planning and the right to continuity of family life (Article 20). Retention failures, therefore, magnify children's vulnerability and weaken the very protections that social work is mandated to uphold.

These systemic risks not only are visible in inquiry reports and court judgments but also play out daily in frontline practice. The following case study illustrates how workforce instability directly undermines children's rights to protection, participation, and family life. Although fictionalised, it is based on common patterns identified in research and practice reviews, showing how high turnover and staff shortages affect both safeguarding and relational continuity.

## Case Study: Workforce Shortages and the Disruption of Child Protection and Contact

### *Context*

In a medium-size local authority in the United Kingdom, the child protection service has faced chronic recruitment and retention difficulties. In the past 2 years, nearly half of the permanent child protection social workers have left, many citing stress, caseload size, and poor supervision. The gaps have been filled with a revolving door of agency workers, many on short-term contracts.

### *The Case of Beth*

Beth is a 7-year-old girl placed under a child protection plan after her school raises concerns about neglect and domestic violence at home. Initially, she is allocated to an experienced social worker, Maria, who undertakes a thorough assessment, establishes regular contact with Beth and her mother, and builds trust. Beth begins to confide in Maria about her experiences at home and expresses, for the first time, her feelings about witnessing violence.

Within 6 months, however, Maria resigns due to burnout and workload pressures. Beth's case is transferred to an agency worker, Tom, who lasts only 3 months. By the time a third worker, Lisa, takes over, Beth has retold her story multiple times. Each transition means delays in assessment updates, inconsistent visits, and disrupted safeguarding planning.

#### *Impact on Beth*

Beth becomes withdrawn in school, stops engaging in play therapy, and tells her foster caregiver: "They don't stay. Why should I tell them anything?" Her right to protection from harm (Article 19) is compromised because the instability in staffing weakens oversight of her case. Her right to participate (Article 12) is also undermined: Although workers try to "hear her voice," the lack of continuity erodes her trust, making her participation tokenistic rather than genuine.

#### *Contact Visits*

Poor staffing affects contact with Beth's family. Court-ordered supervised visits with her father have to be cancelled on several occasions because no staff members are available to supervise them. This disrupts Beth's right to family life and continuity of relationships (Article 20). It also causes confusion and distress: Beth begins to believe she has done something wrong when contact does not happen.

#### *Wider Organisational Impact*

For the remaining staff members, caseloads increase dramatically. Newly qualified workers are left to manage complex cases with little support, whereas managers spend time firefighting rather than providing reflective supervision. The team culture becomes one of crisis response, with little capacity for meaningful relationship-based practice.

#### *Implications for Children's Rights*

This case highlights how workforce instability is not merely an employment issue but also a children's rights issue. A revolving door of workers led to fractured relationships, undermined participation rights (Article 12), destabilised care and family connections (Article 20), and placed protection from harm (Article 19) at risk. The lack of staff members to supervise contact also breached Beth's rights to family life. The failure was systemic, not individual: austerity cuts, high caseloads, and limited retention strategies combined to create unsafe conditions for both workers and children. In short, continuity, protected time for direct work, and reflective supervision were eroded, hollowing out participation (Article 12), protection (Article 19), and stability (Article 20) in practice.

**Box 12.1 Reflective Questions for Social Workers: Workforce Considerations**

How might stable staffing and effective retention strategies have changed the trajectory of Beth's case?
In what ways does workforce instability directly breach children's rights under the UNCRC?
What organisational strategies could managers introduce to protect relational continuity for children in situations of high turnover?
How should policymakers balance cost pressures with the moral and legal duty to uphold children's rights?
What supports do practitioners themselves need to sustain trust-based relationships with children like Beth?

## Structural and Political Constraints: How Systems Hollow Out Rights

The frontline harms described here are not random; it is our view that they are structured by administrative, managerial, and fiscal choices. Neoliberalism has reshaped welfare systems around cost control and measurable outputs, narrowing the scope of social work and diverting attention from the rights and needs of children.

One key impact of this context is chronic underfunding. Austerity policies have systematically reduced budgets for child and family services, leading to rising caseloads, staff shortages, and precarious working conditions. These resource constraints undermine social workers' capacity to practise in line with the UNCRC. They limit the time needed to listen to children and ensure their participation in decision-making (Article 12), disrupt the stability of placements and family life (Article 20), and weaken the protective role of social work by stretching practitioners so thinly that risk goes undetected (Article 19). They also compromise children's right to development (Article 6) by narrowing opportunities for holistic support and restricting interventions that would allow children to flourish. Under austerity, children's rights are not denied outright but instead hollowed out in practice because social workers lack the resources to make those rights meaningful.

Another effect of neoliberal reform has been the rise of managerialism and a culture of performance measurement. Complex relational practice is increasingly reduced to compliance with bureaucratic targets—visits completed, reports submitted, deadlines met. Although accountability is important, the dominance of measurable outputs distorts priorities. It incentivises speed over depth, efficiency over engagement, and paperwork over relationships. This shift erodes children's right to be heard and express their views freely (Articles 12 and 13), to receive consistent and stable care (Article 20), and to have their best interests treated as a primary consideration in all decisions (Article 3). In such systems, children are at risk of becoming data points rather than active participants in their lives.

This shift is evident in the prioritisation of performance targets—such as the number of visits completed or assessments closed in a specified time-frame—over the quality of relationships or the voices of children. Practitioners often describe how the pressure to demonstrate compliance with these metrics leaves little time for the slow, trust-building work that genuine participation (Article 12) requires. At the same time, chronic underfunding driven by austerity policies has reduced staffing levels, leaving remaining workers overstretched and unable to sustain the consistent contact necessary for protection (Article 19) and stability in care (Article 20).

The language of efficiency also reconfigures how success is defined. Services are judged by whether they meet output-based indicators rather than by whether children feel safe, listened to, or supported in their development. This market logic obscures the central moral purpose of social work and risks hollowing out its rights-based foundations. For children, the consequences are concrete: delayed access to therapeutic services (Article 24), disrupted placements that undermine their right to family life (Article 20), and decisions driven by budgetary constraint rather than their best interests (Article 3).

The culture of blame that accompanies neoliberal reforms has further consequences. When systemic failures occur, such as in high-profile cases of child death or abuse, individual practitioners are often scapegoated rather than governments or agencies being held accountable for structural under-resourcing. This dynamic not only drives workers out of the profession but also compounds their sense of moral distress. High turnover in this context undermines children's right to protection from violence, neglect, and exploitation (Article 19); their right to privacy and family life (Article 16); and for children in care proceedings, their right to a fair hearing and access to justice (Article 40). The result is a workforce that is demoralised and depleted, precisely when children most need continuity and protection.

Finally, austerity-driven cuts have directly curtailed children's access to services that are essential to their health and development. Reduced funding for mental health provision, education support, and preventive programmes undermines children's right to the highest attainable standard of health (Article 24), their right to an adequate standard of living (Article 27), and their right to education (Articles 28 and 29). In practice, this means longer waiting lists for vital services, fewer opportunities for early intervention, and an increased reliance on crisis-driven responses. Children whose needs could have been addressed through timely, holistic support often face escalation of harm instead.

Unless these structural forces are addressed directly, reforms to improve retention will remain partial, and breaches of children's rights will continue to be reproduced structurally rather than prevented. The challenge, therefore, is not only to improve leadership, supervision, and professional development in social work but also to resist the policy frameworks that strip social work of its relational and rights-based foundations. Without such resistance, children's rights risk being undermined not by neglect or oversight but by design—embedded in systems that value efficiency over humanity and cost savings over the holistic realisation of the UNCRC.

International comparisons show that these dynamics are not inevitable. In several Nordic countries, for example, investment in universal family support and preventive services has created conditions wherein social workers can focus on relational practice rather than crisis management. In Norway, child protection is resourced to ensure lower caseloads and greater stability, which enables consistent visits and deeper engagement with families. Similarly, in Finland, municipal child welfare teams are supported by legislation that emphasises early intervention, with strong cross-agency collaboration to uphold children's rights to development (Article 6) and well-being (Article 24). These approaches demonstrate that when governments resist austerity-driven logics and embed children's rights in funding and practice frameworks, workforce retention and rights-based outcomes are mutually reinforced.

In contrast, where neoliberal reforms dominate, retention reforms—such as improved supervision, manageable caseloads, and rights-based training—cannot be fully effective without tackling the wider policy frameworks that shape practice conditions. Unless cost-efficiency and bureaucratic accountability logics are directly challenged, even well-intentioned reforms will remain partial, leaving children's rights precarious and unevenly realised.

The structural challenges described here are not abstract; they are felt daily in the lives of children and the practice realities of social workers. When funding cuts reduce services, performance frameworks dominate priorities, and managerial cultures reward compliance over relationships, the impact is experienced most acutely by children, whose rights rely on consistent, relational practice. The following case study illustrates how these pressures play out in everyday child protection work. It shows how a young person's right to participation, stability, and best interests can be quietly eroded—not through deliberate neglect but through systemic demands that leave practitioners rushing, overstretched, and morally compromised.

## Case Study: Target-Driven Practice and the Erosion of Children's Participation

### *Context*

In another local authority, austerity policies have intensified the pressure on children's services to demonstrate measurable outcomes. The department operates under strict performance frameworks: Managers are required to report on the percentage of visits completed on time, the speed of case closure, and the volume of assessments completed. Workers report that "hitting the target" often takes precedence over engaging with families.

### *The Case of Jayden*

Jayden is a 14-year-old boy living with foster caregivers after being removed from his mother's care due to neglect and substance misuse. Jayden is bright but struggles with anxiety and low self-esteem. He is keen to have a say in his care plan, especially regarding decisions about school, contact with his siblings, and long-term placement options.

His social worker, Anika, is committed to rights-based practice and wants to spend time helping Jayden express his views in ways that feel safe and meaningful. However, organisational demands frequently interfere. Anika is expected to complete a set number of statutory visits each month and input detailed reports into the system within 24 hours. As a result, her time with Jayden is often reduced to rushed visits during which she ticks boxes to evidence compliance.

On one occasion, Anika arranges a session with Jayden to explore his wishes about sibling contact using creative methods. The session has to be cut short because her manager calls, reminding her of a deadline for data submission. Jayden later tells his foster caregiver: "She asks me what I think, but she doesn't really listen. It's like she's in a hurry all the time."

#### *Impact on Rights*

Jayden's right to participation (Article 12) is undermined when his views are solicited in ways shaped by administrative timescales rather than his needs. His best interests (Article 3) risk being sidelined by organisational priorities. Similarly, the drive to close cases quickly may jeopardise his right to stability in care (Article 20) because decisions are made with insufficient attention to long-term planning.

#### *Wider Implications*

This case illustrates how neoliberal reforms and managerial targets can distort practice priorities. When children become data points, the relational and participatory essence of social work is lost. Rights such as those outlined in Article 12 (participation), Article 3 (best interests) and Article 20 (family and stability) are not intentionally denied but rather hollowed out in practice. Workers like Anika are left in untenable positions, trying to reconcile their ethical commitments

**Box 12.2 Reflective Questions for Social Workers: Performance Metrics versus Rights**

How do performance targets and bureaucratic demands affect the authenticity of children's participation?

What changes could managers implement to ensure that these targets support, rather than undermine, children's rights?

How can practitioners resist or creatively adapt to bureaucratic pressures while still prioritising children's best interests?

In what ways do neoliberal policy frameworks create systemic risks to children's rights?

What role should policymakers play in shifting the balance from compliance to relational, rights-based practice?

with the managerial demands of the system. Here again, the mechanisms are visible: Protected time is displaced by throughput pressure, continuity falters as hurried contacts accumulate, and the lack of reflective supervision compounds moral distress—undermining participation (Article 12), best interests (Article 3), and stability (Article 20).

### Operationalising Rights: A Practical Matrix and Indicators

To reduce repetition and sharpen accountability, we propose a concise mapping from practice mechanisms to UNCRC rights and indicative metrics (Table 12.1).

### Recommendations and the Imperative of Upholding Children's Rights

Addressing social work retention is not solely a workforce concern; it is a fundamental requirement for upholding children's rights under the UNCRC. Social workers' ability to provide stable, informed, and rights-based care is directly

*Table 12.1* Matrix of Practice Metrics

| *Mechanism* | *Practice Effect* | *UNCRC Articles* | *Example Indicators* |
|---|---|---|---|
| Caseloads and continuity | Missed visits, relationship churn, drift | Articles 12, 19, and 20 | Percentage of children with two or more worker changes per year, warm handover rate, average visit interval |
| Protected time for judgment | Defensive practice, escalation, delays | Articles 3 and 19 | Median caseload, direct work of 35% or more, late-visit rate |
| Reflective supervision | Improved planning, coordinated services | Articles 6, 24, 28, and 29 | Supervision frequency and quality, continuing professional development completion, time-to-service access |
| Career pathways and continuing professional development | Retention of expertise, assessment quality | Articles 19 and 24 | Progression availability, complex-case allocation |
| Relational continuity policy | Child trust, reduced retelling of trauma | Articles 12 and 20 | Named-worker guarantee, percentage of warm handovers |

shaped by the environments in which they work, the training they receive, and the structural support available to them. Strengthening retention, therefore, requires coordinated action across policy, education, and practice. Each recommendation here is designed to restore continuity, protect time for judgment and direct work, and strengthen reflective supervision—the three levers through which retention translates into rights.

#### *Policy Level*

Governments must legislate manageable caseloads and enforce minimum supervision standards to ensure that social workers have the time and support needed to engage meaningfully with children and families. Such measures are central to protecting children from harm (Article 19) and enabling their participation in decisions about their lives (Article 12). Reversing austerity-driven funding cuts is equally vital: Without adequate resources, services cannot retain experienced staff members or provide the relational continuity that children need to enjoy stability and family life (Article 20). Policy frameworks should also make explicit the link between workforce conditions and the realisation of children's rights, embedding Articles 12, 19, and 20 into guidance and regulation. Crucially, regulatory systems should reward quality, rights-based engagement rather than narrow compliance with administrative targets, which too often crowd out the relational time needed to hear children's voices.

#### *Education Level*

Social work programmes should prioritise rights-based and trauma-informed education that prepares students for the ethical and emotional complexities of child protection practice. Students must be equipped to understand not only children's rights (Articles 12, 19, 20, 24, and 28) but also the political and economic contexts in which those rights are pursued. Supporting early professional identity development—centred on advocacy, justice, and empowerment—strengthens motivation and long-term commitment, whereas peer learning and mentorship reduce professional isolation and promote resilience. These educational practices can help future practitioners sustain rights-based engagement even under systemic pressure.

#### *Organisational Level*

Practitioners and leaders in organisations also carry responsibility. Embedding human-centred leadership models that provide psychological safety, professional autonomy, and reflective supervision is critical. Such practices enable social workers to manage stress, navigate ethical dilemmas, and keep children's best interests (Article 3) at the heart of decision-making. Peer support networks and team-based resilience strategies further reinforce morale and professional identity, making it more likely that children experience continuity and stability in their care (Article 20). Employers should also ensure that staff members have time for genuine relational work with children, rather than allowing performance targets to reduce children to statistics. Tailored professional development and career progression opportunities at all stages of practice are necessary to sustain motivation and help workers uphold children's rights to protection (Article 19), participation (Article 12), health (Article 24), and education (Article 28).

Together, these measures demonstrate that retention is best addressed through an integrated approach across policy, education, and practice. However, even well-designed reforms face significant barriers in the current neoliberal policy climate. Chronic underfunding, cost-efficiency logics, and a culture of blame have reshaped public services in ways that undermine social workers and weaken children's rights. Neoliberal reforms reduce complex relational practice to bureaucratic compliance, eroding children's right to be heard (Article 12), fragmenting placements that undermine stability (Article 20), and prioritising cost savings over protection (Article 19). Austerity-driven cuts have limited children's access to education (Article 28) and health (Article 24) while shifting responsibility for systemic failures onto individual workers. Unless these structural forces are challenged, reforms to improve retention will remain partial and breaches of children's rights will continue to be structurally reproduced rather than prevented.

Although these recommendations set out a pathway for improving workforce stability and strengthening rights-based practice, they cannot be considered in isolation from the broader political and economic context in which social work operates. The structural environment—shaped by funding decisions, welfare reform, and dominant policy ideologies—either enables or constrains the capacity of social workers to uphold children's rights. To understand fully why retention remains such an entrenched challenge, it is necessary to consider how neoliberal reforms, austerity measures, and managerial cultures have reshaped the conditions of practice and, in turn, the realisation of the UNCRC.

## Conclusion

Workforce retention in child protection is not simply a matter of human resources management or professional well-being; it is a core issue of children's rights. A stable and motivated workforce is essential to ensuring that children are heard (Article 12), protected from harm (Article 19), supported in their family lives (Article 20), and provided with health (Article 24), education (Articles 28 and 29), and opportunities for development (Article 6). Without such stability, these rights are not fully realised but become fragmented, inconsistently applied, or hollowed out in practice.

This chapter has shown that improving retention requires action across organisational, personal, and structural domains. At the organisational level, supportive leadership, reflective supervision, and manageable caseloads are indispensable in enabling social workers to practise ethically and relationally.

At the personal level, strong professional identity, peer support, and opportunities for ongoing learning help practitioners sustain their motivation and resilience. At the structural level, sustained investment and fair resourcing create the conditions in which rights-based practice can flourish.

Yet reforms in these domains cannot be divorced from the wider political and economic context that shapes the profession. Neoliberal and austerity-driven policies continue to erode the foundations of relational practice by privileging cost efficiency, measurable outputs, and managerial accountability over human dignity, relational trust, and children's voices. These policy logics not only stretch workers to a breaking point but also structurally reproduce breaches of the UNCRC, embedding inequalities into the very systems meant to protect children.

To move forward, children's rights must be understood not only as the moral compass of social work but also as its practical foundation. Embedding rights into retention strategies means recognising that workforce stability is a precondition for fulfilling children's entitlements to protection, participation, provision, and development. It requires governments to legislate and resource in ways that ensure continuity, organisations to cultivate cultures that value relationships as much as compliance, and educators to prepare practitioners who can hold rights at the centre of practice, even under systemic pressure.

In this sense, retention is not only about sustaining the profession but also about delivering justice for children. A workforce that is supported, valued, and retained is one that can stand with children in the most difficult of circumstances, amplify their voices, and safeguard their futures. To achieve this, investment in the workforce must be reframed as an investment in children's rights—ensuring that provision, protection, and participation remain the living, everyday realities at the heart of this book's vision.

## Key Messages: Workforce Retention as a Children's Rights Issue

Workforce stability is a rights issue, not only a workforce issue. Retention is essential to upholding children's rights to protection (Article 19), participation (Article 12), family life (Article 20), health (Article 24), education (Articles 28 and 29), and development (Article 6).

Retention requires action across multiple domains. Supportive leadership, reflective supervision, strong professional identity, manageable caseloads, and sustained investment are all necessary to enable ethical, rights-based practice.

Structural context cannot be ignored. Neoliberal and austerity-driven reforms undermine the conditions for relational work, prioritising cost-efficiency and outputs over children's voices and best interests. Without addressing these systemic forces, reforms to improve retention will remain partial.

Investment in the workforce is an investment in children's rights. A stable, motivated, and skilled workforce is the foundation of meaningful provision, protection, and participation. Retention strategies, therefore, must be understood as central to realising the UNCRC in practice.

## References


Anderson, D. G. (2000). Coping strategies and burnout among veteran child protection workers. *Child Abuse & Neglect*, *24*(6), 839–848. https://doi.org/10.1016/S0145-2134(00)00143-5

Astvik, W., Welander, J., & Larsson, R. (2020). Reasons for staying: A longitudinal study of work conditions predicting social workers' willingness to stay in their organisation. *The British Journal of Social Work*, *50*(5), 1382–1400. https://doi.org/10.1093/bjsw/bcz103

British Association of Social Workers. (2023, December 7). High vacancy rates, poor staff retention—It feels like a "crunch point" in social work. *Professional Social Work*. https://new.basw.co.uk/about-social-work/psw-magazine/articles/high-vacancy-rates-poor-staff-retention-it-feels-crunch

Burns, K., Christie, A., & O'Sullivan, S. (2020). Findings from a longitudinal qualitative study of child protection social workers' retention: Job embeddedness, professional confidence and staying narratives. *The British Journal of Social Work*, *50*(4), 1363–1381. https://doi.org/10.1093/bjsw/bcz083

Carter, R. (2019). *Most children in care experienced at least one change of social worker last year, report finds*. Community Care. https://www.communitycare.co.uk/content/news/most-children-in-care-experienced-at-least-one-change-of-social-worker-last-year-report-finds

Children Act. (1989). U.K. Pub. Gen. Acts, c. 41 (1989). https://www.legislation.gov.uk/ukpga/1989/41/contents

Coffey, M., Dugdill, L., & Tattersall, A. (2004). Stress in social services: Mental well-being, constraints and job satisfaction. *The British Journal of Social Work*, *34*(5), 735–746. https://doi.org/10.1093/bjsw/bch088

Cook, L., Carder, S., & Zschlomler, D. (2022). *Retaining and supporting experienced social workers in child protection: Research briefing*. Centre for Research on Children and Families. https://ueaeprints.uea.ac.uk/id/eprint/89334/1/Retaining_and_Supporting_Experienced_Child_and_Family_Social_Workers_in_Child_Protection.pdf

Cook, L., Carder, S., & Zschomler, S. (2025). "Being a social worker … it's in my DNA": Retaining experienced child and family social workers: The role of professional identity. *Child & Family Social Work*, *30*(4), 996–1005. https://doi.org/10.1111/cfs.13233

Department for Education. (2020). *Longitudinal study of local authority child and family social workers* (Wave 2; DFE-RR989). https://assets.publishing.service.gov.uk/media/5f296a93e90e0732dbca7a54/Longitudinal_study_of_local_authority_child_and_family_social_workers_Wave_2.pdf

Department of Health Northern Ireland. (2022). *Social work workforce review Northern Ireland*. https://www.health-ni.gov.uk/publications/social-work-workforce-review-northern-ireland-2022

deVaron Reynolds, J., Costello, T., & Edwards, M. T. (2008). The study of workload in child protective and child welfare services. *Protecting Children*, *23*(3), 3–5. https://ncwwi.org/files/Job_Analysis__Position_Requirements/The_Study_of_Workload_in_Child_Protective.pdf

Ewalt, P. (1991). Trends affecting recruitment and retention of social work staff in human services agencies. *Social Work*, *36*(3), 214–217. https://doi.org/10.1093/sw/36.3.214

Gomez, R. J., Travis, D. J., Ayers-Lopez, S., & Schwab, A. J. (2010). In search of innovation: A national qualitative analysis of child welfare recruitment and retention efforts. *Children and Youth Services Review*, *32*(5), 664–671. https://doi.org/10.1016/j.childyouth.2010.01.001

Harlow, E., Berg, E., Barry, J., & Chandler, J. (2013). Neoliberalism, managerialism and the reconfiguring of social work in Sweden and the United Kingdom. *Organization*, *20*(4), 534–550. https://doi.org/10.1177/1350508412448222

Healy, K., & Oltedal, S. (2010). An institutional comparison of child protection systems in Australia and Norway focused on workforce retention. *Journal of Social Policy*, *39*(2), 255–274. https://doi.org/10.1017/S004727940999047X

Human Rights Act. (1998). U.K. Pub. Gen. Acts, c. 42 (1998). https://www.legislation.gov.uk/ukpga/1998/42/contents

Independent Review of Children's Social Care. (2021). *The case for change*. https://fdac.org.uk/wp-content/uploads/2021/06/case-for-change.pdf

Independent Review of Children's Social Care. (2022). *The independent review of children's social care: Final report*. https://assets.publishing.service.gov.uk/media/640a17f28fa8f5560820da4b/Independent_review_of_children_s_social_care_-_Final_report.pdf

Koprowska, J. (2024). *Communication and interpersonal skills in social work* (6th edn.). Learning Matters.

McCafferty, P., Duffy, J., & Hayes, D. (2021). Permanency decisions in child welfare: A qualitative study. *The British Journal of Social Work*, *51*(6), 2134–2154. https://doi.org/10.1093/bjsw/bcab095

McCafferty, P., & Taylor, B. J. (2020). Risk, decision-making and assessment in child welfare. *Child Care in Practice*, *26*(2), 107–110. https://doi.org/10.1080/13575279.2019.1703369

McFadden, P. (2020). Two sides of one coin? Relationships build resilience or contribute to burnout in child protection social work: Shared perspectives from Leavers and Stayers in Northern Ireland. *International Social Work*, *63*(2), 164–176. https://doi.org/10.1177/0020872818788393

McFadden, P., Campbell, A., & Taylor, B. (2015). Resilience and burnout in child protection social work: Individual and organisational themes from a systematic literature review. *The British Journal of Social Work*, *45*(5), 1546–1563. https://doi.org/10.1093/bjsw/bct210

McFadden, P., Maclochlainn, J., Manthorpe, J., Naylor, R., Schroder, H., McGrory, S., Ravalier, J., Nicholl, P., Currie, D., Kirby, K., Davies, H., Mullineux, J., McColgan, M., & Mallet, J. (2024). Perceptions of safe staffing, self-reported mental well-being and intentions to leave the profession among UK social workers: A mixed methods study. *The British Journal of Social Work*, *54*(5), 1965–1987. https://doi.org/10.1093/bjsw/bcae014

McLaughlin, H., Scholar, H., McCaughan, S., & Pollock, S. (2023). "Should I stay or should I go"? The experiences of forty social workers in England who had previously indicated they would stay in or leave children and families social work. *The British Journal of Social Work*, *53*(4), 1963–1983. https://doi.org/10.1093/bjsw/bcac191

Mor Barak, M. E., Nissly, J. A., & Levin, A. (2001). Antecedents to retention and turnover among child welfare, social work, and other human service employees: What can we learn from past research? A review and metanalysis. *The Social Service Review*, *75*(4), 625–661. https://doi.org/10.1086/323166

Peart, V. (2024, July 4). Social work is political: For you and your clients' sake, you must vote today. *Social Work News*. https://www.mysocialworknews.com/article/social-work-is-political-for-you-and-your-clients-sake-you-must-vote-today

Redmond, B., Guerin, S., Nolan, B., Devitt, C., & Egan, A. (2010). *The retention of social workers in the health services: An evidence-based assessment*. https://norma.ncirl.ie/1695/1/UCD_Retention_of_Social_Workers.pdf

Research in Practice. (2022). *What is early help? Concepts, policy directions and multi-agency perspectives*. Ofsted. https://www.gov.uk/government/publications/early-help-concepts-policy-directions-and-multi-agency-perspectives

Research in Practice. (2025). *National Workload Action Group—Final report: Research and recommendations on reducing social worker workload*. https://www.gov.uk/government/publications/national-workload-action-group-reports-on-social-worker-workload

Rycraft, J. (1994). The party isn't over: The agency role in the retention of public child welfare caseworkers. *Social Work*, *40*(2), 316–328.

Samuel, M. (2025). *A quarter of children in care had at least three social workers in 2023–2024, DfE reveals*. Community Care. https://www.communitycare.co.uk/content/news/a-quarter-of-children-in-care-had-at-least-three-social-workers-in-2023-24-dfe-reveals

Social Workers Union. (2024). Social workers' concerns about welfare not dealt with by authorities. https://swu-union.org.uk/2024/04/social-workers-concerns-about-welfare-not-dealt-with-by-authorities/

Stevenson, L. (2015). *High Court fines council after social worker turnover breaches child's rights*. Community Care. https://www.communitycare.co.uk/content/news/high-court-fines-council-after-high-social-worker-turnover-breached-child-s-rights

Strolin-Goltzman, J., Kollar, S., & Trinkle, J. (2010). Listening to the voices of children in foster care: Youths speak out about child welfare worker turnover and selection. *Social Work*, *55*(1), 47–53. https://doi.org/10.1093/sw/55.1.47

United Nations. (1989). *Convention on the rights of the child*. https://www.ohchr.org/en/instruments-mechanisms/instruments/convention-rights-child

Webb, C. M., & Carpenter, J. (2012). What can be done to promote the retention of social workers? A systematic review of interventions. *The British Journal of Social Work*, *42*(7), 1235–1255. https://doi.org/10.1093/bjsw/bcr144

# Conclusion

## A Call to Conscience—Reclaiming Children's Rights in Social Work

*Paul McCafferty*

### Introduction

Throughout this book, we have traversed the intellectual, ethical, and practical landscapes that define children's rights in social work. Across four key sections—theory, protection, participation, and provision—we have interrogated the values, practices, and structures that shape whether and how these rights are upheld. This final chapter does not aim to summarise what has gone before, but rather to distil its lessons and extend its points. It reflects on what it truly means—and what it demands of us—to centre children's rights in social work across practice, law, and policy and to move forward with integrity, courage, and collective purpose.

This conclusion is not simply a closing note. It is a call to conscience. It is an invitation—and a provocation—to ask: What kind of social work do we want to practise, and what kind of society are we trying to build? Are we content with a profession that manages risk, monitors behaviour, and administers systems? Or do we strive for a social work that disrupts injustice, centres the voices of those who are silenced, and champions the rights and dignity of every child? These are not abstract questions. They go to the heart of our daily decisions, our institutional cultures, and our collective aspirations.

The pages of this book have illustrated the theoretical foundations, systemic barriers, ethical tensions, and practical innovations that shape children's rights in social work. But this closing moment is not the end of the conversation; it is a threshold. It is a space where we pause to consider what we have learned, what remains unresolved, and what actions we are prepared to take. It is a reminder that every time we sit with a child, write a report, design a policy, or teach a class, we are making choices that reflect and shape our values. To move forward from this threshold demands not only reflection but also moral clarity and collective resolve. The values we choose to act upon must align with a deeper truth: that children's rights are not optional add-ons but the very foundation of our practice.

DOI: 10.4324/9781003582410-18

## Reaffirming the Moral Imperative

Children's rights are not abstract aspirations. They are urgent, immediate, and non-negotiable. Yet the contrast between the ethical clarity of these rights and the ambiguity of their implementation is stark. We speak the language of rights but all too often fail to live its values in practice. The United Nations Convention on the Rights of the Child is clear: Children have the right to protection, to participation, to provision, and to be treated as full people in the present, not as future citizens-in-waiting. Yet our professional cultures, institutional routines, and public discourses continue to treat these rights as conditional—to be honoured when convenient, postponed when challenging, and overridden when adult interests prevail.

This book has shown that social work is not immune to these patterns. Despite our rhetoric of empowerment and child-centredness, we too often default to paternalism, compliance, and a cautious culture that privileges procedure over principle. These tendencies are not simply the result of individual failings or time pressures. They are structural and cultural. They reflect how we, as a profession and a society, continue to see children—not as equals but as problems to be managed, voices to be mediated, and futures to be shaped on their behalf.

To confront this reality, we need more than better guidance or training. We need a collective reckoning with how deeply adultism is embedded in our thinking and how profoundly it limits the potential of our work. If we are serious about rights, then we must be serious about recognising children's moral worth, agency, and capacity in the here and now.

## Learning from What Has Been Offered

The contributors to this book—scholars, practitioners, and young people—have offered rich insights into the conditions that enable or obstruct rights-based practice. In Section I, we saw how social theory can help us make sense of the forces that shape childhood and social work. Honneth's theory of recognition reminds us that rights are meaningless without social validation. Bourdieu's work challenges us to look at how power circulates in subtle, taken-for-granted ways. The sociology of childhood repositions children as social actors, not passive dependents.

In Section II, we confronted the realities of protection—how children's safety is compromised when systems are fragmented, underresourced, or adversarial. From Hayes' analysis of the dichotomy between family support and child protection to the international lens offered by Alfandari and Reichenberg and the complexities of adoption explored by MacDonald and McCaughren, a central theme emerged: Protection must be relational, rights-based, and integrated into a broader commitment to children's well-being.

Section III reminded us that participation is not a luxury. It is a litmus test for whether we truly respect children's rights. From Mercado García's and

McCafferty's systematic review to Edman and McCafferty's six-dimensional model and Ducca Cisneros and Arias Astray's grounded work with adolescents, we are reminded that participation is more than being consulted—it is about being heard, understood, and taken seriously. It requires time, trust, and a redistribution of power that many systems still resist.

Finally, Section IV turned our attention to provision—the entitlements of children to education, health, identity, and support. Marshall and McCafferty's chapter on residential care asks us to reconsider how recognition is embodied in everyday settings. McColgan and McCafferty's global analysis shows how far we have to go in addressing structural inequalities. And the closing chapter by Tanner, McCafferty, and Hayes points to one of the profession's greatest internal threats: a workforce under siege, where children's rights are undermined not by ideology but by exhaustion and instability.

Together, these chapters weave a tapestry of challenge and hope. They are grounded in rigorous scholarship, but they also speak from practice and lived experience. They offer critique but also creativity. They show that another way is possible—if we are willing to choose it.

## Facing the Contradictions—And the Possibilities

There is no denying that progress has been made. The language of rights is now embedded in many policies and organisational missions. Participation frameworks like Lundy's model have helped operationalise children's voices. International instruments have raised the bar for accountability and advocacy.

But alongside these gains, there are stubborn gaps. Rights-based practice remains uneven and often tokenistic. Children from marginalised backgrounds—whether due to poverty, disability, ethnicity, care status, or immigration—continue to be overlooked and underserved. Interventions that are meant to protect can retraumatise. Mechanisms for listening can become rituals of compliance. Services designed to include can exclude by design.

These contradictions do not mean we should give up on rights. They mean we must deepen our understanding of what rights require. Rights are not about checking boxes or managing risks. They are about creating the conditions where children can flourish—emotionally, socially, politically. They are about challenging the very systems and assumptions that make rights fragile in the first place.

To that end, we must see children's rights not only as legal entitlements but also as a radical reimagining of how power operates in social work. A rights-based approach requires us to move from intervention to co-creation, from assessment to accompaniment, from doing for to doing with. It demands that we see our professional authority not as something to be defended but as something to be shared.

This is not easy. It involves uncertainty, discomfort, and conflict. It means we must sit with complexity, hold competing rights in tension, and resist the urge to retreat into defensive routines. But it is also a practice of hope. To work from a place of rights is to work from a belief that change is possible—not only in the lives of individual children but in the systems and cultures that surround them.

As educators, we must ask whether our curricula prepare students to navigate these tensions. Are we teaching values or only competencies? Are we offering students space to reflect on power, identity, and ethics? Are we modelling the kind of practice we hope they will go on to deliver—one rooted in respect for rights, rather than routinised compliance?

As leaders, we must create conditions in which rights-based practice is possible. That means investing in high-quality supervision, recognising emotional labour, and advocating systems that support reflection, not only output. It means challenging a performance culture that prizes efficiency over empathy and safety over justice. Leadership is not about avoiding risk but about enabling ethical courage.

As policymakers, we must ensure that legislation does more than set minimum standards. It must actively promote inclusion, participation, and equity. We must centre children's voices not only in frontline services but also in the design, delivery, and evaluation of the systems meant to serve them. Accountability must be relational, not merely procedural; it must ask whether we are honouring children's rights in spirit and form.

As practitioners, we must resist the drift towards bureaucratic detachment and reclaim the relational heart of social work. Listening deeply, sharing power, challenging adultist assumptions, and making time for meaningful engagement are not extras—they are the core of ethical practice. Upholding children's rights means questioning the status quo, especially when it is defended in the name of protection, risk, or institutional necessity.

As researchers, we must take seriously our responsibility to generate knowledge that matters. This means centring children's voices in research design, questioning dominant paradigms that pathologise or marginalise, and producing findings that are accessible and actionable. And we must move beyond studying children as subjects to engaging them as co-researchers—partners in the creation of knowledge that shapes the systems they must navigate. We must also hold institutions to account by asking uncomfortable questions: Whose knowledge counts? Who is left out of the evidence base? And are we studying children or studying with them?

## A Vision for the Future

So, where do we go from here?

We begin with values. With a conviction that children are not only in our care; they are in our community. With an understanding that their rights are not negotiable, and that honouring those rights is the bedrock of ethical practice.

We continue with action. With the courage to challenge injustice, speak up when systems fail, and try new ways of working even when it feels risky. With the humility to learn from children, share power, and be transformed in the process.

And we end with hope. Not a naïve hope that things will get better on their own but a determined hope that things can be better—if we make them so. That hope is not soft. It is fierce. It is rooted in love, in solidarity, and in a refusal to accept that this—what we have now—is the best we can do.

## A Final Invitation

To all who have read this book: Thank you. Thank you for sitting with the complexity, for staying open to discomfort, and for walking alongside us on this journey. I hope that something within these pages has stirred your thinking, affirmed your values, or challenged your assumptions.

But more than that, I hope it moves you to act—in your practice, your teaching, your policymaking, your research, and in your daily life. Because every child matters. Every voice counts. And every right must be upheld.

Let us begin, together, and let us begin now. Because the future of children's rights does not lie in tomorrow's promises but in today's decisions.

# Index

Pages in **bold-*italics*** refer to boxes and pages in **bold** refer to tables.

For Product Safety Concerns and Information please contact our EU representative GPSR@taylorandfrancis.com
Taylor & Francis Verlag GmbH, Kaufingerstraße 24, 80331 München, Germany

www.ingramcontent.com/pod-product-compliance
Ingram Content Group UK Ltd.
Pitfield, Milton Keynes, MK11 3LW, UK
UKHW022043061126
477531UK00009B/518
*9781032949253*